WORDS OF ETERNITY

WORDS OF ETERNITY
BLAKE AND THE POETICS OF
THE SUBLIME

VINCENT ARTHUR DE LUCA

PRINCETON UNIVERSITY PRESS

PRINCETON, NEW JERSEY

Copyright © 1991 by Princeton University Press

Published by Princeton University Press, 41 William Street,

Princeton, New Jersey 08540

In the United Kingdom: Princeton University Press, Oxford

Library of Congress Cataloging-in-Publication Data

De Luca, V. A., 1940-

Words of eternity : Blake and the poetics of the sublime / Vincent Arthur De Luca.

p. cm.

Includes index.

ISBN 0-691-06874-7

1. Blake, William, 1757–1827—Criticism and interpretation.

2. Sublime, The, in literature. I. Title.

PR4148.S92D4 1991 821'.7—dc20 90-9076 CIP

This book has been composed in Linotron Galliard

Princeton University Press books are printed on acid-free paper,
and meet the guidelines for permanence and durability of the
Committee on Production Guidelines for Book Longevity of the
Council on Library Resources

Printed in the United States of America by Princeton University Press,
Princeton, New Jersey

3 5 7 9 10 8 6 4 2

In memory of Northrop Frye

The Breath Divine went forth over the morning hills Albion
    rose
In anger: the wrath of God breaking bright flaming on all
    sides around
His awful limbs: into the Heavens he walked clothed in
    flames
Loud thundring, with broad flashes of flaming lightning &
    pillars
Of fire, speaking the Words of Eternity in Human Forms

—*Jerusalem* 95.5–9

CONTENTS

ILLUSTRATIONS

All illustrations are by Blake unless otherwise designated.

ACKNOWLEDGMENTS

THE INITIAL RESEARCH for this book was undertaken during a Leave Fellowship sponsored by the Social Sciences and Humanities Research Council of Canada, and the manuscript was completed through the timely assistance of a Research Grant from the same agency, which afforded me an indispensable year of release time from teaching and other university duties. I am grateful also to the Research Board of the University of Toronto for a series of smaller grants to cover incidental travel and other expenses incurred during the preparation of this book. A number of libraries extended to me the privilege of consulting their collections; for their help and courtesy I want to thank the staffs of the British Library, the British Museum, the Rosenwald Collection of the Library of Congress, the Pierpont Morgan Library, the University of Toronto Library, and the Yale Center for British Art. I am especially grateful to the Huntington Library and Art Gallery, and the Houghton and Widener Libraries of Harvard University for granting me extended periods of readership, and for generously providing considerable assistance during my stays.

Brief portions of this work incorporate or adapt material from essays of mine that have previously appeared in print—notably, "Blake and Burke in Astonishment!" in *Blake/An Illustrated Quarterly* 23 (Fall 1989), 100–104; "Proper Names in the Structural Design of Blake's Mythmaking," *Blake Studies* 8 (1978), 5–22; "Ariston's Immortal Palace: Icon and Allegory in Blake's Prophecies," *Criticism* 12 (Winter 1970), 1–19; "A Wall of Words: The Sublime as Text," in *Unnam'd Forms: Blake and Textuality*, ed. Nelson Hilton and Thomas Vogler (Berkeley: University of California Press, 1986), 218–41; and "Blake and the Two Sublimes," in *Studies in Eighteenth-Century Culture*, vol. 11, ed. Harry T. Payne (Madison: University of Wisconsin Press, 1982), 93–105. I am grateful for receiving such permissions as were necessary to allow me to reprint selected material from these essays.

It would be futile to attempt to name all the scholars and critics whose work has influenced and enlarged my understanding of Blake and of the sublime tradition; I have tried to acknowledge as many specific debts as possible in my notes. One such debt, however, should be singled out here: I first read Northrop Frye's *Fearful Symmetry* just over twenty-five years ago, and the experience profoundly affected the direction my scholarly career was to take, transforming my understanding of a Blake whose dimensions I had hitherto only dimly grasped, and leading ultimately (although not without divagations along the way) to the making of this study. In an important sense, this study may be considered a large-scale unfolding, in an updated critical context, of concerns contained explicitly or implicitly in a few dozen lambent and groundbreaking pages in the chapter of *Fearful Symmetry* called "Tradition and Experiment"—which remains the best succinct summary of Blake's position in the aesthetic context of his age. Since coming under his early influence, I have profited from Professor Frye's teaching, his collegiality, and his support of my work, and I most gratefully dedicate this book to his memory.

Among debts of more recent standing, I want to acknowledge the one owed to my graduate students in various seminars on the Romantic and eighteenth-century sublime at the University of Toronto. These students engaged and helped to refine my ideas, and through these interactive seminars the specific form and argument of this book began to take shape. In particular, I want to thank my former students and present colleagues John Pierce and Dena Bain Taylor, whose dissertations under my supervision overlapped some of the concerns in this book, and who certainly taught me as much as I can only hope to have imparted to them. For providing advice, encouragement, or material aid during the course of researching and writing this book, I am extremely grateful to such colleagues and friends as G. E. Bentley, Jr., Stuart Curran, David V. Erdman, Robert F. Gleckner, Morton D. Paley, Richard Teleky, John C. Villalobos, and Joseph A. Wittreich. To Robert N. Essick and Nelson Hilton, who each read the entire manuscript as it approached its final form, I owe a special debt of gratitude for a multitude of helpful comments and apt suggestions for improvement. In the final stages of manuscript preparation, Jonathan Cutmore's sharp-eyed editorial assistance saved me from many a careless error, and Robert E. Brown and Lauren Oppenheim of Princeton University Press were most generous with their help.

Finally, I want to express my profound gratitude to my mother and my late father for their constant encouragement of my scholarly work, to Mary V. Seeman for giving the most valuable kind of advice at the most crucial time, and to Richard Bishop for helping me with a number of tasks and problems connected with this project, tangible and intangible; it is enough to add that when he was needed, he was there.

TEXTS AND ABBREVIATIONS

M Y QUOTATIONS of Blake are taken from *The Complete Poetry and Prose of William Blake*, newly revised edition, ed. David V. Erdman, with Commentary by Harold Bloom (Garden City, N.Y.: Anchor Press/Doubleday, 1982), and are cited in the text as follows: by plate and line numbers for engraved poetry, by manuscript page and line numbers for *Vala* or *The Four Zoas*, by line numbers for other poetry, and otherwise by E, followed by the page number(s) in the Erdman edition. Quotations from Chapter 2 of *Jerusalem* are cited in the order found in E (based on the pagination of Copies A, C, and F), unless otherwise indicated. The following abbreviations are used to cite some of Blake's works:

Am	*America, a Prophecy*
AnnoRen	Annotations to the *Works* of Sir Joshua Reynolds
AnnoW	Annotations to Wordsworth's *Poems*
BA	*The Book of Ahania*
BL	*The Book of Los*
BU	*The [First] Book of Urizen*
DC	*Descriptive Catalogue*
Eur	*Europe, a Prophecy*
FR	*The French Revolution*
FZ	*Vala* or *The Four Zoas*
J	*Jerusalem*
Lao	*[The Laocoön]*
M	*Milton, a Poem*
MHH	*The Marriage of Heaven and Hell*
NNR	*There is No Natural Religion*
SE	*Songs of Experience*
SI	*Songs of Innocence*
SL	*The Song of Los*
Thel	*The Book of Thel*
VDA	*Visions of the Daughters of Albion*
VLJ	*[A Vision of the Last Judgment]*

The Bible is quoted from the Authorized (King James) Version, with citations incorporated in the text.

WORDS OF ETERNITY

INTRODUCTION

W ILLIAM BLAKE never doubted his status as a "sublime Artist" (E 544), nor did he conceal his aspirations to create "the Most Sublime Poetry" (E 730). Even so, the revival of interest in the sublime evident in eighteenth-century and Romantic criticism of the past two decades—an interest that brought the sublime within the orbit of sophisticated modern theory[1]—has largely neglected Blake, while Blake criticism during these years has not derived much of its intellectual substance from the renewed thinking about the sublime. This is a curious but not entirely inexplicable situation. On one hand, the conventional idiom and imagery of the eighteenth-century sublime saturates Blake's writings; for example, on the first plate of text in *Jerusalem*, we find him telling us that his living forms are "Giant," his numbers "terrific," his exertions "energetic," and his supreme visions beheld "with trembling & amazement" (*J* 3). This idiom is so pervasive in Blake's works that it may strike some critics as a sort of background buzz, not especially interesting in itself, and in any case too widely diffused to seem an appealing subject for analysis. On the other hand, Blake is thought to have had little patience for certain key paradigms of the sublime experience, embodied in scenes of man trembling in awe before the might of an omnipotent God, or before the grandeurs of external Nature; the poet's stated hostility to Edmund Burke (see E 660), the leading theoretician of such scenes, seems to confirm this idea. Critics therefore may easily assume that Blake's involvement with sublimity is mainly a matter of surface stylistic effects, habitually deployed, and not something engaging his deeper aesthetic and intellectual concerns.

This book aims to demonstrate that Blake's relation to the sublime is not superficial but profound; it argues that traditions of the sublime extant in his time play a major influential role in his aesthetics, the style and organization of his chief poetical works, and indeed, his outlook on the world. I suggest that when Blake calls himself a "sublime Artist" or speaks of "the Most Sublime Poetry," the adjective carries for him serious weight and meaning—meaning that is rewarding to explore. This exploration leads us on to larger questions: how, for example, does the concept of sublimity help to explain and justify the difficulties that Blake's writings continue to pose? How might it provide an intelligibly unified frame of reference for

---

[1] See, e.g., Thomas Weiskel, *The Romantic Sublime: Studies in the Structure and Psychology of Transcendence* (Baltimore: Johns Hopkins University Press, 1976); Harold Bloom, *Poetry and Repression: Revisionism from Blake to Stevens* (New Haven: Yale University Press, 1976); and Neil Hertz, *The End of the Line: Essays on Psychoanalysis and the Sublime* (New York: Columbia University Press, 1985).

certain features of the writings that are usually considered separately—for example, odd strategies of style and narrative construction, special patterns of imagery and symbolism, or insistent displays of arcane learning? What, finally, can Blake's understanding and use of the sublime tell us of his place in the larger discourse of eighteenth-century and Romantic aesthetics?

A problem of definition arises at the outset. The sublime is a term of ever-shifting reference, not only because of its varying usage by different writers of the period, but also because even for any given writer it can embrace so many different things. The sublime can mean a period style, a rhetorical strategy, a psychological experience, a quality of external phenomena, or a goal of transcendent spiritual attainment—and often we find no sharp distinctions separating these senses. These senses are, moreover, all intimately connected to one another: the psychological experience is usually necessary for the achievement of the spiritual goal, as is the aesthetic stimulus (whether artificial or natural) for the psychological experience, and a context of period conventions for recognizing the stimulating aesthetic signs as such. As Stephen K. Land has aptly stated, "the sublime is an elusive and fluid concept which cannot be confined to either the word or the mind or the world but which is somehow realized in the meeting of all three."[2] It is best, therefore, to consider the sublime not as a single conceptual entity capable of succinct definition, but rather as a field, like the force fields of physics—a region of indeterminate boundaries, in which cause-and-effect relations of all kinds conform to the bent of special operating conditions in a recurrent and recognizable way. And if the sublime is a field, then it is indeed a kind of "unified field," to continue the physics terminology, embracing art and nature, subject and object, matter and spirit; hence, it is a concept broad enough to serve as the basis of a sophisticated and serviceable poetics.

This study maintains that Blake indeed evolved a poetics based on the premises and strategies of the sublime, and that this poetics governed his aims and practices as a working poet. More than is commonly acknowledged, Blake shares with the mainstream of theory stemming from Longinus two central assumptions about the purpose and practical operation of the sublime mode: that it aims to produce a feeling of elevation or self-apotheosis, akin to a religious experience, and that it works dialectically through the intervention of an agency or "sublime object" that shatters expected human norms, posing against those norms something incommensurate, something that exceeds the grasp of our ordinary powers of apprehension and control. In eighteenth-century theorizing, this incommensurate element is diversely represented: it may manifest itself as a dif-

[2] *From Signs to Propositions: The Concept of Form in Eighteenth Century Semantic Theory* (London: Longman, 1974), 38.

ficult point of passage, as something hidden, as a barrier, an irresistible energy, a vacancy, a plenitude, a multiplicity, a vast uniformity, or a loss. The array of possibilities is broad enough to encompass the uniform, unbounded sublime of Addison, Burke's sublime of terror and obscurity, and Kant's sublime of sensory difficulty, to cite a few representative examples. Nor would it take a reader long to discover virtually all these agencies of sublime effect in Blake's works, reproduced either in the content or in the formal properties of the poetry and designs. The remarkable thing about Blake's relation to the sublime traditions of his age is not his distance from their main assumptions, tropes, and dialectical procedures of analysis, but rather the depth of his involvement in them.

Yet one must acknowledge that it is an uneasy involvement. As his poetry and designs persistently reveal, the inherited storehouse of eighteenth-century sublime effects amply supplies Blake's works with scenes and images of excess that his imagination cannot resist, but that his intellectual allegiances force him to repudiate. In particular, his persistent impulse to summon up dark settings, dire actions, and monstrous powers are marks of a taste closely associated with Burke's theory of the sublime, but clearly at odds with Blake's own radical humanism, which takes as an affront any manifestation of external power that diminishes man or curtails the clarity of human vision. While retaining notions of the sublime dynamic widely held by his contemporaries, such as the dialectical route to transcendence and the tense juxtaposition of norms and excess, Blake needs to find a pure ground for sublimity in his work, unsullied by antihumanistic stances. This ground must be constituted of everything that Burke's sublime is not; instead of obscurity, indefinite vastness, and threatening power, there must be determinacy, concentration, and intellectual play. It must provide an element of difficulty and awe without signaling man's impotence or his diminished state. As the present study shows, by the time Blake's career reaches its culmination in *Jerusalem*, this new scheme is well established, with an elaborated theoretical basis and an array of practical manifestations in the poetry and designs. Once established, however, Blake's alternative to the Burkean sublime gives to the latter a certain covert sanction, by making it safe for poetic articulation; its lurid grandeurs, to which his imagination remains attracted, need not lack voice if they can be presented as an antithetical negative, the object of a critique.

Blake's well-known quarrel with Burke, then, is also an internal debate, enacted within the arena of the poet's own works. If one major theme of this book is to show how much common ground Blake shares with his contemporaries in their construct of the sublime, a second is to establish, as his special contribution to the construct, a theory founded on ideals of determinacy and concentrated precision, formulated in deliberate opposition to prevailing Burkean views, yet sharing several cognate features with them. As a result, I would argue, sublimity never manifests itself in Blake's writings as an amorphous body of vague concepts and conventional terms, but rather resolves itself into two strongly delineated and differentiated sublimes. As a poet, Blake entertains both sublimes even as he prefers one, and their ongoing debate in his poetry has far-reaching effects on specific features of its style, organization, images, and motifs. The interplay of these two modes of sublimity forms a running motif of this book, linking the subjects of the work's three main divisions.

These divisions consider Blake's relation to the sublime from three related perspectives: theoretical, stylistic, and thematic. The first section of the book, "Theory," introduces some key terms of Blake's diction, and then deals specifically with his explicit opinions on the sublime as expressed in letters, marginalia, and other expository prose (with some occasional glances at references in the poetry). Blake's observations on the subject are here consolidated and set against the background of opinion in his age to show where he is one with it (as in his requirement of a mechanism of difficulty or sensory discontinuity for the sublime effect) and where he is original (as in developing a sublime of determinate signifiers in which the text itself functions as the sublime object). The second section, "Style," turns to Blake's poetry itself and shows how the interplay of the two sublime modes reconstitutes itself on the stylistic level, giving rise to what I call a "bardic" style and an "iconic" style. The first is characterized by devices appropriate to temporal chronicle and to the achievement of effects of flux, boundlessness, and indefinite extension. The second, which is hieratic, incantatory, and self-enclosed, tends, in contrast, to arrest narrative and to collapse temporality into a hard-edged "now" of intellectual intensity. In the conclusion to this section of the book, I examine how the clashes of these alternative stylistic modes, in their various permutations, significantly determine the chief forms of narrative organization found in Blake's major sublime poems. The third section of the book, "Worldview," marks the juncture of Blake's specific stylistic gestures, such as his choice of imagery, with his larger thematic interests. It takes as its basis Blake's poetic use of stock imagery of the literary sublime, particularly those classes of images that make up a background setting—images of natural grandeur and catastrophe, ruins, architectural splendors, the scene of the North, and the like—and shows that his view of the external world, the workings of the Creation that these images of setting mirror in their sum, is shaped by the same sublime dynamic (including the antagonistic play of the two sublimes) that informs his aesthetics. I suggest further that certain strands of thought that attracted Blake's interest and are reflected in his poetic settings—such as eighteenth-century natural philosophy, the speculations of mythographers on the dispersal of ancient nations, and various kinds of hermetic or quasi-Kabbalistic traditions promoting a hieroglyphic conception of reality—are most readily perceived as an imaginative unity when their mechanisms are seen as displacements of thinking in the sublime mode.

The argument of this book, as the reader may have already gathered, advances less in a linear than in a kind of spiral fashion: its range of reference outwardly expands as it proceeds from aesthetic ideas, narrowly defined, to works, to worldview—but in its progress, it deliberately rounds again and again on certain key ideas (such as the confrontation of the normal and the incommensurate or excessive, the recovery of origins at the moment of sublime exaltation, and the dialectic play of the two sublimes), observing them at each new encounter in a changed and widened context. I have chosen this schematic and achronological method of exposition for the sake of a comprehensive and integrated overview. Eventually a series of commentaries on individual works, showing how Blake's principles of sublimity operate in his practice as it develops over time, could form a useful complement to this study, but such a project, I believe, would be a premature undertaking when the principles themselves are yet to be established—a full task in itself, as I have found. Even so, my approach has not precluded close attention to many individual passages of poetry, and I have devoted some consideration to entire works (especially in the discussion of narrative structure in Chapter IV). Local particularities are thus respected, even if my mainly synchronic organization means the sacrifice of a detailed tracing of changes, nuances, and fluctuations in Blake's ideas of the sublime and their poetic application. As useful as such an inquiry might be, I have preferred, however, an exposition that emphasizes, in Blake's handling of the sublime, the broad consistencies rather than the local variations. (By "consistency" I of course do not mean uniform simplicity; in Blake's case, it is the persistent continuity of a complex dialectic of ideas and poetic strategies.) This emphasis is appropriate if only because the consistencies are genuine and central to the nature of his work. There is a larger context, moreover, that is best explored by considering that work synchronically: the context of the age and the discourse on sublimity that it perpetuated. Within this context, Blake's career as a sublime poet and theorist looks more like a single unified moment than a line of temporal changes—an inclusive moment reflecting and responding to key elements in a whole century's aesthetic ideals.

The sublime discourse of the age is of course a weave of many different voices, often at variance with one another, yet generally forming a recognizable pattern of concerns. I have tried to make room for these voices in this book by quoting liberally from other works of the period, both discursive and imaginative, that help set the context for Blake's sublime. These are offered as a representative sampling rather than an exhaustive survey of the background scene. Although no special claims are made for their direct influence on Blake, I have generally restricted these selections to works in English (including translations) that he could conceivably have read (the use of Kant in Chapter I, included for his heuristic value, is a notable exception). I have of course been alert to evidences of influence where they seem to present themselves. Burke in particular gets special and repeated attention, since he is not only the one writer on the sublime whom we know that Blake read early and attentively, but also the chief goad to Blake's formulation of a countertheory. If my choice of texts seems heavily weighted in favor of examples from the eighteenth century and the first decade of the nineteenth, this is because it is an important part of my purpose to show Blake's handling of the sublime as a response to an *immediate* aesthetic context—that is, as the response of a conscious practitioner in a living, developing mode.

One unavoidable consequence of this choice is that such giants of sublime literature as the Bible, Milton, and Shakespeare play a smaller role in my study than their undoubtedly vast influence on Blake might seem to warrant. If they are giants, however, they are giants before the flood—the flood of aesthetic self-consciousness, of the awareness of the sublime as a named thing, a describable mechanism, that set in with Boileau's translation of Longinus in 1674 and continued through the rest of the succeeding century, making it impossible for any post-Miltonic poet with pretensions to sublimity to proceed with critical naiveté.[3] Milton's influence is like a universal atmosphere, felt everywhere and hence not readily subjected to a narrow analytical account. In contrast, figures such as Gray and Macpherson, while no Miltons, lay a special claim on our interest as poets of a programmatic literary movement, and their works self-consciously derive from and contribute to a theoretical discourse, as do Blake's. Blake indeed holds a special place in this movement, even if it went unrecognized by his contemporaries; he is the authentic strong Bard of the eighteenth-century sublime. Gray and Collins yearned for such a figure to succeed the giants of the past and despaired of his arrival; Macpherson and Chatterton needed this Bard so desperately that they took to manufacturing him; in Blake this desired figure is realized, and his career represents the first flowering of the sublime aesthetic into major poetry. That in itself is sufficient

---

[3] In his still-essential study of the sublime, Samuel H. Monk points out that although Milton was casually aware of Longinus (editions of the *Peri Hupsous* printed in England were available from 1636 onward), he revealed no sign of responsiveness to those emphases on grandeur and transports that gave the treatise its later fame: "It is a strange paradox that the most sublime of English poets should not have caught from Longinus the suggestion of the sublime as the expression of ultimate values in art. . . . He did not; and it was left to the propounders of an adolescent aesthetic in the next century to find in John Milton's poems . . . the supreme illustration of whatever particular type of sublime they advocated" (*The Sublime: A Study of Critical Theories in XVIII-Century England* [New York: Modern Language Association, 1935], 20).

reason for a study such as this to localize the context of comparison to the age out of which his achievement grew.

In emphasizing the importance of historical context here, I do not mean to suggest that this study is to be an old-fashioned survey of sources and analogues or an intellectually neutral foray into the history of ideas. It is intended as a work of criticism, with Blake always as the point of focus, and I have written it with the recognition that any interpretation of past systems of thought—especially a system so loosely organized as the theory of the sublime—must be to some extent a critical reconstruction. This is *a fortiori* the case with Blake's version of the theory, which exists not in any systematic account but rather in a series of disconnected utterances. Criticism needs informed period-based contexts to avoid reproducing formal analyses in a vacuum—"unprolific, self-closd, all-repelling" (*BU* 3.2–3)— as well as to curb the unchecked imposition of purely modern notions on old texts. Nonetheless, even these past contexts must be represented in formulations of our own choosing, and this choice is always problematic. In general, I have been content to describe the assumptions and goals of Blake's aesthetic project in the terms of an expansive, idealized subjectivity that he and many other writers in the sublime tradition would have found familiar—terms belonging, in short, to what Jerome J. McGann has skeptically called "Romanticism's own self-representations."[4] I am certainly aware that the sublime ideology is a historically situated phenomenon like any other and that, as a rampantly idealizing mode, it has rendered itself a particularly inviting target of critique by various demystifying systems of present-day analysis. In what is, however, the first extensive study of Blake's connections with the sublime tradition, in which the primary goal is an alignment of bodies of texts (the poet's and the tradition's) not usually considered in the same context, a more conservative approach seems to me advisable—one in which the parties to be introduced to one another are presented in terms at least recognizable to themselves.

At the same time, one must acknowledge that one's perception of these terms is itself historically situated, and that the critic cannot evade the pressures of his own moment. If, for example, the present work reveals more preoccupation with such topics as language and textuality, discontinuity, indeterminacy, and the regress of origins than one would have found in Monk's landmark study of the sublime more than half a century ago, then the preoccupations of the recent critical past obviously bear some responsibility. These preoccupations have not dictated my approach but they have sensitized me to elements present in eighteenth-century theories of the sublime that would have been, at best, subsidiary to Monk, given his

[4] See *The Romantic Ideology: A Critical Investigation* (Chicago: University of Chicago Press, 1983), 1.

own critical context. The insights afforded by applying contemporary critical concerns to an older body of thought cut both ways, of course. One thing this study implicitly reveals is how much the terminology of recent schools of criticism, with its imagery of blocks, gaps, abysses, labyrinths, postponements, and the like, forms a belated sublime rhetoric, hinting at its intellectual roots in the same strands of post-Enlightenment dialectical thought that gave rise to theories of the sublime. These theories were initially developed in order to come to terms with the difficult, the indeterminate, the incommensurate, and the dialectical elements of aesthetic experience, and there is less anachronism than one might initially imagine in attributing certain kinds of critical understanding characteristic of the poststructuralist era to Blake's sensibility and the tendencies of the tradition in which he works.

To conclude these preliminary observations, some words about the "Words" of my title may be in order. For my purposes, "Words of Eternity" can mean either words *about* sublime objects and ultimate things, or words that function *as* sublime objects and as thresholds to ultimate things—but in any case, they are words. As my references in this introduction to poets and poetics must have indicated by now, this is a study focused on Blake's poetry, not on his visual art. It has become so customary in recent Blake criticism to consider the poetry and the designs as artistically inseparable that any decision to concentrate on only one medium of his work calls for some explanatory comment. It should be clear, of course, that no absolute separation of treatment is possible. First of all, most of Blake's ideas on the sublime apply equally to poetry and visual art, and I therefore have not hesitated to treat statements pertaining to a visual context (the annotations to Reynolds's *Discourses*, for example) as relevant to the poetic. Moreover, there are points in his work at which the two media intersect so inextricably, at which language takes on so many of the attributes of spatial form, and visual images seem so much an extension of words, that it becomes impossible to discuss the verbal medium without discussing the pictorial. Blake's designs also provide at times a marvelous diagrammatic shorthand for discursive concepts and thematic patterns, and where it has seemed appropriate I have gladly invoked such designs as illustrations to my argument. But, on the whole, there are good reasons for separate studies of the two media as sublime modes. There is, of course, a Blakean sublime in visual art, with debts to contemporaries such as Fuseli and great ancestors such as Michelangelo (to name but two out of a legion of influences). This tradition runs a distinct course from the history and theory of the poetic sublime; each has its own special vocabulary, its own characteristic iconography (the nude, for example, can often be a sublime image in art, but is rarely so in poetry), its own leading figures, and its own particular operative devices that often lack equivalents in the other medium. The Blakean visual sublime is rich enough in itself, and draws on a sufficiently full background to deserve its own study, uncomplicated by a divided focus.

The same may be said of Blake's poetic sublime, which, I think it is safe to assert, would remain one of the great achievements of English letters even if its creator had never drawn a picture in his life. If my critical predilections and qualifications lead me to a study of the poetry, these inducements are strengthened by a concern that the poetic rather than the visual component of his composite art is in greater need of emphasis at this stage of Blake criticism. A formalism of the New Critical period that neglected Blake's major achievements, an evangelical humanism of the 1960s and 1970s that exalted these achievements but neglected poetic technique in favor of thematic commentary, and a more recent proliferation of ground-breaking studies oriented toward the concerns of art history have all contributed to this need. Despite what is now some forty years of intense critical interest in Blake, the elaboration of a Blakean poetics remains an incomplete project. If they can contribute to bringing this project closer to fruition, then the words of this book, though scarcely "of Eternity" themselves, will have their fit place in the ongoing discourse of Blake studies.

PART ONE

THEORY

Chapter I

BLAKE'S CONCEPT OF THE SUBLIME

SUBLIME WONDER: THE MOMENT OF ASTONISHMENT

> Terrified at the sublime Wonder, Los stood before his Furnaces.
> And they stood around, terrified with admiration at Erins Spaces
> For the Spaces reachd from the starry heighth, to the starry depth.
>
> *(J 12.21–23)*

IT IS NOT consistently easy to know what Blake means when he speaks of the sublime. The term appears often enough in his work (as either adjective or noun), although not always in clarifying contexts. Yet it turns up prominently on those occasions when he seems most profoundly stirred to define and explain the principles of his own craft—such as the passage in the *Descriptive Catalogue* in which he declares himself to be a "sublime Artist" (E 544); or when, writing to Butts about his newly finished "Grand Poem," he offers his "Definition of the Most Sublime Poetry" (E 730); or in his annotations to Reynolds's *Discourses*, where he specifies the conditions that establish the "Foundation of the Sublime" (E 647); or when he begins an early version of the first plate of *Jerusalem* with comments on the separation of the sublime and the pathetic. Although Blake offers no systematic theory of the sublime such as we find in Burke or Kant or even in the incipiently theoretical writings of, say, Addison or John Dennis, we should not therefore assume that he lacks a cogent and complex idea of the subject. Like any developed body of thought, Blake's concept of the sublime arises out of a historical context of competing concepts—which, in an ongoing dialogic process, it assimilates, contests, modifies, or completes. We are certain that Blake read Burke's *Philosophical Enquiry into . . . the Sublime and Beautiful*, and there is a strong likelihood that he was familiar with contributions to the developing theory of the sublime made by such writers as Dennis, Addison, Hugh Blair, and Robert Lowth. Even where influence is not specifically demonstrable, it remains a simple matter to observe how thoroughly suppositions about sublimity general to his age pervade his own ideas and creative work.

The passage in *Jerusalem* quoted above is a case in point. It encapsulates a Burkean scenario, and in it several crucial terms in eighteenth-century discussions of sublimity gel. Los and other observers catch sight of something exceedingly vast, perceiving it less as an object than as an affect (a "Wonder"). The sight is both uplifting (sublime) and terrifying, and part of the terror is directed toward the observers' own powerful response of awe ("admiration," the Latinate cognate of "wonder"). The outer vastness somehow modulates into an inner power, mediated by a feeling labeled "terror" (but mixed up with awed surprise and uplift) that attaches itself to both the outer and the inner state. Here is an exemplary instance of what Thomas Weiskel, codifying a scheme out of the speculations of Burke, Kant, and Wordsworth, has termed "the sublime moment," a threefold episode of consciousness, in which a state of radical disequilibrium intervenes between a prior state of ordinary awareness and a final state of transcendent exaltation.[1]

In eighteenth-century parlance, the favorite technical term for this state of disequilibrium is "astonishment." Burke begins the second part of his *Philosophical Enquiry*, an analysis of the sublime proper, with a definition of this term:

> The passion caused by the great and sublime in *nature*, when those causes operate most powerfully, is Astonishment; and astonishment is that state of the soul, in which all its motions are suspended, with some degree of horror. In this case the mind is so entirely filled with its object, that it cannot entertain any other, nor by consequence reason on that object which employs it. Hence arises the great power of the sublime, that far from being produced by them, it anticipates our reasonings, and hurries us on by an irresistible force.[2]

Writers throughout the century refer to astonishment in similar terms.[3] But however much these formulas are repeated, perplexities abound. The psychological state itself seems curiously resistant to straightforward discursive explanation, as Burke's own highly figurative language demon-

---

[1] See Thomas Weiskel, *The Romantic Sublime*, 11 and 23–24. Morton D. Paley notes elements of the Burkean sublime in the "sublime Wonder" passage of Jerusalem, in *The Continuing City: William Blake's "Jerusalem"* (Oxford: Clarendon Press, 1983), 61.

[2] Edmund Burke, *A Philosophical Enquiry into the Origin of our Ideas of the Sublime and Beautiful*, ed. J. T. Boulton (London: Routledge and Kegan Paul, 1958), 57.

[3] Addison, for example, tells us that "our imagination loves to be filled with an object, or to grasp at anything that is too big for its capacity. We are flung into a pleasing astonishment at such unbounded views"; according to Johnson, "[The sublime is] that comprehension and expanse of thought which at once fills the whole mind, and of which the first effect is sudden astonishment, and the second rational admiration." Here is a sampling of similar contemporary opinions: "The sublime . . . takes possession of our attention, and of all our faculties, and absorbs them in astonishment"; "[the sublime] imports such ideas presented to the mind, as raise it to an uncommon degree of elevation, and fill it with admiration and astonishment"; "objects exciting terror are . . . in general sublime; for terror always implies astonishment, occupies the whole soul, and suspends all its motions." See, respectively, *Works of Joseph Ad-*

strates. There is a marked ambiguity in the play of these figures. At the moment of astonishment, when the power of the sublime manifests itself, the mind becomes utterly open to the influx of what it beholds ("filled with its object"), and yet this flood of power into the mind produces no kinetic transfer of energy to the mind's faculties, but rather the reverse—a suspension of internal motion, a total arrest. At first appearing entirely permeable, the mind instantly becomes impenetrable, like a container packed to the choking point ("so entirely filled with its object, that it cannot entertain any other"). The mind is quite stopped ("suspended"), only to be "hurried"; its internal density becomes crushing, and yet finally it is easily carried along. "Astonishment," then, cannot be described so much as circumscribed by a ring of mutually canceling figures such as motion/arrest, penetration/resistance, heaviness/lightness. The figures are drawn from physical mechanics, but they compose no mechanics that Newton would recognize. Here the continuum of cause and effect breaks down; outward forces have unpredictable inward consequences. As Burke presents it, "astonishment" marks the intervention of sharp discontinuities in the spheres of both nature and mind: nature suddenly manifests itself in so overwhelming a fashion that <u>normal relations of subject and object are abolished</u>; at the same time, the mind loses its consistency of operation and becomes a thing of paradox, of self-contradictory extremes.

The "terror" that Los feels at the "sublime Wonder" of Erin's Spaces is probably not any sort of conventional fear, but rather a form of astonishment. Blake displays a surprisingly persistent allegiance to Burkean conceptions and diction, revealed in his willingness to link sublime wonder with terror,[4] and in his attachment to the term *astonishment* and its variant

---

dison, 6 vols. (London: T. Cadell and W. Davies, 1811), vol. 4, 340; Samuel Johnson, "The Life of Cowley," *Lives of the English Poets*, ed. George Birkbeck Hill, 3 vols. (Oxford: Clarendon Press, 1905; reprint, New York: Octagon Books, 1967), vol. 1, 20–21; James Usher, *Clio: Or, a Discourse on Taste*, 2d ed. (London: T. Davies, 1769), 102; Hugh Blair, "A Critical Dissertation on the Poems of Ossian," in *The Poems of Ossian*, trans. James Macpherson, 2 vols. (London: W. Strahan and T. Cadell, 1773), vol. 2, 422; and Alexander Gerard, *An Essay on Taste* (London: A. Millar, 1759), 19.

[4] It is worth recalling Burke's well-known formulation here: "whatever is in any sort terrible, or is conversant about terrible objects, or operates in a manner analogous to terror, is a source of the *sublime*; that is, it is productive of the strongest emotion which the mind is capable of feeling" (*Philosophical Enquiry*, 39). Just as Burke's sublime rides on an aesthetics of darkness and deprivation, pain and terror, so in Blake's vocabulary *dark* prevails numerically over *light*, *night* over *day*, *death* over *life*. More notably, the word *terror(s)* and its co-derivatives *terrible*, *terrific*, and *terrified*, taken as a collectivity, would rank within the dozen most frequently used words in his concorded vocabulary (David V. Erdman's *Concordance to the Writings of William Blake* [Ithaca: Cornell University Press, 1967] records a total of 393 appearances of these terms). Despite his stated aversion to Burke, Blake so closely associates the sublime with the terrific that the terminology of the latter often acquires an honorific luster in his work. Thus we have such phrases as "Terrified at the sublime Wonder," cited

forms. Terror and astonishment are kindred states, as Burke makes clear in an etymological aside: "The Romans used the verb *stupeo*, a term which strongly marks the state of an astonished mind, to express the effect either of simple fear, or of astonishment; the word *attonitus*, (thunderstruck) is equally expressive of the alliance of these ideas; and do not the french *étonnement* and the english *astonishment* and *amazement*, point out as clearly the kindred emotions which attend fear and wonder?"[5] Being struck by lightning is literally a form of astonishment, for etymologically the word means "thunderstruck." Perhaps the prestige of the term "astonishment" in eighteenth-century aesthetics derives ultimately from Longinus, who tells us that "the Sublime, when seasonably addressed, with the rapid force of Lightning has born down all before it, and shewn at one stroke the compacted Might of Genius."[6] The two metaphors that Longinus employs here for the onset of the sublime, the stroke of natural lightning and the blow of intellectual power, imply a hidden and prior third, one that connects the forces of nature to the forces of mind. This mediating figure is of course that of a divine being, like the Jove and Jehovah of myth and scripture, at once the author of both natural thunder and human inspiration. Hence, the word *astonishment* encompasses two contradictory aspects of the sublime that shall remain with us throughout this study; it immobilizes or releases, destroys or raises up. One is either struck by the divine power and "hurried" on to participate in its glories, or one is struck dead as a stone.

Blake uses the term *astonishment* more frequently than any other major poet in the period from 1660 to 1830,[7] but always with careful discrimination. Extraordinarily sensitive to the possibilities of wordplay,[8] he is quick to see the "stone" in *astonishment*,[9] a word that could thus easily

---

previously (the Spaces of Erin are beautiful to Los—see *J* 11.8–15), "terrible Blake in his pride" ("When Klopstock England defied," line 2), an uncharacteristically affectionate Enitharmon's "Lovely terrible Los wonder of Eternity" (*FZ* 90.15), the "terrors of friendship" (*J* 45.4), and the "terrific Lions & Tygers" that "sport & play" before the Great Harvest at the end of *Milton* (*M* 42.38). In these instances *terror* loses most of its terrors, and one gets the sense that in such cases Blake is paying tribute less to the signified *feeling* of terror than to the signifier, a vocabulary of the sublime fondly preserved from the fashions of his youth.

[5] *Philosophical Enquiry*, 58.

[6] Dionysius Longinus, *Essay on the Sublime*, trans. William Smith (London, 1756), 3.

[7] There are fifty-one uses of terms from the collectivity *astonish(ed)(es)(ing)(ment)* in Blake's poetry. Among poets of comparable stature, range, and sublime interests, Milton's poetry yields only six instances; Wordsworth's, seventeen; and Shelley's, eleven. Pope draws upon this cluster of terms sixteen times, almost entirely for his translations of Homer, and Dryden, eleven times, mostly for the *Aeneid*.

[8] See Nelson Hilton, *Literal Imagination: Blake's Vision of Words* (Berkeley and Los Angeles: University of California Press, 1983), 16–17, and especially 239–57.

[9] This connection is reinforced by the older sense of *astonished* (or its variant *astonied*) to connote deathlike paralysis and insensibility; thus the *OED* on *astonied*: "Stunned; made in-

encompass the whole program of Urizen, armed with "his ten thousands of thunders" (*BU* 3.28), to bring about a "solid without fluctuation," "a wide world of solid obstruction" (*BU* 4.11, 23). Hence to experience astonishment means, in one sense, to turn to stone, to be "filled," as Burke would say, with the inducing power—and filled solid. Thus in *Urizen*, "Wonder, awe, fear, astonishment, / Petrify the eternal myriads" (*BU* 18.13–14). Since it is the fate of overweening deities in Blake to be struck by their own thunder, as soon as Urizen manifests himself in all his pride, he is struck down and stunned (from *étonnement*) into "*a stony* sleep" (*BU* 6.7) or, elsewhere, into "*a stoned* stupor" (*FZ* 52.20). The moment of astonishment is, then, the moment *par excellence* when, in Blake's famous formula, one becomes what one beholds. Beholding Urizen's stony sleep, mentioned previously, Los is "smitten with astonishment" (*BU* 8.1). But whose astonishment is alluded to here? Los's own or that of Urizen, whom he beholds lying stunned? There is no meaningful way of sorting out distinctions of this nature. Astonishment astonishes, and the petrified petrifies. Thus in *Jerusalem*, seeking the Minute Particulars, Los is again "astonishd he beheld only the petrified surfaces" (*J* 46.5); two lines earlier, we read that "Los was all astonishment & terror: he trembled sitting on the Stone." Los is now filled with his stony object and is *all* astonishment; we see all as stone in these regions. From becoming all astonishment it is easy to become a thing that *causes* astonishment, as in Los's statement, "I now am what I am: a horror and an astonishment" (*J* 8.18). The abstract noun becomes a stony particular, substituting itself for an individuality now petrified and soon to petrify others.

But as there is a thunder that immobilizes and petrifies, there is also a thunder that cracks open the stones, releasing our buried powers to freedom, a "crack of doom" for a sullen old dispensation. In contrast to the "inarticulate thunder" that Urizen booms at his misshapen children in *Vala* (*FZ* 70.39), we have the articulate thunder of that true God who "To Man the wond'rous art of writing gave," and who "speaks in thunder and in fire! / Thunder of Thought, & flames of fierce desire" (*J* 3.4–6). There is also the awakened Albion, "Loud thundring, with broad flashes of flaming lightning & pillars / Of fire, speaking the Words of Eternity in Human Forms" (*J* 95.8–9). And there are the Zoas, fraternal at last, who "conversed together in Visionary forms dramatic which bright / Redounded from their Tongues in thunderous majesty" (*J* 98.28–29). In contrast to the obliterating power of the Urizenic thunder, the power of this thunder resides in its incisive capacity to clarify and reveal. It does not stun with an

sensible, benumbed, paralyzed (1611)"; cf. also Milton on Satan's legions, who "lie thus astonisht on th' oblivious Pool" (*Paradise Lost* 1.266, in John Milton, *Complete Poems and Major Prose*, ed. Merritt Y. Hughes [New York: Odyssey Press, 1957]; further citations of *Paradise Lost* are incorporated in my text and abbreviated as *PL*).

avalanche of sound, but rather cleaves through darkness and obstruction, employing as its cutting tools those instruments that inscribe the definite lines of Blake's "writing," "Words", and "Forms."

It follows that the "astonishment" produced by this clarifying thunder encompasses the moment when surfaces and opacities are burst to reveal an infinite potential within. Thus, when Eno in *The Four Zoas* "took an atom of space & opend its center / Into Infinitude & ornamented it with wondrous art / Astonishd sat her Sisters of Beulah to see her soft affections" (*FZ* 9.12–14). A similar response to visionary revelation appears in Blake's ecstatic report of his first days at Felpham:

> In particles bright
> The jewels of Light
> Distinct shone & clear—
> Amazd & in fear
> I each particle gazed
> Astonishd Amazed
> For each was a Man
> Human formd.
>
> (Letter to Butts, 2 October 1800, lines 15–22, E 712)

If visions of nature humanized bring astonishment, then so too do the recognition and recovery of unfallen portions of humanity within the self: "Los embracd the Spectre first as a brother / Then as another Self; astonishd humanizing & in tears" (*FZ* 85.29–30).

Images of barriers broken, of visions glimpsed through sudden openings, of obdurate forms melting down and flowing together, attend this form of astonishment: "Then Los said I behold the Divine Vision thro the broken Gates / Of thy poor broken heart astonishd melted into Compassion & Love" (*FZ* 99.15–16). Finally, in the single instance in Blake's poetry where astonishment is modified by the adjective *sublime*, Jerusalem recalls ancient days before Albion's dreadful separation: "I taught the ships of the sea to sing the songs of Zion. / Italy saw me, in sublime astonishment: France was wholly mine" (*J* 79.38–39). The response of the nations embraces the full paradox of the sublime moment; arrest is freedom here, for to be filled with the object, is, in this case to be filled with a being who is "called Liberty among the Children of Albion" (*J* 54.5).

Blake's wide-ranging use of the term *astonishment* provides a good index of his understanding of the problematic dynamics of the eighteenth-century sublime. Not only does astonishment occupy a gap between polarized states of experience, but it also unfolds within itself alternate destinies of the sublime moment. Two possible sublimes quiver in the indeterminacy of the moment of astonishment: one, the sublime of terror and deprivation most closely associated with Burke, and the other, a sublime of desire and plenitude. Blake's imagination is repeatedly drawn to the Burkean sublime, but he appears skeptical that it can serve as a mode of genuine elevation and access to a liberating power. Burke would have us believe that the moment of disequilibrium, suspension of faculties, and immobilization of will arises from the access of an overwhelming external power or magnitude. Blake reads such scenes otherwise: encountering "terrific" objects, his protagonists reel not at a magnitude of power made present, but rather at the magnitude of power lost, at the degree of petrifaction revealed in so-called powers by the time they present themselves as natural "terrors."

Blake seeks a less melancholy sublime, and if as a poet he is to gratify desire and recover plenitude, he must attempt some sort of redemption of astonishment. As his own usage of the term clearly indicates, he has no intention of abandoning the drama, the clash of oppositions, and the suspense inherent in Burke's account. Blake is willing to exploit Burke's evocations of giddiness and irresistible rush since they so easily consort with his own imagery of centers opening up, gates broken down, and forms melting. There is a need, however, to relocate the scene of this drama, away from a point of humiliating encounter between the experiencing mind and some thunderous externality. As Blake's own notions of the sublime become more fully articulated, the encounter is seen to take place between a lesser and a greater faculty of the mind, made manifest through the mediation of the poetic text. Blake not only represents scenes of astonishment in his work, but also seeks to create fresh moments of astonishment in the encounter of poem and reader, offering a petrific text to stony understandings and a field of openings for the receptive. The space of the poem itself becomes the site of sublime wonder.

"THE MOST SUBLIME POETRY": CORPOREAL LIMITS AND MENTAL INFINITIES

Blake uses the phrase *sublime poetry* only once in his writings, but it is on a momentous occasion. In the famous letter to Thomas Butts of 6 July 1803, he defines his idea of "the Most Sublime Poetry," asserts his highest literary aspirations, and announces the completion of "the Grandest Poem that This World Contains." The letter is, by any standard, the *locus classicus* for any extended consideration of Blake's idea of the sublime. Its central passage is justly familiar:

> Thus I hope that all our three years trouble Ends in Good Luck at last & shall be forgot by my affections & only rememberd by my Understanding to be a Memento in time to come & to speak to future generations by a Sublime Allegory which is now perfectly completed into a Grand Poem. I may praise it since I dare

not pretend to be any other than the Secretary the Authors are in Eternity I consider it as the Grandest Poem that This World Contains. Allegory addressd to the Intellectual powers while it is altogether hidden from the Corporeal Understanding is My Definition of the Most Sublime Poetry. it is also somewhat in the same manner defind by Plato. (E 730)

Several of the key terms in this passage are problematic, *Allegory* perhaps the most conspicuously so, if the attention it has received from Blake's critics is indicative. But we are not likely to understand what Blake means here by Allegory unless we have come to understand the meaning of the twice-repeated word *sublime*. Is it merely a vague term of superlative praise, or does it have technical and theoretical specificity? If the latter is true, what is the theoretical import of making the definition of "the Most Sublime Poetry" turn on the issue of reception? In particular, why is a division in the audience or faculties of reception a necessary condition for sublimity? And what does concealment (the "altogether hidden") have to do with this division?

As he writes to Butts, Blake is of course much preoccupied with Hayley's response to the "Grand Poem," probably an early version of *Milton*. It is undoubtedly gratifying to Blake's self-esteem to find in Hayley's incomprehension, or "Genteel Ignorance" (E 730) as he calls it, evidence of the poem's authorship in Eternity. In an earlier letter, Blake had made a similar response to objections of the benighted Dr. Trusler: "You say that I want somebody to Elucidate my Ideas. But you ought to know that What is Grand is necessarily obscure to Weak men. That which can be made Explicit to the Idiot is not worth my care The wisest of the Ancients considerd what is not too Explicit as the fittest for Instruction because it rouzes the faculties to act. I name Moses Solomon Esop Homer Plato" (E 702) In the letter to Butts, however, distinctions among classes of men—the weak and the strong, ignorant and wise, idiots and geniuses—are not at issue. The Corporeal Understanding and the Intellectual Powers are faculties within any mind, and not designations for the minds of different persons. Blake strives not to separate the elite from the vulgar as social groups, but rather to uncover the intellectual gifts that we all potentially possess. This is to be done by presenting to the mind artifacts that sift it, separating out the dull from the bright, the stony from the buoyant, so that what is imaginative and visionary within us can outwardly manifest itself. The sublime poem, then, is a thing that can effect a sharp division of the mind into two faculties of opposing capacities. The term *sublime* is precisely appropriate here, for a similar act of division is central to every sophisticated theory of sublimity in Blake's period.

Within the tripartite structure of the sublime moment, discussed earlier, a hiatus of indeterminacy or discontinuity divides a prior moment of normal consciousness from a subsequent moment of idealized restoration or elevation. But it appears that the indeterminacy of the central hiatus is itself the product of a nascent division of emotions and faculties. In Burke, the dichotomy is one of pain and fear on one hand and "delight" on the other, the delight arising from a secondary recognition of our actual safe remove from the sources of apparent pain.[10] Dr. Johnson's sequential formulation is similar: "the first effect [of the sublime encounter] is sudden astonishment, and the second rational admiration."[11] But astonishment itself, as we have seen from Blake's own usage, tends to divide into a phase of incapacity and paralysis, and a phase of momentum and revelation. When the visionary aesthetician James Usher tells us that the passion that the sublime "inspires us with is evidently a mixture of terror, curiosity, and exultation,"[12] we recognize a tripartite structure opening up; the first phase is attached to incapacity and repulsion, the last to the attained height of the sublime proper, and the middle is an indeterminate state of attraction toward the object (and therefore the antithesis of terror), without a fully acquired comprehension of it. In short, within the moment of astonishment are born two states of mind—one that wants to go forward and one that wants to hold back. In more drastic versions of this dialectic, the second state is one that is *held back* whether it wants to go forward or not. In these versions, the division of the mind falls into two unequally privileged faculties—one consigned to pain and deprivation, the other admitted to an exalted sphere of delight.

This division of powers entered the discourse of the sublime as a scene of theophany, in which the unequally privileged powers are those of God and man in confrontation. One of the clearest expressions of this confrontation comes from the Hebraist Robert Lowth, in his *Lectures on the Sacred Poetry of the Hebrews*. Speaking of a description of God's attributes in the Psalms, he comments:

> Here the human mind is absorbed, overwhelmed as it were in a boundless vortex, and studies in vain for an expedient to extricate itself. But the greatness of the subject may be justly estimated by its difficulty; and while the imagination labours to comprehend what is beyond its powers, this very labour itself, and these ineffectual endeavours, sufficiently demonstrate the immensity and sublimity of the object. . . . Here the mind seems to exert its utmost faculties in vain to grasp an object, whose unparalleled magnitude mocks its feeble endeavours.[13]

[10] See Burke, *Philosophical Enquiry*, 37 and 40.

[11] *Lives of the English Poets* vol. 1, 21.

[12] *Clio*, 102.

[13] Robert Lowth, *Lectures on the Sacred Poetry of the Hebrews*, trans. G. Gregory, 2 vols. (London: J. Johnson, 1787), vol. 1, 353.

This passage revels in the language of human abasement, as Lowth stretches himself to find terms sufficient to express how overwhelmed, vain, incapacitated, ineffectual, enfeebled, and mocked our condition is when compared to God's. Burke abbreviates and intensifies the same scenario, stating that when we contemplate the attributes of God, "we shrink into the minuteness of our own nature, and are, in a manner, annihilated before him,"[14] and this language of humiliation becomes part of the standard idiom of the sublime.[15]

In certain more sophisticated theories of the sublime, this drama of unequal outward confrontation moves inward, with one part of the mind taking on the role of incapacitated humanity while another is substituted in the position of God. Wordsworthians are intimately familiar with that moment in *The Prelude*, Book VI, when the poet, "halted, without an effort to break through" records the failure of the "light of sense," while simultaneously Imagination, "that awful Power," rises up to reveal its home in infinitude.[16] The most radical formulation of this separation of faculties, one curtailed in powers, the other unrestricted, appears in Kant's *Critique of Judgment,* in his discussion of the sublime of magnitude: "The feeling of the Sublime is therefore a feeling of pain, arising from the want of accordance between the aesthetical estimation of magnitude formed by the Imagination and the estimation of the same formed by Reason. There is at the same time a pleasure thus excited, arising from the correspondence with Rational Ideas of this very judgment of the inadequacy of our greatest faculty of Sense."[17] For Kant, an intuitive comprehension of the infinite is "altogether hidden," as Blake would say, from the Imagination, the "greatest faculty of sense"—but it is precisely this inaccessibility that provokes the mind to recognize its possession of transcendent powers that can so intuit: "that magnitude of a natural object, on which the Imagination fruitlessly spends its whole faculty of comprehension, must carry our concept

---

[14] *Philosophical Enquiry*, 68.

[15] Thus Usher remarks in *Clio* that the more violent manifestations of nature cause in us "an humiliating awe, surprise, and suspense: the mind views the effects of boundless power with still amazement" (111). Decades later, in his ms. treatise "The Sublime and the Beautiful," Wordsworth speaks in similar fashion of "a humiliation or prostration of the mind before some external agency which it presumes not to make an effort to participate but is absorbed in the contemplated might in the external power" (*Prose Works of William Wordsworth*, ed. W.J.B. Owen and Jane Worthington Smyser, 3 vols. [Oxford: Clarendon Press, 1974], vol. 2, 354).

[16] *The Prelude* (1850), 6.592–605, in *Poetical Works of William Wordsworth*, ed. Thomas Hutchinson, rev. Ernest de Selincourt (London: Oxford University Press, 1936; reprint, 1961).

[17] Immanuel Kant, *The Critique of Judgment*, trans. J. H. Bernard (London: Macmillan, 1914), 119–20. The best compact exposition of Kant's views on the sublime remains that of Monk, *The Sublime*, 6–9.

of nature to a supersensible substrate (which lies at its basis and also at the basis of our faculty of thought)."[18] One need only substitute the term "Intellectual Powers" for Kant's Reason, "Corporeal Understanding" for Kant's incapacitated Imagination, and "Sublime Allegory," for the "magnitude of a natural object," in order to recognize that Blake's and Kant's defining conditions for the sublime have, *mutatis mutandis*, an identical structure. What is a barrier to the faculty allied with sense is an avenue to its more privileged counterpart—and, paradoxically, the avenue becomes available only if the barrier is posed. The sublime stimulus then operates as a kind of psychic traffic light, beckoning one power of the mind to come forth only when another is blocked. Such a principle would explain why, in the letter to Butts, Blake deems a privilege afforded to one of the two faculties more sublime than privileges afforded to both ("My Definition of the *Most* Sublime Poetry" [my emphasis]). Without the thwarting of the Corporeal Understanding, there apparently can be no manifestation of the Intellectual Powers as such, for the latter do not always know themselves in an unmediated fashion. A terminal failure of the understanding is required to throw the intellect into relief, and that sudden manifestation serves to replenish man's sense of his own greatness.

These Kantian conceptions are important to the study of Blake's sublime, not because Kant's thought is interchangeable with Blake's (which is hardly the case), but because it indicates so clearly the particular theoretical tradition in which Blake operates. Kant is useful here because he posits with such uncompromising rigor a mental sublime that rests on a dialectic of plenitude and deprivation for its dynamics. By attacking Burke, who did most to establish this dialectic, Blake has obscured his own adherence to it. More recently, Thomas Weiskel has attempted to divorce Blake rigorously and entirely from the whole Burkean-Kantian-Wordsworthian conception of the sublime, but the fact of the similarity remains.[19] The argu-

---

[18] *Critique of Judgment*, 117.

[19] Weiskel, the most acute and unsparing critic of the Kantian sublime, would have it otherwise: "Blake hated the indefinite, rejected the numinous, and insisted on the primacy of the imagination. His work makes a profound critique of the natural sublime"; in particular, Blake is an enemy "to the inscrutability which always attends the numinous" (*The Romantic Sublime*, 7). In making these claims, Weiskel ignores Blake's definition of "the Most Sublime Poetry" as involving something "altogether hidden." He also passes over those occasions in Blake on which the poet celebrates the incomprehensible (e.g., "The Four Living Creatures Chariots of the Humanity Divine Incomprehensible/ In beautiful Paradises expand" [*J* 98.24–25]) or insists on numinous awe (Blake takes Wordsworth himself to task, for example, for not showing *enough* awe when the latter speaks of passing "Jehovah . . . unalarmed" [*AnnoW*, E 666]). Weiskel appears, moreover, to discount the fact that the terms "Imagination" and "Reason" have mutually reversed connotations in Kant and Blake. That Blake attacks certain emphases on humiliation and deprivation in contemporary theories of the sublime is not in dispute, and Weiskel offers keen insights concerning this critique (see *The Romantic Sublime*, 63–79).

ments for Blake's repudiation of the tradition are based on partial evidence, or evidence not fully considered in a comprehensive context. A more judicious account would stress how Blake manages to reinvest the deprivation-plenitude structure with new emphases, and adapt it to new ends. For instance, he shows little interest in applying his formulation of the sublime to any object connected with nature, with material power or magnitude. Rather, he slips the poetic artifact into the privileged position of the sublime object or stimulus. But he undertakes no quarrel with the opacities, bafflements, and deprivations endemic to the sublime tradition, and, in his scheme, the mental faculties continue to divide into unequally endowed portions.

Blake also shares with such contemporaries as Kant and Wordsworth the notion that the sublime resides in an identification of a desired infinite with the quester's own intellectual being. Blake's grasp of this concept may be illustrated in some of his earliest etched lines, the last three propositions of *There Is No Natural Religion*:

> V If the many become the same as the few, when possess'd, More! More! is the cry of a mistaken soul, less than All cannot satisfy Man.

> VI If any could desire what he is incapable of possessing, despair must be his eternal lot.

> VII The desire of Man being Infinite the possession is Infinite & himself Infinite. (NNR, E 2)

If man is infinite, it must be because he *is* capable of possessing the "All" that alone satisfies. Indeed he does possess it, for despair does not in fact rule human life. "Mistaken souls" cry "More! More!" when they in fact already have "All." Their mistake is that of the Corporeal Understanding, which grasps at finites and seeks to accumulate them. But in comparison with the infinite, no amount of accumulation will seem anything but immeasurably small: "the many become the same as the few, when possess'd." As Kant remarks, "the infinite is absolutely (not merely comparatively) great. Compared with it everything else (of the same kind of magnitudes) is small."[20] An infinite possession therefore cannot result from any process of accumulation, no matter how extended, but must exist in the mind whole and a priori. In the same passage as that just quoted, Kant continues: "And what is most important is that to be able to think it as a whole indicates a faculty of mind which surpasses every standard of Sense. . . . Nevertheless, *the bare capability of thinking* this infinite without contradic-

---

But a critique of a tradition by no means indicates a divorce from that tradition, particularly in the case of one so dialectically motivated as Blake.

[20] *Critique of Judgment*, 115–16.

tion requires in the human mind a faculty itself supersensible." Blake's "All," like Kant's "whole," is an object of desire that only the mind of the desirer can furnish.

Blake's letter to Butts about the Intellectual Powers is only one instance of his habitual association of the sublime with a manifestation of intellect and a flight from the corporeal. Thus in the Proverbs of Hell, "Pathos," "Beauty," and "Proportion" are assigned to the heart, genitals, and limbs respectively, but "the head [is] Sublime" (*MHH* 10.61). Elsewhere, the images in the "Writings of the Prophets" are "sublime & Divine" because they illustrate how "the Imaginative Image returns by the seed of Contemplative Thought" (*VLJ*, E 555). In stressing the sublime as a mental greatness, Blake aligns himself with a venerable tradition of thought, beginning with Longinus, who tells us that "the Sublime is an Image reflected from the inward Greatness of the Soul."[21] In the eighteenth century, there are many echoes and variations of this idea before it reaches the extreme subjectivity of self-apotheosis suggested by Kant when he tells us that "sublimity does not reside in anything of nature, but only in our mind."[22] James Usher expresses the concept as well as any: "at the presence of the sublime, although it be always awful, the soul of man seems to be raised out of a trance; it assumes an unknown grandeur; it is seized with a new appetite, that in a moment effaces its former little prospects and desires; it is rapt out of sight and consideration of this diminutive world, into a kind of gigantic creation, where it finds room to dilate itself to a size agreeable to its present nature and grandeur."[23] We are reminded here of James Beattie's quirky derivation of *sublime* from *super limas*, "above the slime or mud of this world,"[24] which in turn glances ahead to Blake's assertion that "I do not behold the Outward Creation & that to me it is hindrance & not Action it is the Dirt upon my feet No part of Me" (*VLJ*, E 565).

Closer still to Blake in his view of a sublime that resides in a power of mind is John Dennis, earlier in the century. When Blake tells us that "The Nature of my Work is Visionary or Imaginative it is an Endeavour to Restore what the Ancients calld the Golden Age" (*VLJ*, E 555), he may be echoing Dennis, who also has a restorative notion of the arts: "The great design of Arts is to restore the decays that happen'd to Humane Nature by the Fall, by Restoring Order."[25] From Dennis, too, Blake probably acquires his illustrative example of what it means "not [to] behold the Outward Creation," when he contrasts the Corporeal view of the sun as "a

[21] *On the Sublime*, 18.

[22] *Critique of Judgment*, 129.

[23] *Clio*, 103.

[24] James Beattie, *Dissertations, Moral and Critical* (London: W. Strahan, 1783), 606; quoted in Monk, *The Sublime*, 129.

[25] John Dennis, *The Grounds of Criticism in Poetry* (London: G. Strahan, 1704), 6.

round Disk of fire somewhat like a Guinea" with his own view of it as "an Innumerable company of the Heavenly host crying Holy Holy Holy is the Lord God Almighty" (*VLJ*, E 565–66). According to Dennis, "the sun mention'd in ordinary Conversation, gives the Idea of a round flat shining Body, of about Two Foot Diameter. But the Sun occurring to us in Meditation, gives the Idea of a vast and glorious Body, and the top of all the visible Creation, and the brightest material Image of the Divinity."[26] Such a transformation of the outward creation, according to Dennis, is a product of Enthusiasm, "a Passion which is moved by the Idea's [*sic*] in Contemplation or the Meditation of Things," and the Enthusiastic passions are noteworthy because "the greater and more violent they are, the more they show the largeness of Soul, and greatness of Capacity of the Writer."[27] Dennis here narrows or virtually effaces the gap between the imagining perceiver and the imagined percept; to recognize the divinity inherent in the image of the sun is tantamount to asserting the divinity of the self that has conceived the image. The sublime becomes the comprehensive term for the state in which this narrowing occurs: "The sublime is . . . never without Enthusiastic Passion. For the Sublime is nothing else but a great Thought, or Great Thoughts moving the Soul from it's Ordinary Scituation [*sic*] by the Enthusiasm which naturally attends them."[28] It is next to impossible to distinguish here between the reader moved and the poet who moves, embraced as they both are by the unifying and apparently free-floating entity of "Great Thought," which generates passions as its operative mode. Dennis takes the terminology of abstract intellect, "Thought," "Contemplation," and "Meditation," to describe a source of the passions and enthusiasm, and it is here that his theory of the sublime is most relevant to Blake.

In Blake's thought, intellect in its fine essence is always connected to the passions. It is through this connection that the Intellectual Powers discover themselves with that total cognition defined as sublime by its idealist theoreticians. In *A Vision of the Last Judgment* Blake declares that "The Treasures of Heaven are not Negations of Passion but Realities of Intellect from which All the Passions Emanate Uncurbed in their Eternal Glory" (E 564). Intellect, then, is the matrix of desire, and generates those passions that, when "uncurbed," are the Alpha and Omega of human happiness. Blake's Intellectual Powers may resemble Kant's supersensible Reason in that both altogether transcend corporeal modes of understanding, but there is this crucial difference: Blake's supreme faculty discovers itself not

[26] Ibid., 17. The resemblance has been noted by John Beer, "Influence and Independence in Blake," in *Interpreting Blake*, ed. Michael Phillips (Cambridge: Cambridge University Press, 1978), 248–49.

[27] *Grounds of Criticism*, 16 and 21.

[28] Ibid., 78.

in the attainment of some cool, absolute rationality but, as the propositions of *No Natural Religion* show, in the infinitude of its desire. An intellect that fails to quicken Enthusiastic Passions—in short, to emanate as love—would be, for Blake, no intellect at all. It is not enough for the Intellectual Powers to possess plenitude; they must be stirred by that plenitude, and seek its realization in an infinite variety of particular forms, such as Dennis's transfigured sun. These forms are "Realities of Intellect"—that is to say, forms made real by intellect to be the objects of its desires.

It follows from this eroticized conception of intellect that "the Most Sublime Poetry" only begins its task when it separates the Intellectual Powers from the Corporeal Understanding. It is not enough for the poem to operate on a logic of negative inference, relying on assumptions that if one faculty is thoroughly baffled, there must be a residual one rising in hidden strength.[29] Merely to posit this other faculty, to display intellect like a statue unveiled, is in no way to "address" the Intellectual Powers. An address manifests itself as such to the extent that it implies a response and provides the opportunities for such response. Sublime poetry addresses the Intellectual Powers by furnishing them with forms of desire, with an ongoing enticement that releases the uncurbed emanation of passion. Intellect is thus revealed not in some abstract fashion but in its desire to read and in the manner of its reading. Similarly, the Corporeal Understanding reveals itself to be that which cannot read. "The Most Sublime Poetry" is, after all, poetry, and if it aims to sunder the faculties so as to manifest them both in their unalloyed forms, then the means for doing so must reside in the text itself.

THE SUBLIME OF READING: BARRIERS AND DISCLOSURES

The Intellectual Powers and the Corporeal Understanding essentially represent two different states of reading, or perhaps more accurately, two choices of reading. The same act of reading may summon both states in varying proportions, and every reader will pass through each state at different times. For the purpose of argument, however, it is more convenient

[29] Cf. Roger R. Easson's comment that "Sublime allegory is designed to arouse the intellectual faculties by its grandly manipulative obscurity so that the individual's humanity may awake and cast off the dominance of reason" ("Blake and his Reader in Jerusalem," in *Blake's Sublime Allegory: Essays on "The Four Zoas," "Milton," and "Jerusalem,"* ed. Stuart Curran and Joseph Anthony Wittreich, Jr. [Madison: University of Wisconsin Press, 1973], 316). This insight has much validity, but it disregards elements of attraction built into the sublime text and assigns too much of a purely negative function to its difficulties, which, in Easson's account, work more by anarchic destructiveness than by love: "Sublime poetry . . . threatens to disorient the reader, to overthrow reason, and to let loose the disintegrating forces of chaos" (Ibid.).

to consider the Intellectual Powers and the Corporeal Understanding as simultaneously presented to the mind, locked in dubious battle, a crisis in reading. Blake's program of displacing the natural sublime object with a text makes manifest what is, according to some recent critics, latent all the time in eighteenth-century and Romantic theories of the sublime. Given our recent critical climate, in which all readings are said to be problematic, and in which we as readers are all situated in an abyss between opacity and translucence, between putative presence and actual deferral, it is not surprising that the sublime experience has attracted attention as a displaced experience of reading and as an exemplary instance of its difficulties.[30] Conversely, modern theory has often used the language of the natural sublime (high barriers, gaps, abysses, labyrinths) as metaphors for certain textual events.

Needless to say, there is nothing new in this displaced usage, since the natural sublime itself merely takes over the language that had long been used to describe a rhetorical effect.[31] Blake's textual sublime derives in part from the tradition of Longinus, in which the sublime is a trope of rhetoric designed to move an audience,[32] in part from traditions of hidden gnosis, scriptural hermeneutics and allegoresis, and their medieval and Renaissance secular derivatives.[33] The latter traditions seek less to transport the

[30] See, e.g., Geoffrey Hartman, *The Fate of Reading* (Chicago: University of Chicago Press, 1975): "The structure of the act of reading . . . is the structure of the sublime experience in a finer mode" (120); in Neil Hertz, "The Notion of Blockage in the Literature of the Sublime," in *Psychoanalysis and the Question of the Text*, ed. Geoffrey Hartman (Baltimore: Johns Hopkins University Press, 1978), we hear of an "ascesis of reading" (70); Frances Ferguson notes that Burke places poetry at the summit of his "ordering of the arts" because he recognizes language as the preeminent site of difficulty and alienation from apprehensible nature ("The Sublime of Edmund Burke, or the Bathos of Experience," in *Glyph* 8 [1981]: 67); Weiskel speaks of sublime objects and perceivers in terms of "signifiers" and "signifieds" and calls the sublime of difficulty and indeterminacy a "hermeneutic or 'reader's' sublime" (*The Romantic Sublime*, 26–31).

[31] R. S. Crane, in his important review of Monk's book on the sublime, was the first to distinguish the naturalized or psychological sublime from the older tradition of the rhetorical sublime (*Philological Quarterly* 15 [1936]: 165–67); Weiskel begins his own approach to his subject "with the hypothesis that the encounter with literary greatness—the so-called rhetorical sublime—is structurally cognate with the transcendence, gentle or terrible, excited in the encounter with a landscape, the 'natural sublime' " (*The Romantic Sublime*, 11).

[32] See Longinus, *On the Sublime*: "the Sublime is a certain Eminence of or Perfection of Language, and . . . the greatest Writers, both in Verse and Prose, have by this alone obtain'd the Prize of Glory, and fill'd all Time with their Renown" (3). A remnant of this view survives in Burke, who, after all, strews his *Philosophical Enquiry* with examples from literary texts, and who, despite his stress on the natural sublime, concedes in the final sentence of his treatise that "words" have a power to "affect us often as strongly as the things they represent, and sometimes much more strongly" (177).

[33] The most useful account of Blake's debt to these traditions appears in Joseph A. Wittreich, *Angel of Apocalypse: Blake's Idea of Milton* (Madison: University of Wisconsin Press,

reader than to make his path difficult and obstacle-ridden; they are designed to exclude the unworthy, and to discipline the worthy and make them hungry for full truth.[34] Elements of this ancient heuristic function undoubtedly figure in Blake's choice of the term *Allegory* to describe the sublime text. But as we shall see, it is the *sublime* of "Sublime Allegory" that bears the heaviest stress in his conception.

The word *allegory*, etymologically an "other-speaking," suggests in its own compound terms "otherness," alienation, and opacity on one hand, and address and disclosure on the other—in short, the different destinies of the divided mental faculties. The text poses itself as a barrier, but at the barrier there is a point of indeterminacy, a state of incomplete disengagement between the Corporeal Understanding and the Intellectual Powers. The barrier seems to flicker equivocally before the eyes, now opaque, now translucent, now forbidding, now yielding. The sublime text must be capable of provoking despair and desire simultaneously, stunned retreat and joyous elevation. Such a text must appear hard to read; it cannot disseminate its meanings easily or transparently. But at the same time that it appears hard to read, it must also present itself as *almost easy* to read—that is to say, it must be filled with all sorts of glancing lusters of language, moments of eloquent simplicity, accessible dicta, and most important of all, innumerable tantalizing hints and tokens of a comprehensive wisdom or *gnosis*, whose full apprehension awaits us, so to speak, just around the bend. It is a text that labors as hard to forestall our indifference to it as it does to hinder its self-disclosure. Such a text may contain "sublime" events, in the conventional sense of the term, as part of its content, but this is not crucial. The crucial sublime event takes place in the actual difficulties of the reading experience.

First, there is the difficulty faced by the Corporeal Understanding. That which is already "altogether hidden" to the Understanding can never be

---

1975), 171–88. Both Hertz ("Notion of Blockage," 69) and Weiskel (*The Romantic Sublime*, 30–31) touch on the connection between the hermeneutic difficulties of sacred allegory and the bafflements of the sublime, but the richest treatment of the connection is that of Angus Fletcher, *Allegory: The Theory of a Symbolic Mode* (Ithaca: Cornell University Press, 1964) 233–61). Fletcher argues, in effect, that the sublime sensibility is simply the eighteenth-century continuation of allegorical modes of thought. If this is true, then Blake's term "Sublime Allegory" epitomizes the transition. The term itself, as has been variously noted, perhaps derives from Lowth, *Sacred Poetry of the Hebrews* vol. 1, 203: "that sublimer kind of allegory," which under a literal meaning "conceals one interiour and more sacred."

[34] As Michael Murrin succinctly puts it, "The allegorical poet affects his audience more in the manner of a Hebrew prophet than in that of a classical orator. Instead of appealing to all the people and attempting to win them over to a particular point of view, the poet causes a division in his audience, separating the few from the many, those who can understand from those who cannot. . ."; see *The Veil of Allegory: Some Notes Toward a Theory of Allegorical Rhetoric in the English Renaissance* (Chicago: University of Chicago Press, 1969), 13.

found—and because it is never found, it must be perpetually sought or guessed at. Hence, difficulties come into being only after the Understanding has been denied access to the infinite. After the brief episode of "indeterminacy," the episode of attraction/repulsion, invitation/rebuff, and arousal/despair, issues of blockage and disclosure become decided; barriers are then transcended all at once or not at all. But it is the fate of the Corporeal Understanding to conceive none of this. By definition capable only of understanding bodies, it knows nothing of the infinite and hence nothing of the fact that the infinite is "altogether hidden" from it. The fact of its blockage registers only as the experience of "difficulties" and the necessity of laborious reading.

How does the Corporeal Understanding try to read? Alexander Gerard describes this fruitless labor as succinctly as any writer in the period: "The mind contemplates, not one large, but many small objects: it is pained with the labour requisite to creep from one to another; and is disgusted with the imperfection of the idea, with which, even after all this toil, it must remain contented."[35] Anyone who has ever grappled seriously with Blake's text can supply further instances from his or her own experience, for not even the fittest Blake scholar can honestly claim a plenary exemption from lapses into this state. We have all puzzled over recondite terminology, narrative instability, inconsistencies among utterances or between stubborn details and "the system as a whole." In what seems to be an endless task, our procedures are additive, as we move painfully from line to line exploring the dens of the text. Unlike the Los of *Jerusalem*, we "Reason & Compare" (*J* 10.21), accumulating much that is useful to our understandings. But the useful is not the sublime. For all our accumulating, it is number, weight, and measure in a year of dearth, the "More! More!" of the mistaken soul who cannot ever find satisfaction thus; in such a state, despair must be our eternal lot.

Against this dire prospect, we can more effectively estimate the privilege afforded to the Intellectual Powers. For the Corporeal Understanding, the text is a kind of wall, against which it presses itself, groping along, trying in vain to peer through chinks in the hard, opaque surface. How, then, do the Intellectual Powers read? Not, as may be imagined, in some imperious act of untroubled seeing, in which the text becomes a wall of glass, a thing annulled before the glory of some "supersensible" totality lying beyond. Again, our personal experience as readers of Blake must be our guide, and it does not ratify such a serenely grandiose scenario. When we find ourselves first attracted and responsive to Blake's text, it is certainly not because we have been afforded a comprehensive a priori vision of its meanings, but rather because we sense the fullness of its potential. The wall of

---

[35] *An Essay on Taste*, 15–16.

words is still there, but something within us responds to the shifting, captivating lusters that glance off it, points of eloquence and concentrated wisdom, atomies of beauty and pathos. The more these are perceived, the more they cast light on others, until the wall as a whole becomes luminous. The Intellectual Powers seek not to abolish the wall of words but to find satisfaction in it.

The wall as an image of a text is of course Blake's own, established in a moment at which the drama of blockage and disclosure becomes aware of itself as a trope:

> I give you the end of a golden string,
> Only wind it into a ball:
> It will lead you in at Heavens gate,
> Built in Jerusalems wall.

> (*J* 77, E 231)

The end of the string is here in these four lines themselves, for the interpretive clues that the reader needs rest in the metaphors "wall" and "gate," which of course represent the sublime alternatives of blockage and disclosure. The key to reading a poem such as *Jerusalem* is to realize the very fact that it provokes opposed modes of reading. The "golden string" offers no decoding device for a deprived Corporeal Understanding. It merely tells us that the text yields itself to the force of trust, curiosity, and desire, and that it fastens itself to the reader at points of little details, felicities tucked away in the crannies of the wall. Each is Heaven's gate, and there are as many golden strings as there are points of entrance, varying from reader to reader.

We are dealing here not with the meaning of the text but with the pleasure of the text: "If the Spectator could Enter into these Images in his Imagination approaching them on the Fiery Chariot of his Contemplative Thought if he could Enter into Noahs Rainbow or into his bosom or could make a Friend & Companion of one of these Images of wonder . . . then would he meet the Lord in the Air & then he would be happy General Knowledge is Remote Knowledge it is in Particulars that Wisdom consists & Happiness too" (*VLJ*, E 560). Happiness consists in particulars, and the particulars are to be approached as "friends" or "companions," or as emblems of good faith and trust, like the rainbow that God presented to Noah as a guarantee that there would be no second flood (see Gen. 9.12–17). "Contemplative Thought" approaches on a "Fiery Chariot," an emblem associated with fierce desire (see *Milton* 1.10–12). The Intellectual Powers are involved in what seems like a kind of Barthian lover's discourse with the text.

To make a friend of the artist's images (and by image, one must include words in their semantic and graphic dimensions as well, for Blake speaks of the principles of verbal art and visual art interchangeably)[36] is, then, to become their familiar, to embrace them as Los does his Spectre in *The Four Zoas*, "first as a brother / Then as another self" (*FZ* 85.29–30). The image becomes, like the ash on Coleridge's grate in "Frost at Midnight," a "Companionable form" to the Intellect, "every where / Echo or mirror seeking of itself,"[37] for the Intellect, as we know, desires an "All" that can only be found within. As a tangible companion, the text is intellect crystallized into visible and particular form. "The Beauty proper for sublime art," Blake tells us in a definitive statement, "is lineaments, or forms and features that are capable of being the receptacles of intellect" (*DC*, E 544). Such lineaments are as much "lineaments of Gratified Desire" as those that "men in women do require" (see E 474). What satisfies intellect best, apparently, is to lodge itself in a defined space (the overtones of a lover's discourse remain in effect here), while remaining free to exercise "uncurbed" its infinite potentialities.

These requirements are met by language itself, "that system of signs," as Maureen Quilligan puts it, "which retrieves for us the process of intellection."[38] Thus a sublime text is one in which the Intellect recognizes (reads) a glory that the same faculty has put (written) into it. The glory is that of the unrestricted majesty and power of human expressiveness and creativity, exemplified in the gift of language, and made manifest in the immense resources of its signifiers.[39] What Thomas Weiskel has said of Wordsworth's celebration of the power of words in Book V of *The Prelude* is applicable to Blake: "The passage is evoking the penumbra of words, the power inherent not in what they mean but in that they mean; or, in what they are, independent of their meaning—in earlier language, the how and not the what of sublimity. . . . Power inheres not in the perceptual form but in language or symbolicity itself."[40] For Blake, language is not only the glory

---

[36] For example, in describing his painting of the Last Judgment, Blake drifts easily into talking about poetry: "The Last Judgment is not Fable or Allegory but Vision Fable or Allegory are a totally distinct & inferior kind of Poetry" (*VLJ*, E 554); conversely, when he praises Chaucer's characters, he does so in the pictorial terms of his own aesthetic: "the characters themselves for ever remain unaltered, and consequently they are the physiognomies or lineaments of universal human life, beyond which Nature never steps" (*DC*, E 532–33).

[37] "Frost at Midnight," lines 19 and 21–22, *Complete Poetical Works of Samuel Taylor Coleridge*, ed. E. H. Coleridge, 2 vols. (Oxford: Clarendon Press, 1912).

[38] See Maureen Quilligan, *The Language of Allegory: Defining the Genre* (Ithaca: Cornell University Press, 1979), 42.

[39] As Christopher Heppner puts it, "it is the human power to signify that is the basis for the sublime, not the sensory properties of the material world"; see "The Woman Taken in Adultery: An Essay on Blake's 'Style of Designing,'" *Blake/An Illustrated Quarterly* 17 (Fall 1983): 56.

[40] *The Romantic Sublime*, 181; see *The Prelude* (1850), 5.595–605.

of our humanity but its essence, and in the apocalypse described at the end of *Jerusalem*, the form of the sign and the human form become one. Albion speaks "Words of Eternity in Human Forms," and "every Word & Every Character / Was Human" (*J* 95.9; 98.35–36). The attraction of the intellect to the text, then, is an attraction to one's native place, and the feeling of sublime elevation comes from the joy of homecoming.

It becomes increasingly apparent that the phrase "Allegory addressd to the Intellectual powers" refers to a scene of self-recognition. "Allegory" means "other-speaking," but in such a state of sublimity as we get at the end of *Jerusalem*, "Sublime Allegory" becomes an "other-speaking" that cancels its own otherness and becomes simply speaking; the only "other" here is the text itself.[41] The text, the signified of its own signifiers, should not be conceived as a shell covering the meaty kernel of meaning, to use a favorite trope of traditional accounts of the allegorical relation. Even the most profound of his critics can lapse into talk of cracking shells and extracting kernels,[42] but Blake never speaks in such terms. Although Blake's works are full of conventional allegorization,[43] Sublime Allegory is not a conventional system of obscured referentiality. Rather, we are to understand it as a discourse that, when it is at its "Most Sublime," addresses itself to a faculty that seeks "companionable forms," not hidden meanings. To be companionable, such forms must be *seen*, must be apprehended in their specific individualities. It is natural, therefore, that in his most extended series of dicta on the requirements of the sublime, Blake makes this particularity the cornerstone of his thought.

[41] Some recent treatments of allegory view the entire mode generally in a similar perspective. For example, Maureen Quilligan observes that "the 'other' named by the term *allos* in the word 'allegory' is not some other hovering above the words of the text, but the possibility of an otherness, a polysemy, inherent in the very words on the page; allegory therefore names the fact that language can signify many things at once" (*The Language of Allegory*, 26).

[42] See Northrop Frye, *Fearful Symmetry: A Study of William Blake* (Princeton: Princeton University Press, 1947), 380. In the same passage in which he speaks of a "sublimer kind of allegory," Robert Lowth refers to the surface subject as a "rind or shell" hiding the deeper and more important meaning (*Sacred Poetry of the Hebrews* vol. 1, 203).

[43] "Note here that Fable or Allegory is Seldom without some Vision," Blake concedes in a famous passage of *A Vision of The Last Judgment* (E 554), in which "Vision" replaces the earlier "Sublime Allegory" as the term for the highest reach of art. But the reverse is also true, as Blake makes obvious in the same essay when he identifies the figures of his painting of the Last Judgment in terms that correspond altogether to the conventional notion of allegory; e.g., "it ought to be understood that the Persons Moses & Abraham are not here meant but the States Signified by those Names the Individuals being representatives or Visions of those States"; "The Figure dragging up a Woman by her hair represents the Inquisition"; "they strip her naked & burn her with fire it represents the Eternal Consummation of Vegetable Life & Death with its Lusts" (E 556, 557–58, 558). Frye, *Fearful Symmetry*, 9–11, is useful in distinguishing the two opposing senses in which Blake uses the term "allegory."

Singular and Particular Detail: The Sublime of the Signifier

Blake's best-known remarks on the aesthetics of the sublime are contained in his annotations to the *Discourses* of Sir Joshua Reynolds. Here we observe him engaged in a running argument that focuses on the grand style itself, in which he is forced consciously to stake out positions on the subject in response to alternatives actually posed before him.[44] It is particularly significant, therefore, that Blake's only recorded reference to Edmund Burke and to the *Philosophical Enquiry into . . . the Sublime and Beautiful* should occur in these marginal jottings. These notes often seem to use Reynolds as the occasion for an attack directed specifically against Burke. While we have observed elements in Blake's views that are compatible with a Burkean framework, or at least with a tradition in which Burke's voice is conspicuous, the radical differences between the two writers' ideas of the sublime inevitably demand consideration.

Blake more or less identifies Burke as the baleful shadow behind Reynolds's own aberrations:

> Burke's Treatise on the Sublime & Beautiful is founded on the Opinion of Newton & Locke on this Treatise Reynolds has grounded many of his assertions. in all his Discourses I read Burkes Treatise when very Young at the same time I read Locke on Human Understanding & Bacons Advancement of Learning on Every one of these Books I wrote my Opinions & on looking them over find that my Notes on Reynolds in this Book are exactly Similar. I felt the Same Contempt & Abhorrence then; that I do now. They mock Inspiration and Vision (E 660)

It is scarcely necessary to dwell here on the obvious revulsion that Blake would feel toward the empiricism, associationism, physiological reductivism, and the psychology of self-interest that underpin Burke's theory of the sublime.[45] These, however, are not Blake's main objects of attack in the

---

[44] It is always important to keep in mind the degree of serious deliberation involved in Blake's annotations to Reynolds. The annotated British Library copy of Reynolds's *Works* (the first volume of the three-volume second edition of 1798) contains page after page on which Blake's comments are drafted lightly in pencil and then retraced carefully in ink. Blake presumably considered his marginalia an "official" combat against Reynolds's errors, waged on the very site of their perpetration.

[45] E.g., as the agency of the sublime experience, Burke proposes "an unnatural tension and certain violent emotions of the nerves," and he accounts for the delight produced by the sublime as "a sort of tranquility tinged with terror; which as it belongs to self-preservation is one of the strongest of all the passions" (*Philosophical Enquiry*, 134 and 136). Blake is perhaps indebted directly to Burke for his phrase "Corporeal Understanding": "It is probable," Burke writes, "that not only the inferior parts of the soul, as the passions are called, but the understanding itself makes use of some fine corporeal instruments in its operation" (ibid., 135).

Annotations to Reynolds. He is more concerned with the epistemological character of Burke's sublime object itself. Burke's conception of sublime poetry as a form of deliberate indeterminacy seems very much on Blake's mind all along as he reads Reynolds. When Reynolds offers obscurity as "one source of the sublime," Burke's famous argument inevitably rises up before us:

> Poetry with all its obscurity, has a more general as well as a more powerful dominion over the passions than the other art [i.e., painting]. And I think there are reasons in nature why the obscure idea, when properly conveyed, should be more affecting than the clear. It is our ignorance of things that causes all our admiration, and chiefly excites our passions. Knowledge and acquaintance make the most striking causes affect but little. It is thus with the vulgar, and all men are as the vulgar in what they do not understand. The ideas of eternity, and infinity, are among the most affecting we have, and yet perhaps there is nothing of which we really understand so little, as of infinity and eternity.

> But let it be considered that hardly any thing can strike the mind with its greatness, which does not make some sort of approach towards infinity; which nothing can do whilst we are able to perceive its bounds; but to see an object distinctly, and to perceive its bounds, is one and the same thing. A clear idea is therefore another name for a little idea.[46]

These remarks are tantalizing because they mingle concepts that would be anathema to Blake with formulations that sound rather like some of his own. Blake would endorse the notion that poetry is a prime locus of the sublime experience. He would agree that "to see an object distinctly, and to perceive its bounds, is one and the same thing"; indeed the terminology is virtually his own. Moreover, according to a dictum from one of his early tractates, "The bounded is loathed by its possessor" (*NNR*, E 2); there is an implied antagonism between the bounded and man's desire for the infinite that consorts comfortably with Burke's view.

A profound gulf, however, separates Burke's notions of infinity from Blake's. As a Lockean empiricist, Burke must insist on our ignorance of infinity and eternity and restrict the understanding only to finite bodies. The infinite, for Burke, is precisely the absence of what we can know. Sublime objects, then, are merely knowable objects that pose as unknowable. They "make some sort of approach towards infinity" by a process of subtraction, by strategically placed concealments of their bounds. Through the mediation of the indeterminate object, at once accessible and inaccessible, the void of the infinite becomes an implied plenum.[47] An undifferentiated

---

[46] Ibid., 61 and 63.

[47] As Weiskel summarizes it, "the soul is a vacancy, whose extent is discovered as it is filled. Inner space, the infinitude of the Romantic mind, is born as a massive and more or less un-

vagueness or generality is therefore useful to Burke's sublime, "because any difference, whether it be in the disposition, or in the figure, or even in the colour of the parts, is highly prejudicial to the idea of infinity, which every change must check and interrupt, at every alteration commencing a new series."[48] An alternative mode of sublimity is to crowd the perceptual field excessively, so that it is all broken lines and broken masses: the poetic equivalents are the "many descriptions in the poets and orators which owe their sublimity to a richness and profusion of images, in which the mind is so dazzled as to make it impossible to attend to that exact coherence and agreement of the allusions."[49]

Blake will have none of this. The "bounded" is indeed to be "loathed" when what is bounded is the understanding itself, conceived by the empiricist as situated in a limited perceptual field of knowable objects circumscribed by a vast unknowable darkness. For Blake, "some sort of approach towards infinity" from this perimeter is no approach worth speaking of; less than all cannot satisfy man. Taken together, Blake's comments on the sublime in the Reynolds Marginalia make the case for a plainly accessible infinite. They all revolve around the principles of particularity, determinacy, and discrimination—qualities essential for making the forms of the artistic surface distinctly visible to the Intellectual Powers:

> Minute Discrimination is Not Accidental All Sublimity is founded on Minute Discrimination (E 643)

> Without Minute Neatness of Execution The Sublime cannot Exist! Grandeur of Ideas is founded on Precision of Ideas (E 646)

> Singular & particular Detail is the Foundation of the Sublime (E 647)

> Broken Colours & Broken Lines & Broken Masses are Equally Subversive of the Sublime (E 652)

> Obscurity is Neither the Source of the Sublime nor of any Thing Else (E 658)

Blake's stress on particularity and distinctness as productive of the sublime may seem, as Weiskel has said, merely "perverse," an attempt to overthrow Burke by depriving his key terms of their ordinarily understood meaning.[50] Hence, it is important to note that within the general aesthetic debates of his time, Blake speaks from a position of relative strength and within a

---

conscious emptiness, an absence" (*The Romantic Sublime*, p. 15). Ernest Tuveson, "Space, Deity, and the Natural Sublime" (*Modern Language Quarterly* [March 1951]: 20–38) traces the eighteenth-century tendency to identify the physical preserves of God with outer space itself.

[48] *Philosophical Enquiry*, 75.

[49] Ibid., 78.

[50] *The Romantic Sublime*, 67.

widely established context. Burke's stance provoked opposition from many quarters, both when the *Philosophical Enquiry* first appeared and several generations thereafter. "Distinctness of imagery has ever been held productive of the sublime," insisted one of the reviewers in response to Burke's famous celebration of obscurity.[51] Similarly, in his "Critical Dissertation on the Poems of Ossian," Hugh Blair tells us that "simplicity and conciseness, are never-failing characteristics of the stile of a sublime writer," and that "to be concise in description, is one thing; and to be general, is another. No description that rests in generals can possibly be good; it can convey no lively idea; for it is of particulars only that we have a distinct conception."[52] Bishop Lowth presses much the same point repeatedly: "the Hebrew poets have accomplished the sublime without losing perspicuity"; their "imagery is well known, the use of it is common, the signification definite; they are therefore perspicuous, clear, and truly magnificent." Lowth goes so far as to make perspicuity part of his definition of the sublime: "that force of composition, whatever it be, which strikes and overpowers the mind, which excites the passions, and which expresses ideas at once with perspicuity and elevation"; and elsewhere he praises a passage in Deuteronomy on the grounds that it "consists of sentences, pointed, energetic, concise, and splendid; that the sentiments are truly elevated and sublime, the language bright and animated, the expression and phraseology uncommon; while the mind of the poet never continues fixed to any single point, but glances continually from one object to another."[53] Lowth senses in Hebrew style a kind of scintillating restlessness, a supercharged *pointillisme* ("sentences pointed, energetic, concise") that reminds us of effects rendered by the Blakean wall of words, discussed earlier, as well as of the luminous potential that Blake tells us resides in particular and determinate forms.

The opinions on this topic of Blake's contemporary, the antiquarian and mythographer Richard Payne Knight, are particularly worth pausing over for their relevance to Blake's own views. Knight's *Analytical Inquiry into the Principles of Taste* directs a stream of argument against Burke's *Philosophical Enquiry*:

> The peculiar business of poetry is so to elevate and expand [its objects] that the imagination may conceive *distinct* but not *determinate* ideas of them; and thus have an infinite liberty of still exalting and expanding, without changing or confounding the images impressed upon it. . . . All obscurity is imperfection; and indeed, if obscurity means indistinctness, it is always imperfection. The more distinct a description; and the more clearly the qualities, properties, and energies

---

[51] See *The Monthly Review* 16 (May 1757): 477n.
[52] Blair, "Critical Dissertation," *Poems of Ossian* vol. 2, 423 and 385.
[53] Lowth, *Sacred Poetry of the Hebrews* vol. 1, 120, 131, 307, and 325.

intended to be signified or expressed, are brought, as it were, before the eyes, the more effect it will have on the imagination and the passions: but then, it should be *distinct* without being *determinate*. In describing for instance, a storm at sea, the rolling, the curling, the foaming, the dashing, and roaring of the waves cannot be too clearly, too precisely expressed: but it should not be told how many yards in a minute they advanced.[54]

In opposing "distinct" to "determinate" ideas, Knight appears from a Blakean standpoint to be taking with one hand what he gives with the other, but the example supplied at the end of the passage alleviates this impression. By "determinate," Knight appears to mean "measured" or "quantifiable" rather than closed or definite. Knight's distinctness is indeed close to Blake's determinacy—and, like Blake, he stresses those elements in the sublime image that give it its *character*, or special form, and eliminates those elements that limit the object to the occasional, the material, or what Blake calls the "Accidental," the stuff of "number, weight, & measure" (*MHH* 7.14). For Knight, the mind is not exalted and expanded by confronting a bloated indefiniteness. Rather, it must be pierced by the sharpness of the image, and only then can it expand in an indefinite liberty.

These various formulations—Lowth's splendid and pointed sentences, Blair's "lively" ideas, or Payne Knight's distinctly clear rolling waves—all pose a sublime based on salience or concentrated force against the Burkean sublime of perceptual deprivation and diffusion. This sublime substitutes intensity for extensiveness—it cuts more sharply and more deeply, vibrates more intensely, and compresses its power more minutely than anything that our ordinary senses provide.[55] This mode subsumes what Morton Paley has called "the sublime of energy,"[56] and it operates not only in energy's domain of the body but also in the domain of the text, or wherever the multiple and the multifaceted are made altogether manifest in a little moment or a little space. In his Annotations to Reynolds, Blake provides the most articulate and cogent formulation of this notion of the sublime. When Lowth or Payne Knight call for perspicuity and distinctness in sublime poetry, they do so in part because they think that it will bring the object more sharply into focus; the poet's style is like a pair of new eyeglasses for the myopic imagination. Blake goes beyond such writers in pro-

---

[54] Richard Payne Knight, *An Analytical Inquiry into the Principles of Taste*, 3d ed. (London: T. Payne and J. White, 1808), 391–92.

[55] Cf. Knight on Greek poetry: "The obscurity of the lyric style of Pindar and the Greek tragedians does not arise from any confusion or indistinctness in the imagery; but from its conciseness and abruptness; and from its being shown to the mind in sudden flashes and corruscations, the connexion between which is often scarcely perceptible" (*Analytical Inquiry*, 401).

[56] See Morton D. Paley, *Energy and the Imagination: A Study of the Development of Blake's Thought* (Oxford: Clarendon Press, 1970), 3–11.

claiming the sublimity of determinacy, particularity, and discrimination for their own sake. They are valued not because they make objects more clear, but because they are the "real" constituents of objects. Indeed, Blake's prescriptions are too rigorous for even the most sharp-edged mimesis of objects to satisfy. Blake calls for a total determinacy, or closure of outline; a total particularity, or representation of all the parts—indeed, all the particles of the image; and a total discrimination or singularity—that is, the separation and differentiation of the image from every other contiguous image. No ordinary perception or ordinary description, however acute, can meet such requirements. In three-dimensional space, objects hide portions of themselves, crowd on one another's outlines, and break their masses, those nearby obscuring those farther away, all distorted by perspective. Nothing in this space can supply the "lineaments, or forms and features that are capable of being receptacles of intellect." There are only crowded absences here, not presence.

In his visual art, Blake's stylistic manner of flattening the picture plane and disposing his figures in a "symmetrical frontality" serves, as W.J.T. Mitchell has pointed out, to minimize these defects of natural seeing. Blake is striving "to undercut the representational appearance of particular forms and to endow them with an abstract, stylized existence independent of the natural images with which they are identified." In essence, as Mitchell's study has effectively shown, "Blake's visual images move toward the realm of language, operating as arbitrary signs, emblems, or hieroglyphics."[57] All lines, pictorial and otherwise, are absorbed into the idea of text, an autonomous structure of writing that is anterior to possible referentiality. The particularity, determinacy, and singularity of language are to be found in its signifers, not in the indefinite plurality and ambiguity of its signifieds. The signifier is finite and, at the same time, "polyvalent," or endowed with a surplus of signifying potential in relation to any given signified.[58] "Not a line is drawn without intention & that most discriminate & particular as Poetry admits not a Letter that is Insignificant so Painting admits not a Grain of Sand or a Blade of Grass Insignificant" (*VLJ*, E 560). Every line, letter, or grain is "significant" in the sense that it is impressed with a self-subsistent signifying power, which is its principal glory. Blake's reference to the letter indicates that his interest here is in the forms as signifers, and not in what they signify (see the famous crux in *J* 3, E 146: "every letter is studied"). The world of artifacts affords nothing more absolutely and exclusively linear, minute, determinate, particular, individuated, and differentiated than a graphic sign or letter. Because it imitates nothing and can-

---

[57] W.J.T. Mitchell, *Blake's Composite Art: A Study of the Illuminated Poetry* (Princeton: Princeton University Press, 1978), 19, 37, and 4.

[58] The best discussion of polyvalence or "polysemy" of signification in Blake is to be found in Hilton, *Literal Imagination*, 10–18.

not be represented at all unless all its parts are inscribed completely, the form of a letter is both perfect and particular, definite and yet open to countless participations in potential reference. We may speak of the determinate sublime, then, as a sublime of the signifier, one in which exhilaration comes from recognition of the creative power of the letter. Behind the letter resides an unnamed and, to fallen eyes, unseen exactitude, for which the abstract term "human intellect" passes as a secular designation.[59]

Problems remain, however, in this account of Blake's sublime. How is one to reconcile, after all, the "indeterminacy" of the sublime moment with the specification that the sublime image must be "determinate"? How indeed does a sublime that requires something "altogether hidden" consort with one that banishes obscurity as its source? For all the harsh attacks on Burke, we may still sense the presence of a Burkean magnetic field tugging at the needle of Blake's aesthetic compass. Conversely, if Burke were to scan some knotty, congested passages from Blake's Prophecies, he certainly could not fault them for lack of obscurity or for a display of "little ideas." Even the characters of Blake's script sometimes fall short of an absolute formal determinacy, so that it is not always easy for an editor to decide what letter or mark of punctuation in a given passage is intended. While Blake's poetic and artistic practice is intellectually directed against Burkean assumptions and precepts, it often betrays a certain fondness for Burkean effects. Compared to Addison, for example, who finds the Roman Pantheon more sublime than a Gothic cathedral,[60] Burke and Blake seem to belong to the same camp: they are unavoidably allied as advocates of a problematic and agonistic sublime.

It is not in the matter of occasion or of agency that Blake and Burke differ in their conceptions of the sublime. They both provide a structure that includes a moment of discontinuity—the episode of "astonishment"— and a psychic effect in which the mind becomes self-divided. They differ in that Blake recognizes the means for a *more thorough* discontinuity and a more radical division of the faculties. Nothing can be more discontinuous with its surroundings than what is altogether determinate, particular, and distinct in itself. The more that Blake withholds from his texts those concessions to referentiality that create the illusion of representing objects

[59] Morris Eaves observes that "metaphors of precision have very close relatives . . . in teleological metaphors of ultimate truth, of final distinctions, in Christian theology. A universal man—a man who is the universe, such as the figure of Christ who appears at the beginning of Revelation as a conglomerate of divinity-humanity-animal-vegetable-mineral—carries out the Last Judgment with a two-edged sword as his organ of discourse"; see *William Blake's Theory of Art* (Princeton: Princeton University Press, 1982), 20. Speaking more specifically of Blake's small units of language—words—Nelson Hilton says that "the more deliberately the word is perceived, the more it begins to assert itself—to spell itself out—in all its associations and etymology, its eternal human form. . . . Every word is a parable about linguistic structure as incarnate human imagination" (*Literal Imagination*, 7).

[60] *Works* vol. 5, 350ff.

known to our understanding—such as syntactic and narrative continuity, familiarity of allusion, and the like—the more his words, letters, and lines take on a distinct intensity of their own, and the more thoroughly they recede from the grasp of the Corporeal Understanding. Yet they do so without any sacrifice to their intrinsic clarity of form. The sublime text must be a clear yet difficult text, its clarity based not on mundane simplicities, but indeed turned severely against them. The element of indeterminacy in the sublime of the text rests not at all with the sublime image itself, but with the expectations of the perceiver, conditioned to encounter signifiers that efface their own presence, the better to operate as servants of referentiality. This is one element of the difficulty involved in the determinate sublime, but obscurity, in the Burkean sense, is not the producer of this difficulty.[61] There is a difference between the obscurity that hides outlines like a formless vapor, demanding difficult and ultimately frustrated labor of attempted penetration, and the burden of a text that imposes on the perceiver the difficulty of apprehending many condensed visions of clarity all at once, none of them hidden; if there is blinding here, it is from an overdeterminate clarity of *presence*.[62] What are present, of course, are the seeds of meaning, not the external meanings themselves. Interpretive labors are still required to fetch these, but if the text is truly efficacious, the sublime event will have occurred before these labors begin. There is difficulty in this event too, perhaps greater than that involved in any of the subsequent labor. This is the struggle with a self that is impatient with discontinuity and paradox, demanding a servitude of language to familiar referentiality. Self-annihilation is the key here, as it is with so much else in Blake. When that is accomplished, paradox becomes visionary freedom and the recalcitrance of the text becomes the autonomy of a respected friend, a companion in the dialectic of desire.

The Poet's Work: His Sublime and His Pathos

"When that is accomplished": it is a tall order. Self-annihilation presumably provides the bridge between "the Most Sublime Poetry" and the altruism of "The most sublime act," which, as Blake states in the Proverbs of

---

[61] See Wittreich, *Angel of Apocalypse*, 188. Wittreich tells us that Blake rejects "obscurity as opacity," the obscurity of the Burkean sublime (187). Blake's work demands a complexity of seeing, but this is not the same thing as hindered seeing, which the term "obscurity" implies. The Corporeal Understanding is hindered not so much by obscurities that the poet imposes as by its own false presuppositions.

[62] In "The Sublime Poem: Pictures and Powers" (*Yale Review* 58 [Winter 1969]: 211), Martin Price, speaking of Blake's occasional pileups of small, sharply visualized details, comments on "the closeness of attention that all but obliterates the outlines of the natural object in its familiar form, finding in it the effluence of vast powers and rising in wonder to a contemplation of those powers through the object."

Hell, "is to set another before you" (*MHH* 7.17). The sublime *experience* must eventuate in a sublime *doing*, or else the interplay of intellect and its self-satisfying desire remains a sterile and narcissistic exercise, quite alien to anything we know of Blake's program. But the subjugation of self and the act of setting another before oneself are problematic processes; to an observer they may as easily provoke a new sublime of terror as provide intimations of altruistic love. Take, for example, Los's famous *agon* with his Spectre in the first chapter of *Jerusalem*:

> Yet ceased he not from labouring at the roarings of his Forge
> With iron & brass Building Golgonooza in great contendings
> Till his Sons & Daughters came forth from the Furnaces
> At the sublime Labours for Los. compelld the invisible Spectre
> To labours mighty, with vast strength
>
> (*J* 10.62–11.1)

Los labors here not in order to achieve the sublime experience but because he has already experienced it; he has had access to the Divine Vision and, indeed, keeps it (see *J* 95.20). His work is both productive and altruistic, simultaneously paternal and maternal, as Blake suggests by projecting from the word "Labours" both the products of the womb ("Sons & Daughters") and those of the wage-earning factory artisan. The language of the passage, however, rigorously excludes any overt hint of the loving, the maternal, the soft, the yielding; it is redolent of the hard, muscular, contentious imagery of a masculine world ("roarings," "iron & brass," "great contendings," "compelld," "mighty," "strength"). If this is a sublime, it is a sublime that meets Burkean prescriptions—or, to use Blake's own words, a Sublime . . . shut out from the Pathos (*J* 90.12).

My general point is that Blake often finds it difficult to depict his actors in anything other than a sublime mode that they themselves are ostensibly trying to transcend. This is part of a larger problem attendant upon any production of sublime poetry that has a redemptive purpose: the recalcitrance of corporeal existence in time to which the poet must return after his own moment of astonishment and transformation. Ideally, "the Poets Work is Done . . . Within a Moment: a Pulsation of the Artery" (*M* 29.1–3), but after that moment has passed, the poet must face the fact that although "the Work" is done, the necessity of further labor is ongoing and unremitting ("yet ceased he not from labouring"). A posture of heroic endurance is required, which tends to bring with it, in what is supposed to be a labor of love, a disquieting rhetoric of force and compulsion. What goes for poets goes for readers alike; too often, after their own sublime encounter with the Blakean text, in their eagerness to spread the good news they turn into aggressive banner-wavers, relentless explicators, or imperious system builders, as anyone acquainted with the history of Blake criticism can easily attest. The essence of the sublime experience is that it offers *all*, a total gratification of desire to the Intellectual Powers, but the communication of that experience (whether by poets or by readers) too readily operates on a principle of *exclusion*, a casting out of the indulgent, the accommodating, the softer "feminine" affections.

Blake is thoroughly aware of this disturbing paradox and the shadow it casts on the efficacy of a "Most Sublime Poetry," and we may conclude this chapter on his conception of the sublime by examining the ways in which he articulates the problem. We are sometimes told that Blake has no distinct concept of the sublime as a separate category of aesthetic experience, that he uses the term as an indiscriminate epithet of praise, and that he conflates the categories of the sublime and the beautiful at will.[63] Although conflations of this sort do occur at certain points in his work, the fact remains that Blake displays a perfect conversance with the terminology of aesthetic categorization in his day. The categories are listed, for example, with their anatomical seats of origin, in this Proverb of Hell: "The head Sublime, the heart Pathos, the genitals Beauty, the hands & feet Proportion" (*MHH* 10.1). Later in his career he develops a strong preoccupation with these categories, particularly the two chief contraries, the sublime and the pathetic (often subsumed in contemporary accounts by the beautiful). Thus we may infer from some cancelled lines on the frontispiece to *Jerusalem* that he originally intended to make the separation of sublimity from pathos the very argument of his great poetic *summa*. This inference is corroborated by a remarkable account in *A Descriptive Catalogue* of a "voluminous" work on "a subject of great sublimity and pathos" (almost certainly *Jerusalem*), which his painting "The Ancient Britons" was designed to illustrate. It is worth pausing over this account, for it reveals more clearly than anything else in Blake's work a sense of the sublime as a category of limitation or exclusion—not an *all*, but a residue of something prior and greater, for which no aesthetic term is available.

The discussion of the Ancient Britons strangely converts a myth of the origins of history into an allegory of the genesis of aesthetic categories; the myth not only projects "sublimity and pathos," it is *about* sublimity and pathos:

> The three general classes of men who are represented by the most Beautiful, the most Strong, and the most Ugly, could not be represented by any historical facts but those of our own country, the Ancient Britons; . . . They were overwhelmed by brutal arms all but a small remnant; Strength, Beauty, and Ugliness escaped the wreck, and remain for ever unsubdued age after age. . . . The Strong man represents the human sublime. The Beautiful man represents the human pathetic, which was in the wars of Eden divided into male and female. The Ugly

---

[63] See Weiskel, *The Romantic Sublime*, 67.

man represents the human reason. They were originally one man, who was four-fold; he was self-divided, and his real humanity slain on the stems of generation, and the form of the fourth was like the Son of God. How he became divided is a subject of great sublimity and pathos. (*DC*, E 542–43)

We are uneasily aware that the "human sublime" offered to us here is something different from notions of the sublime discussed earlier in this chapter, as deduced from the letter to Butts or the annotations to Reynolds. In those instances, the sublime appears to be a term for an absolute height of value toward which all art must tend; here, it merely connotes one *kind* of aesthetic value among others, existing on a par with other competing values, such as those of the beautiful and the pathetic. In the latter case, the sublime serves as a term of differentiation, just as the terms "male" and "female" differentiate subsets of humanity. Some background is useful at this point. Throughout the eighteenth century, ideas of the beautiful and the pathetic tend to separate out from the idea of the sublime.[64] At the same time, as Monk has shown, the pathetic comes increasingly to signify the softer affections aroused by the pitiable and the endearing.[65] Meanwhile, the beautiful tends to lose its ancient conventional association with harmony and proportion, and to acquire feminine sexual connotations. Burke's treatise on the sublime and the beautiful is particularly influential in this latter development. He specifically rejects proportion as the source of beauty and locates it instead in the small, the physically unthreatening, the smooth, and the gently curvaceous, all essentially female attributes that, he writes, comprise "the physical cause of love." The pathetic and the beautiful thus converge upon a common eroticized femininity. Massive, strong, threatening, rugged, and angular, the sublime is obviously conceived as a contrasting male counterpart.[66] Blake himself shows a post-Burkean understanding of beauty when, in the Proverb from the *Marriage* quoted previously, he specifically divorces proportion from beauty, and locates the latter in the genitals. Likewise, in the account of the Ancient Britons, he accepts the assimilation of pathos and beauty: "The Beautiful man represents the human pathetic," and in the fall, this Ancient Briton

[64] For Longinus, the Pathetic "or the Power of raising passions to a violent and even enthusiastic degree" was an extremely important, though not a necessary, constituent of the sublime (see *On the Sublime*, 17–18). By the first decade of the eighteenth century, John Dennis so fully identifies the sublime with the "Enthusiastick Passion" that he even takes Longinus to task for suggesting that the sublime can do without it (see *Grounds of Criticism*, 78). Late in the century, however, the sublime and the pathetic have become quite distinct, as Johnson's comment on the Metaphysical poets serves to indicate: "Nor was the sublime more within their reach than the pathetick" (*Lives of the Poets* vol. 1, 20).

[65] See Monk, *The Sublime*, 13 and Paley, *The Continuing City*, 58. Paley provides a good account of Blake's references to the pathetic, particularly with regard to *Jerusalem* (see *The Continuing City*, 58ff.).

[66] On female beauty, physical love, and masculine traits, see, respectively, *Philosophical Enquiry*, 115, 151, and 124–25.

evolves a female double. Blake substitutes *pathos* for Burke's beauty as the effective contrary term to the sublime ("the human *sublime*," "the human *pathetic*"), but he perpetuates the identification of the contraries as masculine and feminine principles.

In his account of the Ancient Britons, Blake categorizes these principles, yet tends to blur the distinctions between them. Among the Ancient Britons there are, after all, no separate females; all three are men. Moreover, some of their attributes tend to slide into one another: the human pathetic is Beautiful, and there is a Beauty "proper to sublime art"—namely, "lineaments, or forms and features that are capable of being the receptacles of intellect" (E 544). Blake describes his Strong man, the human sublime itself, "as a receptacle of Wisdom, a sublime energizer; his features and limbs do not spindle out into length, without strength, nor are they too large and unwieldy for his brain and bosom. Strength consists in accumulation of power to the principal seat, and from thence a regular gradation and subordination; strength is compactness, not extent nor bulk" (E 545). Strength is, of course, a conventional attribute of the Burkean sublime, but here it is difficult to distinguish from Beauty; if one is a "receptacle of intellect," the other is a "receptacle of Wisdom." Moreover, the description of Strength, focuses, oddly enough, almost entirely on classical proportion ("regular gradation and subordination")—the traditional criterion for beauty itself, until Burke banished it in favor of a quasi-feminized form. Beauty is thus defined in terms that belong properly to the sublime ("the head Sublime"), and the human sublime is described in terms traditionally proper to beauty. They interpenetrate in a latently erotic union, as compact strength energizes itself within a receptacle of lineaments—lineaments of gratified desire, perhaps.

They interpenetrate, and yet they do not. If the sublime, the beautiful, and the pathetic are one, why establish them as separate personifications in the first place? And why attach these figures to a myth that discovers them to be already diminished forces? For the Strong man, the Beautiful man, and the Ugly man "were originally one man, who was fourfold; . . . and the form of the fourth was like the Son of God." If the Strong man is the human sublime, who is this fourth, who, according to the myth, vanished "In the last Battle of King Arthur [when] only Three Britons escaped" (E 542)? Indeed, who is the "one man" whose "real humanity" was slain? The "human" of the terms "human sublime" and "human pathetic" appears to be something less than "real humanity," just as three is an inescapable reduction of four.

Blake would like to have it both ways on this matter. He would like to imagine the three Britons as a small, indefatigable remnant, perpetuating in corporeal time and space the plenary powers of humanity that existed before the fall: "a small remnant; Strength, Beauty, and Ugliness escaped the wreck, and remain for ever unsubdued, age after age" (E 542). Thus when he comes to "say something concerning his ideas of Beauty, Strength and Ugliness," (E 544) he presents at least two of these in the interchangeable terms that would have been proper to their ideal status in eternity. The Ugly man, meanwhile, has already taken on the look and actions of lupine or tigerish savagery prominent in the eighteenth-century sublime of terror: "approaching to the beast in features and form, his forehead small, without frontals; his jaws large; nose high on the ridge, and narrow; . . . The Ugly Man acts from love of carnage, and delight in the savage barbarities of war" (E 544–45).[67] Clearly, there is no perpetuation of a prelapsarian sensibility here. Blake's painting of the ancient Britons thus depicts gradations of fallenness; some residues of the fall have separated farther from the lineaments of intellect and gratified desire than others, but all are separate and diminished to some degree. It is only a matter of time before the Strong man, the human sublime, becomes no more than the brawny, cavern-dwelling "*strong* Urthona" (*Eur* 3.10) depicted in the early Lambeth books, or the raging, despairing, indefinitely formed Tharmas, "Parent *power* darkning in the West" (*FZ* 4.6). These are mock strengths and mock powers—for the human sublime when it is cut off from pathos, or the love of intellect for form, becomes an elaborate masquerade for despair.

This latter stage of separation is presented in two important passages from *Jerusalem*, briefly cited previously. One of these is from the cancelled inscription on the frontispiece:

> His Sublime & Pathos become Two Rocks fixd in the Earth
> His Reason his Spectrous Power, covers them above
> Jerusalem his Emanation is a Stone laying beneath
>
> (*J* 1.4–6)

Another version of this scene appears late in the poem:

> no more the Masculine mingles
> With the Feminine. but the sublime is shut out from the Pathos
> In howling torment, to build stone walls of separation, compelling
> The Pathos, to weave curtains of hiding secresy from the torment.
>
> (*J* 90.10–13)

[67] Dennis is seminal in considering ferocious wild beasts—"Monsters, Serpents, Lions, Tygers"—as appropriate subjects for arousing "Enthusiastick Terrour" and, hence, the sublime (*Grounds of Criticism*, 87–88). The sublime, Burke tells us in remarks perhaps not lost on the author of "The Tyger," "comes upon us in the gloomy forest, and in the howling wilderness, in the form of the lion, the tiger, the panther, or rhinoceros." He adds that "on account of their unmanageable fierceness, the idea of a wolf is not despicable; it is not excluded from grand descriptions and similitudes" (*Philosophical Enquiry*, 66 and 67). Burke may have in mind the famous and bloodcurdling passage on the ravenous mountain wolves, in Thomson's "Winter," lines 388–413 (James Thomson, *Poetical Works*, ed. J. Logie Robertson [London: Oxford University Press, 1908]).

These passages raise the paradoxical idea of a *deprived* sublime, one that is "shut out" from other forms of sensibility, a sublime that is petrified and, in short, fallen. In the first of these passages, the human reason has advanced to sovereignty over the other faculties. In the second, the "stone walls of separation" and the curtain of secrecy that the sublime and the pathos place before one another look suspiciously like those thwartings, or barriers, or obscurities that figure so largely in eighteenth-century accounts of the sublime as a mode of deprivation—a view found in its most rationalist form in Burke. A sublime of deprivation becomes automatically a sublime that puts itself in reason's spectrous power, for it requires that we reason the idea of strength or power into being through negative tokens—withdrawals, resistances, incomplete disclosures. But what has really withdrawn is not "the great" (as Addison called the sublime experience), but rather something so deeply hidden that its absence is unremarked because its appeal is buried (like the Emanation Jerusalem "laying beneath") or forgotten. The mind's deep quest is for receptacles of intellect, the total gratification of desire in definite, permanent form.

Weiskel has found anxiety at the core of the eighteenth-century fascination with the sublime, "the anxiety of nothingness, or absence. In its more energetic rendition the sublime is a kind of homeopathic therapy, a cure of uneasiness by means of the stronger, more concentrated—but momentary—anxiety involved in astonishment and terror."[68] But the unease is never really cured, which is why sublime poems of the period often have to repeat their heightened moments again and again.[69] It is not cured because the true source of the mind's deprivation is concealed from it. The mind is induced into believing that it is deprived from access to "the great," and so it dreams up strategies for discovering itself equal or superior to this "great"—empty strategies from Blake's point of view, for this great does not exist, it is "not extent nor bulk." All the while, however, the anxiety, the unease, the stirrings of an unacknowledged desire continue, prompting the mind to ever-renewed feats of grandeur, new "highs." The Burkean sublime is despair ("howling torment") that thinks itself to be a plenitude of strength.

The masculinist language of the Burkean sublime is important in this context. When Blake paraphrases the separation of the sublime and the pathos as "no more the Masculine mingles with the Feminine," he refers, of course, not to actual men and women. If the masculine mingles no more with the feminine, it is not for lack of physical congress, but rather for lack of something more truly fulfilling. The masculine and feminine principles

---

[68] *The Romantic Sublime*, 18.

[69] See, for example, Thomson's unappeasable appetite for introducing catastrophe after catastrophe in *The Seasons*, even in the generally benign contexts of "Spring" and "Summer"; on the verbal level, a similar effect is achieved by the jerky, unremittingly exclamatory style of Young's *Night Thoughts*.

within the self, which comprise the love dialogue between creative intellect and formal lineaments, have become sundered, so that love is sought in one place and transcendence or the sublime in another, in a masculinist framework divorced from the fulfillment of erotic desire. More accurately, the desires are not quelled, but simply shifted elsewhere. Burke speaks of the softer affections with considerable condescension: "love approaches much nearer to contempt than is commonly imagined," and Frances Ferguson has noted Burke's oddly ennervating conception about sexual arousal and the effects of beauty.[70] One reason for this is that the full language of Eros is transferred to another encounter—that with the masculine sublime. Admiration, and then erotic intensity, become attached to strength and bulk. When Burke, describing "the passion caused by the sublime," tells us that it "hurries us on by an irresistible force" and leaves a mind "entirely filled with its object,"[71] he employs the language of ravishment and reveals the latently homoerotic discourse that underpins much of his aesthetics. In the fall, one forgets what one loves—even though the desire for it remains. To vie in muscular, rocklike strength against the vast rock-face of "the great" allows one to forget one's loss; it is a transaction that can assimilate desire in a form in which it need not be recognized as such.

As is frequently noted, Blake, too, privileges masculine imagery in his designs and masculine forms of action in his poetry. Even his type of the human Pathetic, is, before an unfortunate postlapsarian division into sexes, a Beautiful *man*. Some recent critics have called attention to homosexual imagery in certain of Blake's designs. Perhaps one purpose of these displays of eroticized male forms in his work is to expose the latent argument of conventional eighteenth-century sublime aesthetics to plain sight.[72] The object of the exposé is not the homoeroticism per se of the Burkean sublime, but rather its structure of subterfuge and displacement. Blake decodes

[70] See Burke, *Philosophical Enquiry*, 67 and Ferguson, "The Sublime of Edmund Burke," 75–76.

[71] *Philosophical Enquiry*, 57.

[72] Martin Price has noted that the "homosexual fantasy" evident in some eighteenth-century Gothic novels ("sublime beauties colored by guilt and ambivalent desire") is connected to "the summoning up of titanic energies from their caves of suppression" ("The Sublime Poem," 205). Lately some note has been taken of homoerotic elements in Blake's own work; e.g., Susan Fox, *Poetic Form in Blake's "Milton"* (Princeton: Princeton University Press, 1976), 228–29, and W.J.T. Mitchell, "Style and Iconography in the Illustrations of Blake's Milton," in *Blake Studies* 6 (Fall 1973): 66–67, raise the question of certain designs in *Milton*; and in her sometimes heavy-handed Freudian study *Blake's Prophetic Psychology* (London: Macmillan Press, 1983), Brenda S. Webster reads these designs as unmistakably homosexual, interpreting them as the poet's quest to acquire the potency of an idealized male muse (261–62). *Milton* is, of course, the work par excellence in which the Poet is overtaken by the "irresistible" force of the sublime moment.

the attraction to male dominance, cloudily concealed in an abstract discourse about "the great," by offering clearly delineated, unadorned masculine images of potency and action.

But there is also a more positive impulse at work in Blake's privileging of male form. Strength, struggle, and contest all play a genuine part in the constellation of qualities that he values, because they are all necessary to break down conventional modes of understanding. In the Edenic state, the sublime and the pathetic presumably disappear as separate modes of aesthetic experience and reappear joined in an intellectual form neither male nor female. But few readers are already in the Edenic state when they come to Blake, nor would they need the mediation of his art if they were so. The figure of the eroticized male mediates by destabilizing conventional norms of gender polarization, and hence it starts to undo the fall. It thus functions like the Blakean text itself. Blake requires a text that evokes a psychology of response similar to that of the Burkean sublime while presenting an altogether different set of rewards. Hence, he is willing to let a kind of separatist or masculinist aesthetic prevail provisionally in his work, one that defers easy gratification and subjects the reader to various forms of muscular rough treatment—assault on the senses, indecorum, deprivation of the corporeal understanding, unending challenge. The well-delineated muscularity of his masculine images thus serves as a visible epitome of this textual activity.

These images, as images, remain nonetheless a mode of sublimity shut out from the pathos. Yet it is not a sublimity that we can afford to pass unalarmed—as Wordsworth, to Blake's dismay, claimed to do with Jehovah and his shouting angels.[73] The human sublime needs the sublime of greatness and potent terror as a necessary foil, as a first term in a process of educative reading. Let us recall the scene from the cancelled frontispiece of *Jerusalem*, in which a spectrous reason hovers over the two rocks of the sublime and the pathetic, imposed on top of a buried Jerusalem. Once located in the position of the keystone over the arch whereby we enter the poem, the lines plausibly may contain hints to direct our own reading of the poem. We are allowed to see the spectre hovering over the rocky landscape as a rationalist reader might pore over the plates of Blake's sublime allegory. What this reader sees are isolated and ill-defined shapes that he can recognize from the context of eighteenth-century aesthetics—a knottily muscular, surly sublime and an unrefined mass of pathos, a bundle of soft, ineffectual emotions. Both forms emerge murkily from the *Jerusalem* text itself, a stone slab, a plate of scratched metal, a table impressed with a crowd of dead signs. What the spectrous reader does not see is Jerusalem the Emanation, the form of gratified desire, which is a living text.

When Blake cancelled this passage from the frontispiece, so that in all extant copies we enter the gate of the poem wordlessly, he deprived us of these emblematic hints of how to read it. It is one thing to be shown the reasoning spectre reading badly, and quite another to be catapulted directly into the work without posted warnings regarding the spectrous reader in ourselves. This spectrous reader must be conjured up time after time until at last, in our floundering reading of the text, we read *him* and read his sublime (which has been ours until this point) as the vast funerary monument to a displaced erotic desire. Blake forces us to reenact these spectrous readings, to relive these ravishments by "the great," or finally to reject them. The arena for these choices and challenges is in that sum of particular signifying acts and forms that we call the poet's style. On the level of style, as well as of idea, there are two sublimes, one darkly mimicking the other—or, rather, in its rough, separately masculine fashion, memorializing the other, namely the lost but potentially recoverable sublime of intellect. Blake treats the Burkean style of the sublime as Los might treat his spectrous brother; it is appropriated, assimilated, hated, and perhaps secretly loved, but ultimately made present as a negation, the better to reveal the outlines of a new, emergent style.

PART TWO

STYLE: SUBLIME EFFECTS

Chapter II

THE BARDIC STYLE

SUBLIME EXTENSION

CONTINUITY AND DISCONTINUITY

BLAKE'S ATTRACTION to a muscular, agonistic, hard-edged and angular sublime entails choices regarding the decorum appropriate to the sublime poem. Should the "great" present a stylistic effect of stronger cohesion than the pettiness of ordinary experience affords, or should it work to violate and sunder the perhaps all too oppressive cohesion of ordinary experience itself? Reynolds would argue that the great style reduces "the variety of nature to the abstract idea" and "improves partial representation by the general and invariable ideas of nature," prompting Blake to brief explosions in the margins (see E 643, 649). Much commentary in the period indeed moves away from the uniformitarian serenity of Reynolds and toward a view of the sublime as a turbulent, subversive, indecorous force, "a surpassing of conventions or reasonable limits," as one modern critic has called it.[1] A massively disordered stylistic surface is the appropriate dress for this conception of the sublime.

Such a style finds sanction in the literary remains of primitive times. In his *Northern Antiquities*, describing the style of the Eddas, Paul Henri Mallet provides an exemplary instance of this taste:

> The style itself, in which the expressions, one while sublime, one while extravagant and gigantic, are thrown together without art; the littlenesses that accompany the most magnificent descriptions; the disorder of the narrative; the uniform turn of the phrases, confirms to all who read this work an idea of a very remote antiquity, and a mode of thinking and writing peculiar to a simple and gross people . . . whose vigorous imagination, despising or not knowing any rules of art, displays itself in all the liberty and energy of nature.[2]

---

[1] Price, "The Sublime Poem," 194; see also Frances Ferguson, who speaks of the requirement of the sublime to preserve "its *difference* from the custom, habit, and fashion which are continually launching insidious assimilative forays upon it" ("The Sublime of Edmund Burke," 71).

[2] Paul Henri Mallet, *Northern Antiquities: or a Description of the Manners, Customs, Religion and Laws of the Ancient Danes, And Other Northern Nations*, trans. Bishop Percy, 2 vols. (London: T. Carnan, 1770), vol. 1, 108–9.

Blake, who assures us that the "British Antiquities are now in the Artist's hands" (E 542), displays a number of these features of style, as we shall see, perhaps in a conscious effort to revive the imaginative vigor of the ancient models. Ossian was certainly one of these stylistic models, and his antiquity, which Blake never doubted (see *AnnoW*, E 665), won a defense from Hugh Blair in the following terms:

> The manner of composition bears all the marks of the greatest antiquity. No artful transitions; nor full and extended connection of parts; such as we find among the poets of later times . . . but a style always rapid and vehement; in narration concise even to abruptness, and leaving several circumstances to be supplied by the reader's imagination. The language has all that figurative cast, which . . . partly a glowing and undisciplined imagination, partly the sterility of language and the want of proper terms, have always introduced into the early speech of nations; and in several respects, it carries a remarkable resemblance to the style of the Old Testament.[3]

The arts of later times are the arts of "transition" and "extended connection," the arts of continuity—which, insofar as they accord with the decorous uniformitarian principles of Reynolds, display the greatest remove from primitivism, real or ascribed. Against this development, Blake seeks to revive the art of discontinuity, a poetry of leaps and haltings, of sudden disjunctions and mismatched interfaces. The example of the "ancients" merely confirms what Blake's principles of the sublime would indicate to him in any case: that poetic continuity is the stylistic equivalent of indefinite form or blurred outline in the visual percept—and, as such, must be similarly repudiated.

A clarification of terms is in order here. What passes for continuity in one frame of reference may seem like discontinuity in another. For example, when Blake cries out that "Broken Colours & Broken Lines & Broken Masses are Equally Subversive of the Sublime" (E 652), it appears as if he himself is repudiating discontinuity in favor of the uniformitarian surface recommended by Reynolds. But from the context, it is clear that Blake is opposing a certain kind of continuous texture, for he is responding to Reynold's commendation of Venetian coloring for its "soft and gradual transition from one [tint] to another."[4] Unbroken lines are of course continua themselves, but Blake endorses them when they assume the form of "bounding line[s]" (*DC*, E 550)—that is, when they enclose shapes that are self-contained and therefore discontinuous with everything adjacent to them. Such bounding outlines direct the eye to the intensive center, whereas "soft and gradual transitions" diffuse attention over an extended

---

[3] Blair, "Critical Dissertation," *Poems of Ossian* vol. 2, 319–20.

[4] *Works* vol. 1, 102.

field. The bounding outline sharply differentiates its enclosed shape from other shapes, but it is spared the innumerable tiny breaks in lines that create, to the undiscerning eye, the illusion of "gradual transition." Such transitional forms are merely lines and masses that are broken before they ever establish themselves to the eye. They share the defects of excessive sameness and excessive differentiation. The more gradual the transition, the more the continuum tends toward absolute uniformity, which is the equivalent of a monotonous vacuity; at the same time, differences too finely subdivided tend, when closely perceived, toward incoherence and an indefinitely inchoate plurality, toward fade-outs and shadows.

Such featureless expanses are strongly established as sites of the sublime for many eighteenth-century tastes.[5] Burke straddles the fence on this issue, requiring a uniform continuity that is periodically vexed or broken:

> To produce therefore a perfect grandeur in such things as we have been mentioning, there should be a perfect simplicity, an absolute uniformity in disposition, shape and colouring. Upon this principle of succession and uniformity it may be asked, why a long bare wall should not be more sublime than a colonnade; since the succession is no way interrupted; since the eye meets no check; since nothing more uniform can be conceived? . . . When we look at a naked wall, from the evenness of the object, the eye runs along its whole space, and arrives quickly at its termination; the eye meets nothing which may detain it a proper time to produce a very great and lasting effect. The view of a bare wall, if it be of a great height and length, is undoubtedly grand: but this is only *one* idea, and not a *repetition* of *similar* ideas; . . . we are not so powerfully affected with any one impulse, unless it be one of a prodigious force indeed, as we are with a succession of similar impulses.[6]

For all Burke's advocacy of the obscure and the indefinite, his system depends for its energy on shock and astonishment, and hence provision is made for definite breaks, for demarcations and pointed effects. Prone to seeing the sublime stimulus as a continuous expanse when he considers it

---

[5] A well-known instance of this taste occurs in Johnson's depreciation of the sublimity of the famous "Dover cliff" passage in *King Lear* on the grounds that such Shakespearean details as "the crows and choughs that wing the midway air" (*Lear* IV.vi.13) and the man gathering samphire from the cliff face break what should be a sense of uninterrupted height: "it should be all precipice," Johnson growls to Garrick, "—all vacuum. The crows impede your fall" (James Boswell, *The Life of Samuel Johnson, L.L.D*, 2 vols. [London: J. M. Dent, 1949], vol. 1, 365). A similar affinity for continuous wholes is expressed by that bellwether of mid-century taste, Alexander Gerard: "Innumerable little islands scattered in the ocean, and breaking the prospect, greatly diminish the grandeur of the scene" (*Essay on Taste*, 15). Addison perhaps stands at the head of this line of taste with his seminal remark that "by greatness, I do not only mean the bulk of any single object, but the largeness of the whole view considered as one entire piece" (*Works* vol. 4, 340).

[6] *Philosophical Enquiry*, 142.

in spatial terms, as soon as a temporal dimension is added, Burke requires a discontinuous, sharp-edged sublime. In this respect, he is closer to Blake than he is to Johnson or Reynolds.

As a temporal idea, continuity implies the binding of particulars into a linked sequence, each point in time or space different from the next, yet inseparably bound to it. This sequential linking is imaged in the description of Los "forging chains new & new / Numb'ring with links, hours, days & years" (*BU* 10.17–18). Wordsworth invokes this form of continuity when, in the epigraph to the "Intimations" Ode, he desires his "days to be / Bound each to each in natural piety"—a desire that Blake explicitly castigates (*AnnoW*, E 665). In Blake's work, temporal continuity more frequently takes the form of an entropic progression, in which each moment is linked to its successor to the extent that it depletes its successors of a certain portion of a full power or vitality that existed when the chain began. This is the situation of Urizen, who, as Nelson Hilton has shown,[7] is bound by a chain of ages that are also ages of change, until nothing is left of his eternal life, which "Like a dream was obliterated" (*BU* 13.33–34). Continuity, conceived as a chain of causes and effects, is unidirectional, an enslavement to steady attrition.

In literary symbolism, the vision of temporal continuity is typically expressed in the figure of the journey, but this figure exists in Blake's work mainly to be parodied and subverted. The hero of *Milton* perhaps comes the closest to enacting a traditional epic journey, but since it consists, strictly speaking, of a single, instantaneous vertical descent, it is as unorthodox a literary journey as one is likely to find. Most of the other travelers in Blake's work are a hapless lot—figures who either wander back and forth over the same stretch of land, like Tiriel,[8] or who go nowhere at all as they yearn for the traveler's destination, like the Sun-flower of *Songs of Experience*, or who travel vicariously through the self-repeating lives of others, like the Mental Traveller, or who simply are lost, like the dreaming Traveller "under the Hill" in the Epilogue to *The Gates of Paradise*. The most purposeful of these travelers is Urizen, in Night VI of *Vala*, who after one of the most arduous journeys in Romantic literature, after struggles with monstrous terrors, climbs and drops, blank vistas and high barriers, discovers he has returned to the place where he started. Most of these travelers are compulsive, obsessed with origins and destinations, and their days are bound each to each with a vengeance.

Readers who read with their Corporeal Understanding are in the position of these unhappy travelers. They come with certain expectations of

---

[7] See *Literal Imagination*, 69–71.

[8] For a lucid account of Tiriel's back-and-forth meanderings, see G. E. Bentley, Jr.'s "Introduction" to his edition of *Tiriel* (Oxford: Clarendon Press, 1967), 10–11.

literary fulfillment and meanings that comfort the cultural suppositions that they have brought to the reading experience, and when they do not find them, their experiences are rather like Urizen's on his journey: "Infinite was his labour without end his travel" (FZ 69.25). Although Urizen's abysses, deserts, and living terrors are standard images from the catalog of the natural or Burkean sublime, it is not a sublime that Urizen seeks, but rather one that is inflicted on him. The more he strives to brush these disturbing interruptions aside and get on with his journey, the thicker they come. Like Urizen, the mind addicted to continuity becomes insensible to interruption and shock, plodding wearily in and out of the bomb craters of discontinuity that pockmark the road of experience. Blake's own narrative surfaces, with their notorious instability of setting, disjunctive narratives, and decontextualized references, form a sort of rhetorical equivalent to the rough topography of the Burkean landscape; on one level it is a kind of facsimile of the surface of the fallen world itself, as seen from the standpoint of vision, stripped of the decorum of "general and invariable ideas of nature" that make that world look like a field of continuity. Those who continue on, reading such a decorum into the surface of things, continue in illusion. Blake's own disordered surfaces may be designed in part to elicit, expose, mock, and cast out such readings.

But there is another possible purpose in this narrative disorder. As we have seen, Burke approves of certain interruptions in uniform fields. Speaking of "a sudden beginning, or sudden cessation of sound," he adds, "in every thing sudden and unexpected, we are apt to start."[9] To be startled by sudden sensory alterations, even by sudden threats or obstacles, alleviates the dullness of mundane continuity—which is one reason why the rough surprises of the Burkean sublime are, in controlled measure, aesthetically pleasing. Yet these interruptions of the ordinary are but small beer when compared to Blake's forms of discontinuity. If events of mundane experience belong to the order of time and history, these intrusive events of his poetry belong to the order of miracle. "Historians," Blake says, "being weakly organized themselves, cannot see either miracle or prodigy; all is to them a dull round of probabilities and possibilities; but the history of all times and places, is nothing else but improbabilities and impossibilities; which we should say, was impossible if we did not see it always before our eyes" (DC, E 543). These historians are like Urizen floundering on his circular journey in Night VI of Vala, or like the reader determined to see cause-and-effect narrative development in Blake's longer poems, or like the critic determined to translate their anomalies into a coherent, all-inclusive line of didactic meaning. The textual discontinuities that inconvenience such schemes might seem to an ideal reader of Blake

---

[9] *Philosophical Enquiry*, 83.

like providential interventions, opportunities to enter new imaginative space.

The ultimate intervention of miracle is, of course, apocalypse—the end to the continuity of time itself. The sound of the last trump is Burke's sudden loud noise raised exponentially to the infinite. Where it counts most crucially, Blake is rhetorically brilliant at manipulating Burkean "cessation of sound" and shocking breaks in expectation to create a sublime effect:

> Over them the famishd Eagle screams on boney Wings and around
> Them howls the Wolf of famine deep heaves the Ocean black thundering
> Around the wormy Garments of Albion; then pausing in deathlike silence
>
> Time was Finished! The Breath Divine Breathed over Albion
>
> (*J* 94.15–18)

"Such sounds as imitate the natural inarticulate voices of . . . animals in pain or danger, are capable of conveying great ideas"; thus Burke,[10] but here the Burkean "great" is turned inside out while its structure of suddenness is preserved. The bestial cries, though part of the paraphernalia of the Burkean sublime are introduced here not as "terrific" intrusions on our complacency, but as the reverse. They themselves are the old continuity, a background of natural wailing caught in the last stages of entropic fade-out, before miracle intervenes and a burst of new utterance proclaims their everlasting abolition. The transformation is as much formal as it is thematic. Against the continuity of the drawn-out lines, paratactic syntax, and weary tone of lines 15–17 there is posed the exclamatory three-word sentence that begins line 18, a disjunction enhanced visually by the empty space that follows the word "silence." At the same time, there are auditory modulations that enforce the change, as "famishd" becomes "finishd," "death" becomes "breath," and the *eas* of *screams* and *heaves* become the ease of *Breathed*.[11]

These breaks and modulations are closer in many ways to musical forms than they are to the norms of most narrative poetry. Although the climactic turning point of *Jerusalem* no doubt has, as its ultimate source, the silence

---

[10] Ibid., 84.

[11] A much larger transformation is encapsulated in these modulations, that of an entire tradition of "dark" sublime literature into the kind of visionary sublime represented by *Jerusalem*. As Molly Rothenberg has noted in "Blake Reads 'The Bard': Contextual Displacement and Conditions of Readability in *Jerusalem*" (*Studies in English Literature* 27 [Summer 1987]: 494–95), the phrase "the famishd Eagle screams" is a quotation from Gray's "The Bard," line 38, in which it functions as part of the Bard's melancholic stance. By reminding us of this stance in the final moments before its eternal abolition in the new dispensation of "time finished," Blake pointedly suggests the supersession of Gray's mode and the advent of a new mode of apocalyptic poetry.

in heaven before the opening of the seventh seal in Revelation (see Rev. 8.1), its rhetorical form is more likely to remind us of the treatment of such apocalyptic moments in the choral music of Blake's own century—for example, such explosive passages as the *et resurrexit* in Bach's B Minor Mass or the *es ward Licht* in Haydn's *Creation*. But the musical analogy may be applied more generally. The broken continuities, stop-and-start development, repetitions, key changes, and tempo contrasts perfected in Haydnesque and Mozartian symphonic form[12] reveal themselves virtually as the integument of the intellectual sublime, in which conception (the sublime) and feeling (the pathetic) consummate their union in a flow of pure signifiers. Tied to the referentiality of language and weighted with the pressure of urgent meanings, Blake's text cannot attain such an unalloyed form, yet it displays, so far as the medium of language permits, nearly all the same devices to ensure the vibrant interplay of continuity and discontinuity. Blake is perhaps the most symphonic of English poets, for he displays musical patterning on a grander scale than his closest rivals in this field, Smart before him and Whitman after. The principles of continuity and discontinuity form the music of the mind, the outline of the contraries, the lineaments of the intellectual wars. They provide the foundations on which Blake's monumental referential structures are built. To unimaginative minds, this opposition of continuity and discontinuity translates into ideas of complacent attachment versus disturbing loss; to the more imaginative, the terms suggest, respectively, enchainment to time and visionary liberation. These are, of course, thematized ways of looking at continuity and discontinuity. The musical analogy directs us instead to their formal functions, to the rhetorical strategies of Blake's art. These strategies suggest a provision of all things to all readers; for the stylistic organization of the text is itself a kind of polyvalent signifier. To one reader, perhaps addicted to "natural piety" or trust in days blended smoothly each in each, the style mirrors the recalcitrant surface of a fallen world, a topography of continual discomfort, anxiety, and alienation; to another reader, it revives the imaginative vigor of ancient bardic poetry; to a third, it presents a new, revolutionary surface studded with prodigies and miracles.

---

[12] For an impressively authoritative study of these musical matters, see Charles Rosen, *The Classical Style: Haydn, Mozart, Beethoven*, rev. ed. (London: Faber and Faber, 1976). Citing such elements as "the classical technique of transition from one kind of rhythm to another, . . . a real dramatic clash in the changes of key, and a sense of periodic phrasing" (43), Rosen makes the general claim that "the second half of the eighteenth century represents an important stage in the centuries-long process of the destruction of the linear aspect of music" (29). We cannot tell what, if anything, Blake knew of the music of the great Viennese classicists (although Haydn's triumphant visits to London in 1791–1792 and 1795 admit the possibility of some knowledge); but the case for Blake's acquaintance with their late-Baroque predecessor Handel and the possible influence of the *Messiah* on the form of *Jerusalem* has been plausibly argued in Paley, *The Continuing City*, 291-94.

To speak of "the text," as in the preceding, is, however, to speak too abstractly and imprecisely. While remaining clearly within the genre of sublime poetry, Blake's various poems convey differing stylistic impressions, and indeed there are stylistic variations within individual works. An organized understanding of this range of styles is perhaps best achieved by discriminating the poles of intention that motivate these differing stylistic effects. The goal of continuity (in subject matter or narrative form) offers one such pole; the goal of a radical self-signifying discontinuity, the other. Inasmuch as the principle of continuity makes possible coherent narrative and the depiction of passing linear time, Blake must bow to the principle when he attempts such things—yet without unduly sacrificing the disjunctive effects required for the achievement of the sublime. The abrupt, artless mode of chronicle practiced by the ancient, primitive bards is apparently Blake's chief model in these attempts, and for this reason I have designated this stylistic pole "bardic." The opposite pole—that aimed at achieving an effect of radical discontinuity and self-referentiality—I call "iconic," for in this mode, as we shall see, the text is foregrounded as text and *is* what it says, and is *seen* for what it is. So long as one recognizes that Blake's individual poems are to be situated on a continuum between these stylistic poles, and that they quite frequently contain mixtures of the opposing modes, these categories should prove useful to a clearer understanding of his sublime style.

THE BARDIC VOICE: UTTERING THE "ARTIFICIAL INFINITE"

Everyone acquainted with Blake knows of the bardic voice and its self-proclaimed powers:

> Hear the voice of the Bard!
> Who Present, Past, & Future sees
> Whose ears have heard,
> The Holy Word,
> That walk'd among the ancient trees.
>
> (*SE*, E 18)

The Bard's authority comes from a divine sanction that enables him to see into the passing epochs of earthly time; the importance accorded to his "voice" comes from a more personal source. "Voice" marks the presence of individuated utterance and thus draws our attention to the Bard's participation in the events chronicled in his own song. Hence, the power of the passions that the song expresses derives in part from their source in the Bard's personal experience; in ancient days he was *there*. The Bard is thus a kind of visionary poet whose comprehensive vision is never wholly separable from an expression of personal concern, even personal crisis. The Bard of the "Introduction" to *Songs of Experience* is, to be sure, a highly generalized figure, and his personal emotional involvement in the events he describes is presented only in a nominal way; but some of Blake's Bards register their involvement in the content of their vision with a heightened, almost novelistic vividness, as in these lines printed in some copies of *America*:

> The stern Bard ceas'd, asham'd of his own song; enrag'd he swung
> His harp aloft sounding, then dash'd its shining frame against
> A ruin'd pillar in glittring fragments; silent he turn'd away,
> And wander'd down the vales of Kent in sick & drear lamentings.
>
> (*Am* 2.18–21)

Impersonality is no more a part of this Bard's sensibility than an immutable understanding of events is part of his visionary powers. He is as much caught up in flux and time's transformations as are the great events of history that it is his vocation to recount.

Behind the melancholy of the Bard in *America* and the lapse of his voice into silence lie the examples of Macpherson's Ossian and the eponymous Bard of Gray's famous Pindaric ode. Macpherson presents Ossian as both the chronicler of his age and a participant in the events chronicled. This is a figure obsessively preoccupied with the passing of time, and his tone is unremittingly elegiac: "Did not Ossian hear a voice? or is it the sound of days that are no more? Often does the memory of former times come, like the evening sun, on my soul. The noise of the chase is renewed. In thought, I lift the spear"; "I look into the times of old, but they seem dim to Ossian's eyes, like reflected moon-beams, on a distant lake. Here rise the red beams of war! There, silent, dwells a feeble race! They mark no years with their deeds, as slow they pass along."[13] The Bard in Gray's poem is also the last of his race—and as he stands on the brink of a dizzying abyss, he also looks back to a dim, magical past of lost Bards:

> Cold is Cadwallo's tongue,
> That hush'd the stormy main:
> Brave Urien sleeps upon his craggy bed:
> Mountains, ye mourn in vain
> Modred, whose magic song
> Made huge Plinlimmon bow his cloud-top'd head.[14]

[13] *Poems of Ossian*, "Conlath and Cuthona," vol. 2, 183; "Cath-loda," vol. 1, 29.
[14] "The Bard: A Pindaric Ode," lines 29–34, in *Thomas Gray and William Collins: Poetical Works*, ed. Roger Lonsdale (Oxford: Oxford University Press, 1977).

But unlike Ossian, this Bard is also obsessed with futurity, and the bulk of his poem is devoted to a prophetic chronicling of the future misfortunes of the Plantagenets and the rise of the Tudors, capped by a more extended penetration into the distant prospect of English poetry, the domain of Milton and his successors:

> A Voice, as of the Cherub-Choir,
> Gales from blooming Eden bear;
> And distant warblings lessen on my ear,
> That lost in long futurity expire.

("The Bard," lines 131–34)

What is significant about the bardic vision here is that it proceeds to no apocalyptic finality, like the visions of futurity of Ezekiel or John of Patmos. Gray's Bard sees future time as one might see objects in a spatial prospect—the more distant receding from sight, and eventually vanishing at an indeterminate point. Beyond Milton's Eden nothing is clear, and there is a telling ambiguity about the "distant warblings" that "lessen" and become "lost in long futurity." Is this a tribute to a poetic vitality so strong that it propagates a line of succession stretching to infinity, or is it another mid-century lament for the post-Miltonic atrophy of poetic inspiration, a reduction and final disappearance of vitality? The ambiguity of Gray's meaning corresponds nicely with the dimness of his Bard's prospect. The poem, its protagonist, and the protagonist's vision all fittingly proceed to the same dying fall; the Bard casts his chronicle into the infinitely diminishing prospects of futurity's abyss before he himself suicidally follows after it at the end of the poem and "plunge[s] to endless night" (line 144).[15]

The vertigo attendant on the Bard's prospects, physical and visionary, reminds us that the eighteenth-century sublime sensibility includes a

---

[15] Harold Bloom identifies the figure of the Bard with the poets of "Blake's own literary age, the time of Sensibility or the Sublime, . . . poets to whom he felt the closest affinity—Thomson, Cowper, Collins, Gray, Chatterton"; regarding these mostly melancholy figures (with Gray's Bard especially in mind), Bloom says, "the theatre of mind dissolves in the endless night of an original chaos, the abyss always sensed in the histrionic mode. . . . The theatre of mind is necessarily a Sublime theatre of the Indefinite" ("Blake's *Jerusalem*: the Bard of Sensibility and the Form of Prophecy," in *The Ringers in the Tower: Studies in the Romantic Tradition* [Chicago: University of Chicago Press, 1971], 68 and 72. The distinction elaborated in Bloom's essay between the Hebrew prophet, shaper of "definite form" (72), and the "bard of sensibility" parallels my own distinction between "bardic" and "iconic" styles of Blakean narration, as defined and discussed in this chapter and the one following. But whereas Bloom reads the opposition in terms of rival voices, one plangent and self-expressive, the other oratorical and audience-directed, I see the rivalry as one of voice and text: the language of continuous speech, necessarily implicated in the temporality of telling, versus language as writing, fixed definitely as spatialized form.

marked taste for abysses that open endlessly within abysses. Deconstructionist theory of recent decades has textualized this interest by terming the experience of reading a *mise en abyme*, or "abyss structure," in which the writing that one confronts yields no access to truth but only a glimpse of an anterior writing, and so on, ad infinitum, as in a hall of mirrors. This abyss structure has some affinities with what Burke calls, in his *Enquiry*, "the artificial infinite." He defines it as a succession of uniformly framed parts stretching so far "as by their frequent impulses on the sense to impress the imagination with an idea of their progress beyond their actual limit." Uniformity and succession create "that uninterrupted progression, which alone can stamp on bounded objects the character of infinity."[16] The artificial infinite is a combination of a severe limit in one set of parameters—a specific size and shape applied uniformly to each object in the succession, with the same finite interval between each of them—and limitlessness in the extension of the whole; Burke's sublime colonnade, cited earlier, would typify this effect. The same scene, finite in itself yet indefinitely repeated in a receding depth perspective, gives the imagination the illusion of grasping infinity in one profound apprehension; endlessness is seen all too *particularly* as endless. The terror of the artificial infinite is that claustrophobia and vertigo emerge from it together, a sense of eternal confinement within the narrow limits of the objects arrayed in a series, combined with a sense of falling through the whole series all at once. One cannot look into such a structure and pass it by at the same time; to look in is to fall in. Our modern infatuation with language as a structure of "undecidability," in which ultimate referential origins are infinitely withdrawn, is perhaps a respectable academic version of the pleasurable *frisson* of falling so often evoked in the imagery and narrative organization of eighteenth-century sublime poetry.[17]

No poet in this mode exploits the falling effect better than Blake. For him, the fall is no mere hypothetical event occurring in an indefinite mythic time, but a palpable experience that he is fond of reenacting in the mold of poetic language itself:

[16] *Philosophical Enquiry*, 74.

[17] See, e.g., Mark Akenside in "The Pleasures of Imagination," describing some of the ecstasies of the soul in full flight through the fields of the void:

She meditates the eternal depth below,
Till, half recoiling, down the headlong steep
She plunges, soon o'erwhelmed and swallowed up
In that immense of being.

See "The Pleasures of Imagination," 1.208–11 in *The Poetical Works of Mark Akenside* (London: C. Cooke, 1795). Johnson's comment on Dover Cliff is worth recalling: "It should be all precipice—all vacuum. The crows impede your fall" (see note 5, this chapter).

Falling, falling! Los fell & fell
Sunk precipitant heavy down down
Time on times, night on night, day on day
Truth has bounds. Error none: falling, falling:
Years on years, and ages on ages
Still he fell thro' the void, still a void
Found for falling day & night without end.

(BL 4.27–33)

In content and style, this is a perfect miniature encapsulation of the artificial infinite. Combining echoes from *Paradise Lost*, such as the fall of Mulciber and Satan's journey through Chaos, all elements in the passage contribute to a single effect. As the pattern of stresses mimes the plunge of a body tumbling end over end, verbal repetition creates, as it were, a paradoxically discontinuous continuity. The whole set of terms produces the effect of an unending series, while each particular term seems to mark a stage or finite quantum of falling, breaking the continuum into a regress of frames.

From a structural standpoint, the bardic style may be viewed as a method of reproducing Burke's artificial infinite as an extended literary effect. The falling sensation that Blake mimics with such skill in *The Book of Los* and elsewhere may arise on a larger scale when the reader is confronted with a narrative that typically avoids the proportionings, subordinations, and buildups necessary for the effects of conventional beginnings, middles, and ends. Instead of comforting closures, bardic narrative offers a continuum of receding vistas and distant glooms, in which images and scenes are but passing stations in an indefinite series, while we are borne along on the swift and unvarying rush of the Bard's voice as it cascades from image to image, event to event. This mode is particularly adaptable to the chronicling of ancient origins, the unfolding of ages, and the prospects of futurity, insofar as these phenomena are viewed as part of a series, as local modulations within an unfathomable abyss of time. The overwhelming flux of time is both a source of the chararacteristic bardic melancholy and a model for the form of the bardic utterance. Ossian, Gray's Welsh Bard, and the "stern Bard" of *America* are all betrayed by the power of time and change, which removes the world they particularly loved, or which reveals old beliefs, once uttered in prophetic sincerity, to be folly. But if these figures typically present themselves as victims of a great force, it is only to reenact a characteristically Burkean scenario, in which the connoisseur of "terrific" objects somehow converts his humiliation into a personal triumph. The great force—here, the abyss of indefinite temporal extension—is assimilated into the Bard's rhetoric and reproduced as an array of stylistic effects. We are enjoined to "hear" the Bard's voice, which has managed to become the very voice of time's cascading flow, and the vertigo that was once his now becomes ours.

This feat is accomplished by subjecting a steadily maintained continuity of narrative to an overlay of the various devices of literary "astonishment." All narrative writers deal with time and change, but the tendency of sublime bardic narrative is either to accelerate the flow of events, so that it descends on us like a cataract, or else to subject it to a kind of reiterative stutter, forwarding it by fits and starts that bring us to new reenactments of what are more or less the same events. Arrest and momentum are thus merged into one experience. Blake is particularly adept at achieving these effects. They depend largely on an emphasis on physical metamorphoses in his imagery, on a profusion of changing tropes and of participial constructions in his diction, and on a conspicuous employment of paratactic sentence structure, repetition, and parallelism in his syntax.[18] Manifestations of these stylistic tendencies are to be found in all his major narratives from *Poetical Sketches* to *Jerusalem*, and they are most conspicuous in those works of the middle period that deal with the history of the ages—namely, the run of Lambeth books from *America* to *The Book of Ahania*, and the epic *Vala* that coalesced from them. Wherever they appear, they mark a strong upsurge of the bardic voice in his poetry. It is not the only mode at his disposal, but it is sufficiently rich in its devices to sustain a closer examination.

SYNTAX: CATALOG AND PARATAXIS

The most prominent feature of bardic syntax is its reliance on a serial arrangement of its constituent elements. Individual nouns, phrases, or whole

[18] Describing Blake's style in the context of late eighteenth-century sublime verse, Josephine Miles comments that "the participial sort of meaning is a major meaning for him, the motion observed in process and seen as qualitative rather than as active"; see *Eras and Modes in English Poetry* (Berkeley and Los Angeles: University of California Press, 1957), 85. In her essay "The Formal Art of *The Four Zoas*," Helen T. McNeil ratifies this observation by noting the frequency of participial constructions used to describe the actions of the Zoas: "Actions described with these participial forms are forced into a kind of continual present. The reader is overwhelmed by a spate of actions all in the process of occurring, but he is rarely relieved by their completion" (in *Blake's Visionary Forms Dramatic*, ed. David V. Erdman and John E. Grant [Princeton: Princeton University Press, 1970], 386). More recently, Ronald Clayton Taylor has noted that "indefinite repetition, in whatever form, is the semantic dynamo of Blake's uneasy motion" and that "Blake's style of unending process is quantitatively the predominant mode, and its overall effect is to entrap its reader continually in the meanderings of Time. It is composed of process predications . . . and by the progressive construction"; see "Semantic Structures and the Temporal Modes of Blake's Prophetic Verse," in *Essential Articles for the Study of William Blake, 1970–1984*, ed. Nelson Hilton (Hamden, Conn.: Archon Books, 1986), 255 and 251.

clauses tend to form a succession of brief, more or less equally weighted elements distributed isochronously along an indefinitely extended line. Rapidity of movement is achieved in the narrative not by subsuming particulars in a generalizing summary, but by reducing particulars, fully itemized, to virtually atomic units of significance; the rapidity is staccato rather than smooth. In her outline of Blake's stylistic affinities with the eighteenth-century sublime poem, Josephine Miles has observed that "nouns must be many, and listable, and cumulative. Verbs must be used mostly to keep the work going; there cannot be much play of subordination, or of reasoning. . . . This was Blake's mode of choice in most of his work, from *The French Revolution* through *Jerusalem*."[19] Miles identifies a number of features that belong to what I am calling the bardic style. It is a style that favors a sensory, even an exclamatory, rendering of experience over a "reasoning" exposition. Hence the Bard, sensitive to the pathos of time's rapid flow, mimics it in his forms and shows scant interest in an analytic unfolding of the circumstances of any given incident. Analysis demands a syntax of subordination, of complex modification and periodic balance—but such a style hinders the effect of flow, of unbounded process. Subordinating syntax creates static structures endowed with centers and dependencies, whereas the isochronous, parallel, and independent clauses in paratactic syntax distribute emphasis evenly over an indefinite continuum; the center is ever-shifting, residing in different objects in the fleeting moment that each passes before the Bard's notice.

This style is particularly suitable for catalogs and inventories, important tools for the bardic task of surveying the phenomena of temporal experience. Blake's poetry is notable for its catalogs—which, in their sweep of the particulars of the creation, sometimes affect the naive simplicity and nonmimetic realism of the lists found in medieval metrical romances:

The barked Oak, the long limbd Beech; the Ches'nut tree; the Pine.
The Pear tree mild, the frowning Walnut, the sharp Crab, & Apple sweet,
The rough bark opens; twittering peep forth little beaks & wings
The Nightingale, the Goldfinch, Robin, Lark, Linnet & Thrush
                    (*FZ* 8; Textual Note, E 824.7–10)

Timbrels & violins sport round the Wine presses; the little Seed;
The sportive Root, the Earth-worm, the gold Beetle; the wise Emmet;
Dance round the Wine-presses of Luvah: the Centipede is there:
The ground Spider with many eyes: the Mole clothed in velvet
The ambitious Spider in his sullen web; the lucky golden Spinner;
The Earwig armd: the tender Maggot emblem of immortality:
The Flea: Louse: Bug: the Tape-Worm: all the Armies of Disease
                    (*M* 27.11–17)

---

[19] *Eras and Modes*, 86.

Living Creatures starry & flaming
With every Colour, Lion, Tyger, Horse, Elephant, Eagle Dove, Fly, Worm,
And the all wondrous Serpent clothed in gems & rich array Humanize

(*J* 98.42–44)

The bardic narrator of these passages bestows his interest equally on the creatures he catalogs, giving an undue emphasis to none. Everything in the verse, from the punctuational halts of colons and semicolons to the vivid descriptive tags attached to some of the creatures, serves to emphasize the isolated particularity of each creature and to minimize the relations they bear to one another. The narrator surveys an indefinitely extended set of life forms, notes certain individual members of the set and passes on; it is the multiplicity or abundance of particulars, not the nature of the particulars that catches his attention. At the same time, it is a fleeting abundance; each particular shines momentarily before the reader's eye, then slips backward and away from the ever-moving present of the unremitting bardic voice.

Like nouns and noun phrases, independent clauses may themselves be strung together into a series, thereby yielding paratactic syntax and the inventorying of actions, just as the simple list is an inventorying of objects. As a verbal artifact, the list accentuates the temporality of narrating and reading by reducing each subject of attention to its briefest form, thus speeding up the process of movement through the whole. Lists composed of successive actions double this emphasis on the temporal, for they attach the rapid pace of a purely verbal movement to the impression one gets of the passage of time within the tale itself, as in this example from the *Book of Urizen*:

7. He form'd a line & a plummet
To divide the Abyss beneath.
He form'd a dividing rule:

8. He formed scales to weigh;
He formed massy weights;
He formed a brazen quadrant;
He formed golden compasses
And began to explore the Abyss
And he planted a garden of fruits

(*BU* 20.33–41)

Lines like these present discrete quanta in an apparently unending series. Urizen's formations could conceivably go on forever here, and even when the catalog of measuring devices in fact ceases, the isochronous paratactic clauses roll on beyond it. Each action in the catalog of particulars presents a new element in a rapid series of changes, with each change contained and completed in its own end-stopped line of verse. The separate events flicker by as in speeded-up movie film, yet there is an unsettling impression that actual temporal progress is held in suspension. The parallel constructions of the clauses, the end-stopping, and the return of the lines again and again to the phrase "he formed" create an effect of dull, relentless repetition appropriate to the real nature of Urizen's character and his makings. For, in one way or another, Urizen seems perpetually in a state of free fall and at the same time locked in an unprogressive formal rigidity. His paradoxical situation, in turn, is a mirror of metronomic or clock time, which these lines mimic in their fashion: a continuum marked only by formal ticking repetitions and lacking both perceivable boundaries and a stable "now" point to serve as a center.

Although there is always an element of disquiet in the paratactic style of narration, in Blake's hands it is a flexible instrument of expression, adaptable to a variety of moods and capable of conveying a variety of effects beyond the mere rendering of chronological succession. To understand this point, as well as to note fundamental stylistic consistencies at work within the distinguishing differences that characterize separate poems, one should look closely at passages of somewhat greater structural complexity than those considered so far. Two passages widely separated in their time of composition, from *The French Revolution* and *Jerusalem* (to take works that Miles has cited as starting and ending points for the main span of Blake's career as a sublime poet), may serve the purpose:

> Rushing along iron ranks glittering the officers each to his station
> Depart, and the stern captain strokes his proud steed, and in front of his solid ranks
> Waits the sound of trumpet; captains of foot stand each by his cloudy drum;
> Then the drum beats, and the steely ranks move, and trumpets rejoice in the sky.
> Dark cavalry like clouds fraught with thunder ascend on the hills, and bright infantry, rank
> Behind rank, to the soul shaking drum and shrill fife along the roads glitter like fire.
> The noise of trampling, the wind of trumpets, smote the palace walls with a blast.
>
> (FR 287–93)

> Reuben return'd to his place, in vain he sought beautiful Tirzah
> For his Eyelids were narrowd, & his Nostrils scented the ground
> And Sixty Winters Los raged in the Divisions of Reuben:
> Building the Moon of Ulro, plank by plank & rib by rib
> Reuben slept in the Cave of Adam, and Los folded his Tongue
> Between Lips of mire & clay, then sent him forth over Jordan
> In the love of Tirzah he said Doubt is my food day & night—

All that beheld him fled howling and gnawed their tongues
For pain: they became what they beheld. In reasonings Reuben returned
To Heshbon. disconsolate he walkd thro Moab & he stood
Before the Furnaces of Los in a horrible dreamful slumber,
On Mount Gilead looking toward Gilgal: and Los bended
His Ear in a spiral circle outward; then sent him over Jordan.

(J 32.1–13)

Each of these passages, with its profusion of separate sequential actions, has a style carefully suited to its subject. These are scenes of continuous motion marked off in a series of stages; in the first passage they are indicated aurally by the drumbeat of the army marching on Versailles and visually by the successive passing of the infantry units, "rank behind rank"; in the second, by the spasmodic series of Reuben's comings and goings, punctuated by the severe interventions of Los. In both passages the syntax virtually does away with subordination (with the very minor exceptions of "all that beheld" and "what they beheld" in J 32.8–9), displaying instead a series of brief independent clauses (eight in the seven lines of *The French Revolution* extract, with nine indicative verbs; fourteen in the thirteen lines of the *Jerusalem* extract, with nineteen indicative verbs—including one in direct address). Verbs of locomotion predominate (cf. Miles: "verbs must be used mostly to keep the work going"). The conjunction "and" provides a loose continuity, joining clauses or predicates six times in the *Jerusalem* extract, and five in the briefer passage from the *French Revolution*. Actions are simple and wholly contained within the clausal unit, and they either repeat themselves (as when Los sends Reuben over Jordan) or are mutually dissociated. The relation of one action to the next is that of contiguous succession, for while the larger action depicted in each passage is comprehensively motivated (Los and the revolutionary army each have a broad purpose), the individual smaller actions, locked into a grammar of independent clauses, do not seem to motivate one another.

The effect of such a style is to render action both linear and fragmentized, to make it a string of moments in an indefinite series. In *The French Revolution* this effect is linked to a movement of liberation; temporal change and a loosening of ties are potent forces for the good, for they bring about the overthrow of old tyrannies in the here and now of material life. Hence the separated, paratactic phrases in the passage quoted move like a series of waves, accumulating power, until they smash into the seawall of the palace in the final line. In the *Jerusalem* scene, change is more dire, simultaneously suggesting both a dispersion and a constriction of potentiality. In particular, the spate of proper nouns in this passage (Reuben, Los, Tirzah, Ulro, Adam, Heshbon, Moab, Mount Gilead, Gilgal, Jordan) enforces the effect of scattered centers, a multiplicity of actors and locales.

The bardic catalog is reinstated here as a series of way stations in a spasmodic progress. But each stage of Reuben's progress leaves him increasingly diminished, a dwindling figure in an expanding panorama of locales.
One can scarcely imagine more diametrically opposed visions of temporal
change than those contained in these two passages, yet they both exhibit
essentially the same stylistic construction. Although the poet's point of
view is never really in doubt, his narrative voice in itself is rarely evaluative.
The same voice may produce hope or horror, but these are responses to
the content of the poem, not to the modulations of the voice. For it is not
the function of the bardic voice to judge the productions of temporality
but rather to reproduce their effects in the mode of telling. Its task is to
render temporality as a sublime trope.

TROPES: METAMORPHOSIS AND RHETORICAL SUBSTITUTION

The idea of temporality is inseparable from the idea of change—which,
according to all orthodox accounts, is a consequence of the fall. From
Blake's somewhat different standpoint, the notion of change is one of the
many illusions that the fall into corporeal perception engenders:

> In Eternity one Thing never Changes into another Thing Each Identity is Eter-
> nal consequently Apuleius's Golden Ass & Ovids Metamorphosis & others of
> the like kind are Fable yet they contain Vision in a Sublime degree being derived
> from real Vision in More Ancient Writings. Lots Wife being Changed into a
> Pillar of Salt alludes to the Mortal Body being rendered a Permanent Statue but
> not Changed or Transformed into Another Identity while it retains its own In-
> dividuality. (*VLJ*, E 556)

If Eternal truth is one thing and Fable another, then most of Blake's bardic
narratives are "Fable . . . in a Sublime degree," for they are heavily
freighted with images and dramatizations of metamorphosis. They are, as
Frye has said of Ovid's poem, tales "of humanized creatures dwindling into
objects of perception,"[20] and they have their mythic foundation in a great
primordial metamorphic event, Albion's transformation from Universal
Manhood into a large rock in the North Atlantic sea. The Burkean landscape of heights and abysses, the topography of the fallen world itself, is
therefore not merely the arena for time's changes, but also the quintessential image of the fact of change. It is, like Lot's wife, the "Permanent
Statue" or mineral residue of heights, depths, and expanses of a former
human vitality.

Within this universal frame of metamorphic reduction, where living

---

[20] *Fearful Symmetry*, 42.

form turns into stone, occasions of transformation in Blake's narratives nevertheless often communicate a sense of busy local vitality. In his early work, metamorphosis displays a generally benign aspect; a sublimating personification can raise the creatures and phenomena of nature to higher status, so that the lion of "The Little Girl Found" turns into "a spirit arm'd in gold" (line 36), the Evening Star of *Poetical Sketches* into a "fair-hair'd angel," and the passing seasons in the opening lyrics of that volume into a set of pastoral divinities. Or else a happily cyclical life force, implied by the turning of the seasons in the *Sketches*, can express itself in such watery transformations as the Cloud celebrates in *Thel*:

> Nothing remains; O maid I tell thee, when I pass away,
> It is to tenfold life, to love, to peace, and raptures holy:
> Unseen descending, weigh my light wings upon balmy flowers;
> And court the fair eyed dew to take me to her shining tent

> (*Thel* 3.10–13)

Here is metamorphosis in Blake at its most benign. Change is presented here as a species of exchange; the flowers will exhale the descended drops in the form of vapor, and thus back to cloud. Exempt from the destructive erosion of time, metamorphosis of this sort means liberation from the fixed form of stony residues.

Metamorphoses so effortless, so agreeable to the expectations of common experience, edge toward that ideal of "soft and gradual transition" that Reynolds commended and away from the rugged discontinuities of the sublime. In ordinary usage, however, the term *metamorphosis* suggests changes of an extreme or even preternatural kind, achieved with unusual speed. In Blake's later work, representations of this sort of transformation are more common and tend to produce that surprise and wonderment so requisite for the sublime effect. These transformations have their own vitality, different from that of the Cloud in *Thel*, for they suggest a perverse life surging up suddenly and terrifically against the background of a deadened landscape, without alleviating its gloom. *Vala* provides some of the most spectacular examples:

> Then he beheld the forms of tygers & of Lions dishumanizd men
> Many in serpents & in worms stretchd out enormous length
> Over the sullen mould & slimy tracks obstruct his way
> Drawn out from deep to deep woven by ribbd
> And scaled monsters or armd in iron shell or shell of brass
> Or gold a glittering torment shining & hissing in eternal pain
> Some [as] columns of fire or of water sometimes stretchd out in heighth
> Sometimes in length sometimes englobing wandering in vain seeking for ease

> (*FZ* 70.31–38)

For the monsters of the Elements Lions or Tygers or Wolves
Sound loud the howling music Inspird by Los & Enitharmon Sounding loud
     terrific men
They seem to one another laughing terrible among the banners
And when the revolution of their day of battles over
Relapsing in dire torment they return to forms of woe
To moping visages returning inanimate tho furious
No more erect tho strong drawn out in length they ravin
For senseless gratification & their visages thrust forth
Flatten above & beneath & stretch out into beastial length

(FZ 102.3–11)

His eyes shot outwards then his breathing nostrils drawn forth
Scales coverd over a cold forehead & a neck outstretchd
Into the deep to seize the shadow scales his neck & bosom
Coverd & scales his hands & feet upon his belly falling
Outstretchd thro the immense his mouth wide opening tongueless
His teeth a triple row he strove to sieze the shadow in vain
And his immense tail lashd the Abyss his human form a Stone
A form of senseless Stone remain in terrors on the rock

(FZ 106.25–32)

In the first of these passages, dire change passes over Urizen's lost children; in the second, over his troops in battle; and in the third, over Urizen himself. These Circean transformations accelerate before our eyes, as if by a kind of sorcery, a process of degradation that the human condition suffers, in any case, in the long cascade of ages since the fall. By this acceleration, however, the bardic narrator injects some local energy, a sublime "excess," in what we know to be a scene of actual human exhaustion. In each case, too rapid a depletion of these figures' real humanity acquires the look of a power gained in the realm of the monstrous. As in the Burkean economy of the sublime of magnitude, in which the infinite is imagined via the absence of the definite, sublime moments are manufactured here out of scenes of excessive loss—a process that depends on the theatricality of the excess to conceal the extent of the loss. Not only do the mutants of these visions become "terrors," sources of astonishment, but, in a grimly ironic fashion, they themselves become subjects of the sublime effect. The "dishumanizd" men of the first passage undergo (as serpents) the experience of incorporating the infinite within the self ("stretchd out enormous length"), or they attain "heighth." In the second passage, which plays brilliantly on the platitude that men become bestial in war, actual beasts momentarily gain elevated brows (or "the head sublime," as one of the Proverbs of Hell puts it) and sublimate into "*terrific* men." The third passage, like the first, displays a grotesque incarnation of the sublime ideal of infinite self-expansion

("Outstretchd thro the immense"), and makes the specific point that this astonishing transformation is a diminishment or depletion ("his human form a Stone").

The sublime of bardic narration relies heavily on the metamorphic image, for metamorphosis merely represents the continuum of change in so condensed a fashion that it seems a monstrosity or discontinuity. Metamorphosis allegorizes change—that is it *speaks* of change in an *other* guise, substituting images of energy to render depletion and images of greatness to speak of loss. In this sense, it is difficult to separate the metamorphic image from the trope, and hence the continuum of Blake's bardic chronicles (which are often nonstop streams of metamorphic events) become a sort of continuous trope, a traditional synonym for allegory itself. What could be more appropriate for a poetry that chronicles the changes of the temporal continuum than a parabolic language of substitutive change? In his widely influential essay "The Rhetoric of Temporality," Paul de Man has pointed out the "constitutive temporal element" in allegorical tropes: "it remains necessary, if there is to be allegory, that the allegorical sign refer to another sign that precedes it. The meaning constituted by the allegorical sign can then consist only in the *repetition* . . . of a previous sign with which it can never coincide, since it is of the essence of this previous sign to be pure anteriority."[21] Because Blake's poems are nonmimetic, there is a blurred distinction between rhetorical figures and scenic dramatizations, where tropes (already by definition "turns") palpably turn into metamorphic beings.[22] In the verbal surface, the second term in a simile suggests the destination of the first, the outcome of a transformation ("his eternal life was like a dream" is not semantically convertible into "a dream was like his eternal life"). Metaphors likewise efface the original images of the objects they represent, yet retain traces of those originals. Take the opening apostrophe of "To the Evening Star": "Thou fair-hair'd angel of the evening." What was once the Evening Star (before poetry set in) is now called a "fair-hair'd angel," yet that angel still lingers starlike in the western twilight. We read "angel" but remember "star," as if the personification substituted itself for something that formerly occupied the same space, shared the same identity, but was altogether different in form. Troping is always a *becoming*, a representation of metamorphosis enacted on the level of

[21] Paul de Man, *Blindness and Insight: Essays in the Rhetoric of Contemporary Criticism*, 2d ed. (Minneapolis: University of Minnesota Press, 1983), 207.

[22] In another essay, de Man notes this turn as a general characteristic of metaphors: "Something monstrous lurks in the most innocent of catachresis. When one speaks of the legs of a table or the face of the mountain, catachresis is already turning into prosopopeia, and one begins to perceive a world of potential ghosts and monsters" (Paul de Man, "The Epistemology of Metaphor," *Critical Inquiry* 5 [Autumn 1978]: 13–30).

style—and, conversely, things that change their form in time are natural tropes.

Few writers, of course, can do without figurative language, and there is no inevitable connection between its employment and the construction of a sublime bardic style. When tropes stream forth in virtually unbroken succession, however, as they often do in the works of such poets as Thomson, Collins, and Macpherson, we have a rhetoric that calls attention to its sublime potential. As a model of sublimity, the example of the Bible lies behind much of this rhetoric. The Hebrew poets, Robert Lowth tells us, "have assiduously attended to the sublimity of their compositions by the abundance and splendour of their figures; . . . for in those poems at least, in which something of uncommon grandeur and sublimity is aimed at, there predominates a perpetual, I had almost said a continued use of the Metaphor, sometimes daringly introduced, sometimes rushing in with imminent hazard of propriety."[23] The sublimity of such metaphors (and by his choice of examples, Lowth includes similes) apparently resides not so much in the individual figures themselves as in the way they rush upon one another boldly and even indecorously. Temporal excitements are evoked here ("perpetual," "continued," "rushing"—a series of terms that increasingly accelerate the temporal continuum as it verges on the momentously "imminent"), as well as prospects of change ("hazard," "introduced"), and the transgression of discrete bounds ("daringly," "propriety"). Lowth offers heady prospects for poets who might wish to indulge their tastes for tropes, and it is not surprising that the more daring and indecorous, such as the young Blake, were quick to accept the invitation.

This poetry is particularly notable for generating its tropes from the same fund of images that composes the actual environment surrounding the dramatic characters, so that the transgression of propriety to which Lowth alludes becomes an actual blurring of the perceived boundaries between person and thing. Here, for example, is a messenger in Ossian's *Fingal*, reporting on the warlord Swaran:

"I beheld their chief," says Moran, "tall as a glittering rock. His spear is a blasted pine. His shield is the rising moon! He sat on the shore! like a cloud of mist on the silent hill! Many, chief of heroes! I said, many are our hands of war. Well art thou named, the Mighty Man: but many mighty men are seen from Tura's windy walls."

"He spoke, like a wave on a rock, who in this land appears like me? Heroes stand not in my presence: they fall to earth from my hand. Who can meet Swaran in fight? Who but Fingal, king of Selma of storms?"[24]

[23] *Sacred Poetry of the Hebrews* vol. 1, 121.
[24] *Poems of Ossian* vol. 1, 220–21.

Swaran's person differs in no essential way from the gloomy Northern landscape that surrounds him. In a sense he is diffused everywhere, "outstretchd thro the immense" like the dragon form of Urizen in *Vala*. Rhetoric like this displays a curious collapsing together of those supposedly opposing tropes metaphor and metonymy. Thus Swaran is first beheld sitting *near* waves ("he sat on the shore"), and then is said to speak "like a wave." He becomes what he is next to. The change of form implied in the simile is really a suffusion of contiguous forms with one another's attributes.

Frye has spoken of the Ossianic style as producing "huge cosmological figures in whom the human and natural words can hardly be distinguished,"[25] and draws the clear connection between these and Blake's "Giant forms." Blake's mythical personae are gigantic precisely because they, too, tend to encompass their surroundings, transforming themselves into it. An early instance is the Ossianic, or perhaps Chattertonian,[26] ballad "Gwin, King of Norway," from *Poetical Sketches*, in which the clash of opposing armies elicits a succession of tropes that combine to make up a cosmos, a conspectus of all the elemental spheres: "Like rushing mighty floods"; "Like clouds, come rolling o'er"; "Like reared stones around a grave"; "Like warring mighty seas"; "Like blazing comets in the sky" ("Gwin," lines 24, 36, 41, 70, and 101). But by the end of the poem, the human forces actually become what they formerly were merely like—or, rather, they are enveloped in the element and annihilated by it, as the flood they so resembled returns *in propria persona*:

> The river Dorman roll'd their blood
> Into the northern sea;
> Who mourn'd his sons, and overwhelm'd
> The pleasant south country.
>
> (lines 113–16)

The catastrophic conclusion of this bardic chant has already been enacted in the Bard's tropes; the deluge of tropes that descends on the human form in this poem both gives and takes away, it magnifies corporeal power and attenuates the human shape, it energizes and drowns.

To illustrate the point about the destabilizing effect of multiplied tropes, images of fire serve as well as those of flood; one may say that a conflagration of tropes consumes its tenor. Orc is a good example, chained to his rock, but burning with a vitality that cannot be confined to the limits of his own circumscribed form:

[25] *Fearful Symmetry*, 176.

[26] See Margaret Ruth Lowery, *Windows of the Morning: A Critical Study of William Blake's Poetical Sketches* (New Haven: Yale University Press, 1940), 179ff., for Chatterton's presumed influence on "Gwin."

His nostrils breathe a fiery flame. his locks are like the forests
Of wild beasts there the lion glares the tyger & wolf howl there
And there the Eagle hides her young in cliffs & precipices
His bosom is like starry heaven expanded all the stars
Sing round. there waves the harvest & the vintage rejoices. the Springs
Flow into rivers of delight.

(*FZ* 61.24–29)

The description continues beyond this point, but these lines sufficiently display the richness of Orc's metamorphic potential. Yet the congestion of proliferating tropes suggests that it is an overrich endowment. Orc's form is manifestly unstable, lost in an excessive distribution of elements—and the hint is already implanted of his actually dramatized metamorphosis not far off in the story, when he will organize into an ultimate slipperiness, a serpent body, a "Self consuming dark devourer rising into the heavens" (*FZ* 80.48). In his self-consuming, he finds his ascension, his sublime.

Burke stalks behind this self-consuming figuration, as we suspect he might. The Burkean sublime, a force dependent on the blurring of discrete outlines as it "anticipates our reasonings, and hurries us on by an irresistible force," finds a particularly congenial residence in poetry in which a hurried succession of tropes renders the perceived form of their referents unstable. The description of Satan reviewing his legions in Book I of *Paradise Lost* provides Burke with a pregnant example:

> he above the rest
> In shape and gesture proudly eminent
> Stood like a Tow'r; his form had yet not lost
> All her Original brightness, nor appear'd
> Less than Arch-Angel ruin'd, and th' excess
> Of Glory obscur'd: As when the Sun new ris'n
> Looks through the Horizontal misty Air
> Shorn of his Beams, or from behind the Moon
> In dim Eclipse disastrous twilight sheds
> On half the Nations, and with fear of change
> Perplexes Monarchs.

(*PL* 1.589–99)

Regarding these lines, Burke comments: "Here is a very noble picture; and in what does this poetical picture consist? in images of a tower, an archangel, the sun rising through mists, or in an eclipse, the ruin of monarchs, and the revolution of kingdoms. The mind is hurried out of itself, by a croud of great and confused images; which affect because they are crouded and confused. . . . The images raised by poetry are always of this obscure kind."[27] In the sublime Miltonic passage discussed here, Satan the archan-

---

[27] *Philosophical Enquiry*, 62.

gel is triply troped into ruin. First, the images representing him—the sun in eclipse, the monarch perplexed, and so forth—are themselves "con-fusions," intermixtures of a passing glory and a coming gloom. Second, each time Satan is troped with an image drawn from the natural, artificial, or political world, the diachronically substitutive features of troping come into play, mediating a "then" of archangelic brightness in eternity and a "now" of dark materiality bound to the changes of time. Third (and here Burke places his particular stress), each dark trope displaces its predecessor trope, but too quickly for the former lineaments to be effaced in the memory, so that all the images heap together or "ruin" together (like the stones of the tower toppling) in a cumulative disfigurement or obscurity. Overcome by a crowding avalanche of images, the mind is swept away into its own darkness, as Satan is into his. The superimposition of images, according to Burke, is thus a subtractive rather than an additive process. Each new trope removes light and clarity from the amassing whole until we are left with a final dark. The tropic style, then, is always in danger of becoming en-tropic, an enactment and celebration of slippage, loss, and depletion—the grim corollaries of a vision of things that places transformation and instability at its center. The kind of poetry that Burke favors merely speeds up the process.

To summarize, the post-Miltonic bardic style, of which Blake is the great master, represents a full adaptation of the narrative voice to Burkean formulas of pacing and expression—the tensely repetitive staccato extensions of the "artificial infinite," the "irresistible" cascade of events that "hurries" us on, the blurring of outline through a profusion of tropes. Paratactic phrasing and swift changes of tropes hurl the reader through bewildering mutations of forms. The succession of changes, like the verbal structure itself, is open-ended, suggesting "diminishing" vistas that are also vistas of human diminishment, leading to a final entropy. Condensations of change, rendered by visions of metamorphosis, evade or forestall the entropic tendency by offering the thrill of the terrific or monstrous. The narrating voice offers no center of stability, no stance outside of flux—for the Bard is a participant in the cascade of time that he chronicles, and his gift is only to see more of it than ordinary men can, but not to see something that differs from it. He has the science of the indefinite but not of the eternal. In this style, then, the indefinite, the vast, the dark, the terrific, and the unstable are reproduced as a mode of telling. Burke reigns here, but none of the territory is alien to Blake. Like many prophetic poets, Blake displays a certain fondness for communicating bad news, and he knows how to luxuriate in all the darkest and most hectic modes of its representation. This ability to encapsulate the Burkean sensibility whole within his bardic form is one major part of his poetic genius; the other is that his art knows ways to a sublimity beyond the Burkean confines.

Chapter III

THE ICONIC STYLE

SUBLIME CONCENTRATION

NEGOTIATING THE VORTEX: A WHIRL OF WORDS

BARDIC vision, as we have seen, yields continued glimpses of the abyss of time and thus supplies one major ingredient of the sublime of astonishment: a constant vertigo or disequilibrium. Meanwhile, inside the abyss, scenes of transformation confront the reader with shocking encounters, with monstrous discontinuities that are equally necessary for provoking the sublime response. But the bardic vision of transformation, whether presented in sudden electric moments or in great receding vistas of imagined time, rarely provides exemplars of the determinate, the particular, and the distinct—the qualities, according to Blake, that alone can deliver the sublime from the antihumane grip of a system fitted to the Corporeal Understanding. Such qualities are supplied by what I have called the "iconic" element in Blake's style. To effect its own sublime, the Blakean textual icon must exhibit not flow but structure, not the metamorphosis of forms but the identification of forms, not linearity but centripetal concentration. More than a mere "speaking picture," the icon is ideally a passage of verse that presents an image of totality, of an "all" concentrated within formal bounds. It must seem definite, yet unfamiliar, unassimilated with the routine continuities of ordinary experience and ordinary thought. It should propagate multifaceted ideas in the observer's mind, yet remain aloof from pat allegorization or ready translation into flat discursive terms. It may, of course, throw off certain glints of referential meaning or derive parts of its composition from a referential background—but the referential significance of the icon is never its most important element and may be present only as a kind of enticement to the reader, or as a tease. Yet while it teases, it also actualizes intimations of the infinite and the eternal by detaching one from all cause-and-effect chains of corporeal existence, from time, sequential logic, and the many kinds of errant traveling.

The famous vortex passage in Book I of *Milton* provides a brilliant example of these effects in operation and thus serves as an appropriate introduction to Blake's iconic mode. We may begin by recalling that before entering the vortex, Milton's "real and immortal Self" (*M* 15.11) is a sleeper in heaven; after passing through the vortex, Milton finds himself in

our fallen world, beholding Albion as the island of Great Britain, "outstretchd and snowy cold, storm coverd; . . . what was underneath soon
seemd above. / A cloudy heaven mingled with stormy seas in loudest ruin"
(*M* 15.37, 42–43). The passage from one state to the other is through the
vortex, and this passage in the spatial sense is enacted by a passage in the
textual sense, an opening in the continuity of the narrative that has suc-
ceeded in spinning around the understandings of reader after reader who
has entered it:

> The nature of infinity is this: That every thing has its
> Own Vortex; and when once a traveller thro Eternity.
> Has passd that Vortex, he percieves it roll backward behind
> His path, into a globe itself infolding; like a sun:
> Or like a moon, or like a universe of starry majesty,
> While he keeps onwards in his wondrous journey on the earth
> Or like a human form, a friend with whom he livd benevolent.
> As the eye of man views both the east & west encompassing
> Its vortex; and the north & south, with all their starry host;
> Also the rising sun & setting moon he views surrounding
> His corn-fields and his valleys of five hundred acres square.
> Thus is the earth one infinite plane, and not as apparent
> To the weak traveller confin'd beneath the moony shade.
> Thus is the heaven a vortex passd already, and the earth
> A vortex not yet pass'd by the traveller thro' Eternity.

(M 15.21–35)

Perhaps no passage (in the textual sense) has received so much explication
from Blake's critics as this one—and notoriously, no two readings coincide.[1] Dissatisfaction with earlier readings may account for the successive

---

[1] A representative sampling of the many critical accounts of the vortex, culled from several
different decades, indicates the extent of disagreement and the interpretive problems involved. Thus Northrop Frye (*Fearful Symmetry*, 350) explains the phenomenon as "an angle
of vision opening into our minds with the apex pointing away from us" and likens passage of
the vortex to "trying to see a book from the book's point of view"—a formulation as mysterious as the original lines it is trying to explain; *ignotus per ignotius*. Harold Bloom in *Blake's
Apocalypse: A Study in Poetic Argument* (Garden City, N.Y.: Doubleday, 1963), endorsing
Frye, adds details of his own: "To pass *through* a vortex [Bloom's emphasis] in this sense is to
see an object from the object's own point of view; . . . in seeing it as first separate, and then
entering it, you pass from the outer ring of the whirlpool it extends towards you to the
vacuum at its center" (358). But of course, Blake actually says "pass [a] Vortex," not "pass
through a vortex"—and, by the same token, Bloom's explanatory machinery of objects seen as
initially "separate," of "outer rings" and "centers," is entirely built on extrapolations nowhere
explicitly endorsed by the imagery of the text. More recently, Donald Ault has reversed the
direction of the vortex, placing the apex in the lens of the eye and aligning the expanding
vortex with the "conical angle" of vision (*Visionary Physics: Blake's Response to Newton* [Chi-
cago: University of Chicago Press, 1974], 160); Susan Fox incorporates both directions,

attempts, but the apparently unquenchable urge of critics to come up with a clear paraphrase of the passage itself demands explanation. Certainly part of its attraction lies in the seductive impression it establishes that final answers will be given here. It opens with a momentous simplicity, a tone of straightforward address; one senses that at last all the recondite mythopoeia of the Bard's Song, all the grand cloudy symbols of the narrative, shall part like a veil, revealing the infinite in a single clear apprehension ("The nature . . . is this"), and in six words: "every thing has its Own Vortex." The rest of the passage takes on the form of a syllogism, one that invites the reader to work out its terms. Once invited, however, the reader soon discovers that the logic is entirely elusive, that it is filled with absent premises and suppressed implications, and that even the premises offered resist paraphrase and unambiguous visualization.[2] The problem is not so much with the key terms such as "infinity" and "vortex," as with the less conspicuous verbs, adverbs, and prepositions. What does it mean to "have" a vortex—"have" in what sense? (To possess, produce, contain, emanate, incorporate, encompass, inscribe, experience?) When one "passes" a vortex, does one pass *through* it or pass *by* the vortices that other things "have"? What direction is the traveler facing if he "perceives . . . backward," yet "keeps onwards"? How does the atemporality of Eternity reconcile itself with the sequentiality implicit in the idea of traveling, with notions of before and after (the "passd already" and "not yet pass'd" of lines 34–35)? Such undecidables that riddle even the unobtrusive verbal support structure of the passage make detailed paraphrase of the scheme as a whole essentially a forlorn project. Basic terms of orientation are either lacking or contradictory.

If it is true that this passage evades paraphrase, it is presumably because Blake has designed it to do so. But critics cannot be blamed for returning to the attempt time after time—for, as part of that Blakean design, the

---

saying that "each observer stands at the point at which two vortices meet"—but, having doubled the number of vortices specified by Blake, she declines to state how they function and retreats instead into high-minded vagueness: "How much he sees depends on how well he looks. If he looks well, if he sees with fourfold Edenic vision, he embraces what he 'sees' as part of himself and there is no distance between perceiver and perceived" (*Poetic Form in Blake's "Milton,"* 71). Finally, Nelson Hilton avoids explaining the vortex itself, calling the first half of Blake's description "straightforward," and devotes his attention instead to an ingenious reversal of standard interpretations of exactly what the "traveller thro' Eternity" sees and what the "weak traveller confin'd beneath the moony shade" (*Literal Imagination,* 211–13). My aim, of course, is not to castigate these various critical attempts, but rather to show how the impulse to paraphrase the unparaphrasable necessitates such evasions and supplementary extrapolations.

[2] Hilton acknowledges the "indefinite" character of the similitudes in lines 28–35 and the "unconvincing" nature of the doubly repeated "thus" ostensibly concluding the syllogism (*Literal Imagination,* 212).

passage presents itself as a locus of unique clarification, a moment of specially privileged understanding. And throughout the passage, Blake maintains a simple vocabulary and a cozy, childlike setting for his similitudes that continue the effect of difficulty made easy. Meanwhile, we have plunged into a spatial tangle that involves spirals, globes, linear paths, infinite planes, limited acres, directions backward and forward, north, south, east, and west. There are too many terms and too few logical connectives between them. We are thus drawn in, held, teased, and disoriented by a system that appears always on the verge of perspicuity without ever quite coming into rational focus. Then, all at once, we find ourselves seeing clearly again—but what we behold is Albion on the rock in the mortal sea of Time and Space. We have passed the verbal vortex and have experienced, with Milton, what it is like to negotiate the difficult passage between Eternity and the corporeal world.

As a text, the vortex passage is clearly iconic (in the sense of an image that, in some fashion, is what it represents), for it enacts the effects attributed to the object it purports to describe. Indeed, this is not a text *about* a vortex; there is in fact no vortex "out there," even as a substitutive trope for some other rational concept (since all critical attempts to recover this concept dissolve in mutually cancelling interpretations); the text *is* the vortex. It is a structure that forces the understanding, as it proceeds forward through the succession of verse lines, to circle continually back on itself. This circling is driven by the equal influences of two diametrically opposed stylistic poles—one communicating firmness and certainty (in the diction, the tone, the syllogistic syntax), and the other communicating indeterminacy (in the suppression of logical connections and the excessive multiplication of terms). Such a text belongs neither to Eternity (which is all determinacy) nor to the corporeal world beneath the "moony shade" (for the text lacks external referentiality) but, rather, fills the opening between them. Texts of this kind are perhaps the literary equivalents of what Mircea Eliade has called the "sacred center," an opening where the disjunctive realms communicate, where (as the Bard in *America* says of the summits of the lost Atlantean hills) "you may pass to the Golden world" (*Am* 10.7).[3] These Blakean artifices of the center tend toward comprehensiveness in a little space, embracing elements of expansion and limitation, the dark and the light, particularity and indeterminacy. They are examples of what Angus Fletcher has called "microcosmic reduction"—images that "contain the

---

[3] See Mircea Eliade, *The Sacred and The Profane: The Nature of Religion*, trans. Willard R. Trask (New York: Harcourt, Brace, 1959), 20–21, 25, and 37. The sacred center, as it appears in Blake's poetry and thought, is examined in Edward J. Rose, "The Symbolism of the Opened Center and Poetic Theory in Blake's *Jerusalem*," *Studies in English Literature* 5 (Autumn 1965): 587–606.

cosmos of those works where they appear."[4] In employing this structure, Blake follows a venerable tradition in mythic literature, as Fletcher has shown. What is original in Blake's use of the pattern is the extent to which the very language and style describing the visionary center imitate its affective attributes. It ritualizes reading by demanding that it reenact the sacred experience presented in its space of words. Thus, even if these words leave our reason baffled in the end, despite their promise to explain "the nature of infinity" or the procedures of a "traveller thro' Eternity," the sublime moment has already become enacted in the verbal artifact, and our traveling is accomplished.

Hieroglyphic Form: The Sublime of the Bible

Although Blake's originality in achieving sublime effects from iconic language is undeniable, he himself is more than ready to claim venerable precedents for his practice. Just as the epics and lays of primitive or pseudo-primitive Northern poetry supply him with his stylistic model for the bardic sublime, so the style of his iconic vision depends on what he calls, in the Preface to *Milton*, the "Sublime of the Bible." We need to know precisely what this phrase means. Nothing is more common in discussions of the sublime, starting with Longinus's famous quotation of the first chapter of Genesis, than recourse to the Bible for instances of terror, power, infinitude, natural grandeur, and other standard items in the catalog of sublime stimuli.[5] Burke himself is quick to illustrate his notions of the sublime with examples from the Bible, particularly from the Book of Job. But if instances of a conventional Burkean sublime are all that Blake has in mind when he uses the phrase "the Sublime of the Bible," then there is little point to the rest of what he has to say in the *Milton* Preface. There he opposes, somewhat intemperately, the biblical sublime to the works of a host of mighty poetic names both classical and modern, including Homer, Shakespeare, and Milton. Such an opposition is scarcely to be

---

[4] *Allegory*, 214 and 219. Elsewhere in the same study, Fletcher points out how the epic hero's passage through such centers—and by extension the reader's (examples from Virgil and Spenser are cited)—functions poetically as an initiation into the world of vision (350–51).

[5] For comprehensive treatments of the relation of the Bible to eighteenth-century literature and aesthetics, see Murray Roston, *Poet and Prophet: The Bible and the Growth of Romanticism* (London: Faber and Faber, 1965) and David B. Morris, *The Religious Sublime: Christian Poetry and Critical Tradition in Eighteenth-Century England* (Lexington: University Press of Kentucky, 1972). For Blake's own connection to eighteenth-century traditions of biblical scholarship and Bible-inspired literature, the most thorough account is in Leslie Tannenbaum, *Biblical Tradition in Blake's Early Prophecies: The Great Code of Art* (Princeton: Princeton University Press, 1982).

found in most eighteenth-century essayists on the sublime; they tend to find the same sublime effects in the great poets that they find in the Bible. It is not for its conventional "effects," then, that Blake elevates the sublime of the Bible and distinguishes it so sharply from secular vessels of the sublime. Elsewhere, Blake specifically excludes the Burkean infinite, the vast, lonely, and indefinite abyss, from anything to do with biblical sublimity: "Many suppose that before the Creation All was Solitude & Chaos This is the most pernicious Idea that can enter the Mind as it takes away all sublimity from the Bible & Limits All Existence to Creation & to Chaos To the Time & Space fixed by the Corporeal Vegetative Eye" (*VLJ*, E 563). The corporeal terrors that other contemporary writers adduce as evidence of biblical sublimity are, in fact, its enemies.

What, then, is the sublime of the Bible? In the Preface to *Milton*, Blake addresses the "Young Men of the New Age," those whom he believes to be particularly fit to appreciate biblical sublimity and to forsake secular models: "Painters! on you I call! Sculptors! Architects!" (*M* 1, E 95). If these seem an unlikely set of devotees for a book that lacks visual designs, we might refer to the literal sense of Blake's famous aphorism that "The Old & New Testaments are the Great Code of Art" (*Lao*, E 274). Nothing in the Bible appears to have fired his imagination more than the notion of Solomon's Temple as the prototype for all grandeur in the iconic arts of painting, sculpture, and architecture[6]—a notion that leads him to conjure a whole lost world of "stupendous originals" existing in an idealized Fertile Crescent: "The Artist having been taken in vision into the ancient republics, monarchies, and patriarchates of Asia, has seen those wonderful originals called in the Sacred Scriptures the Cherubim, which were sculptured and painted on walls of Temples, Towers, Cities, Palaces, and erected in the highly cultivated states of Egypt, Moab, Edom, Aram, among the Rivers of Paradise" (*DC*, E 530, 531); likewise, the Laocoön sculpture is really a copy of "the Cherubim of Solomons Temple" (*Lao*, E 273), and even "Jesus & his Apostles & Disciples were all Artists Their Works were destroyd by the Seven Angels of the Seven Churches in Asia" (*Lao*, E 274).[7] If the Bible is the great code of art, then it once shared that status with codes that were visual and architectural as well as verbal; a book in words, yet filled with images that "the Spectator could Enter" (*VLJ*, E 560) as he might through a gate, is the only intact surviving relic of the glories of that halcyon age. Hence, Blake is particularly attracted to those passages in the

---

[6] For an exposition of this idea, see Anthony Blunt, *The Art of William Blake* (New York: Columbia University Press, 1959), 18.

[7] Morton Paley has extensively discussed these and similar Blakean passages in their historical and aesthetic context in "Wonderful Originals—Blake and Ancient Sculpture," in *Blake in His Time*, ed. Robert N. Essick and Donald Pearce (Bloomington: Indiana University Press, 1978), 170–97.

Bible that attempt to burst beyond the preeminent domain of words—narrative and discourse—to capture the felt experience of visionary architecture. Such visions as that of the chariot and temple in Ezekiel, or of the New Jerusalem in Revelation—discrete and formal, measured and specific, yet always exuberantly inventive—make the words that describe them hieroglyphic (literally, "sacred sculptures"), a verbal replication of the high art of the temple walls themselves.

Several influences may have helped to shape Blake's association of the biblical sublime with hieroglyphic form. There is, for example, the Renaissance tradition, convincingly drawn by Joseph Wittreich, of regarding the Book of Revelation as a "picture prophecy," a series of visual impressions that the Evangelist then translated into words.[8] Another likely influence, not specifically pictorial yet deeply involved with formal or iconic arrangements of words, is Robert Lowth's conception of the sublime of the Bible in his famous Lectures. Stating that the "Hebrew poets have accomplished the sublime without losing perspicuity,"[9] Lowth discovers this perspicuity and much of the Bible's sublimity in the formal organization of Hebrew poetry, in the patterning of syntax in parallel constructions, in the formulaic character of the imagery, and in the presentations of the Godhead in terms drawn from ritual. According to Lowth,

> The Hebrew poets frequently express a sentiment with the utmost brevity and simplicity, illustrated by no circumstances, adorned with no epithets (which in truth they seldom use); they afterwards call in the aid of ornament; they repeat, they vary, they amplify the same sentiment; and adding one or more sentences which run parallel to each other, they express the same or a similar, and often a contrary sentiment in nearly the same form of words. . . . They dispose the corresponding sentences in regular distichs adapted to each other, and of an equal length, in which, for the most part, things answer to things, and words to words, as the Son of Sirach says of the works of God, *two and two, one against the other.*[10]

These highly structured patterns of language provide the abstract model for the schematized unfolding of visual images, such as the description of the New Jerusalem in Revelation. Iconic syntax seeks to recover the precision, formality, and concentration of sacred ritual—from which, most probably, this rhetorical style is ultimately derived.[11] We apprehend the verse not as a stream of passing signs but as a single consolidated sign, a

---

[8] See Joseph A. Wittreich, Jr., *Visionary Poetics: Milton's Tradition and His Legacy* (San Marino, Calif.: Huntington Library, 1979), 19–26.

[9] *Sacred Poetry of the Hebrews* vol. 1, 120.

[10] Ibid., 100–101, quoting Ecclesiasticus 23.15. For connections between Lowth's antiphonal theory of Hebraic verse and Blake's practice, see Paley, *The Continuing City*, 45–47, and Tannenbaum, *Biblical Tradition in Blake's Early Prophecies*, 25–27.

[11] See Lowth, *Sacred Poetry of the Hebrews* vol. 2, 24–32.

magnified word to celebrate the Word, as its order is in itself an encapsulated portion of the Divine Vision.

A third possible influence, reconciling Blake's dual interest in the pictures and words, are those venerable biblical traditions that claim for scripture "not a Letter that is Insignificant." According to Kabbalist doctrines that Blake may well have known, God is supposed to have fashioned the alphabet before he fashioned the world, using the visual shapes of the former as architectural blueprints to construct the latter.[12] In this view, God's creative power is indistinguishable from the creative power inherent in the Hebrew letters of his name, the unutterable Tetragrammaton. Such a view possibly informs that passage in *Milton*, in which creation, the "Woof of Six Thousand Years" (*M* 42.15), is presented as a tissue of "woven letters," and "the Writing / Is the Divine Revelation in the Litteral expression" (*M* 42.13–14). The Temple of Israel, and, after it, the New Jerusalem of John, according to various commentators, are not merely the supreme exemplars of visible art, but are also, like the eternal letters, microcosms of the creation.[13] In their exactitude of shape and outline, these iconic forms are magnified reflections of the primordial letters, and by a tertiary act of reverse formation, it should be possible out of words and letters themselves to build those visionary structures anew. Hence, for Blake, the special sublimity of the Bible—the sublime unavailable to bardic chronicle—resides in its daring venture into the recreation of pure iconic form out of words.

Mere vivid description or "realistic" word painting is not involved here; the form of the icon is reenacted in the form of the style. When Ezekiel describes the chariot of the Living Creatures in the first chapter of his prophecy, the impression of formal precision and authentic visionary presence is a feat of his language (or, to speak more strictly, the language of the Authorized Version that Blake imbibed from his earliest youth):

Now as I beheld the living creatures, behold one wheel upon the earth by the living creatures, with his four faces. The appearance of the wheels and their work was like unto the colour of a beryl: and they four had one likeness: and their appearance and their work was as it were a wheel in the middle of a wheel. When they went, they went upon their four sides: and they turned not when they went. As for their rings, they were so high that they were dreadful: and their rings were full of eyes round about them four. And when the living creatures went, the wheels went by them: and when the living creatures were lifted up from the earth, the wheels were lifted up. Withersoever the spirit was to go, they went,

[12] See the concluding chapter of this study, 207–15, for a fuller discussion of this tradition and its connection to Blake's sublime.

[13] See Paley, *The Continuing City*, 136ff., for instances of this tradition. The image of the Temple, according to Paley, "becomes an analogy of an analogy, the microcosm of the world city, with its gates, walls, courtyards, and towers" (136–37).

thither was their spirit to go: and the wheels were lifted up over against them: for the spirit of the living creatures was in the wheels. When those went, these went; and when those stood, these stood; and when those were lifted up from the earth, the wheels were lifted up over against them: for the spirit of the living creatures was in the wheels (Ezek. 1.15–21)

Of Ezekiel's visionary style, Lowth remarks, "His diction is sufficiently perspicuous, all his obscurity consists in the nature of his subject."[14] For all the prophet's recording of detail, we certainly do not see the chariot clearly in any mundane sense. There is a congested maze of fours and ones, creatures and faces, faces and wheels, rings and eyes. The perspicuity lies entirely within the order of language—particularly as it is deployed to create an impression of intellectual order. The imagery is rich with figures of radial symmetry (the four directional points, the concentric wheels, the one central spirit) and geometrical exactitude. The prophet's tone—relentless, almost pedantic in its declarative insistence—communicates a conviction of an absolute irreducible *something* that has been seen. Parallelism and antithesis in the syntax ("when those went, these went; and when those stood, these stood") enhance the effect of balanced order, while the repetition of phrases becomes formulaic and produces the effect of incantation, of language pointing not so much to its subject but to its own properties as a detached body of signifiers. Hence, the character of the divine presence—its order, its precision, its authenticity, its transcendent autonomy—is rendered in the manner of the telling, and Ezekiel's words thus remain more powerful than any attempted visual illustration of them might be.

When Blake comes to describe the city of Golgonooza on plates 12–13 of *Jerusalem*, a passage explicitly modeled on Ezekiel's visions, he too endeavors to produce not an easily visualizable description of the city but a vision of order that the mind, rather than the bodily eye, can perceive:

> And the Four Points are thus beheld in Great Eternity
> West, the Circumference: South, the Zenith: North,
> The Nadir: East, the Center, unapproachable for ever.
> These are the four Faces towards the Four Worlds of Humanity
> In every Man. Ezekiel saw them by Chebars flood.
> And the Eyes are the South, and the Nostrils are the East.
> And the Tongue is the West, and the Ear is the North.
>
> (J 12.54–60)

Here, Blake concentrates the resources of a world of signifiers—names, numbers, directional orientations, syntactical correspondences, formulaic repetition, rhythmic incantation—to describe Golgonooza. "Describe," however, is perhaps not the best word; these things *are* the city, for Gol-

---

[14] *Sacred Poetry of the Hebrews*, vol. 2, 94.

gonooza is nothing but the sovereign attributes of intellect gathered into a definite presence—and the manifest presence of intellect is language itself. Golgonooza is the sum of the words used to make its existence known to us, an anagrammatic reassembling of the "living word," *logon zooas*, as Nelson Hilton has suggested.[15] Indeed, its walls and towers are present wherever words manifest their power to form an order of freestanding autonomy, transcending mere descriptiveness.

THE VISIBLE TEXT: A WALL OF WORDS

If a work such as *Jerusalem* is both a "city" and a verbal artifact, then the walls of the city are its hundred plates. As noted in Chapter I, Blake makes the connection explicit when he speaks of "Jerusalem's wall," in a quattrain that paraphrases imagistically the differentiated fortunes of the Intellectual Powers and the Corporeal Understanding. Walls frequently function as sublime objects, because if they are sufficiently grand, they supply not only "height," but also resistance and challenge to penetration. If they circumscribe a city, they also provide it with a definite outline and a compact, concentrated form. Words form walls when they are massed in certain ways—that is, when the visual or iconic dimensions of texts, their height, breadth, and density of figuration, are foregrounded. As soon as words become *seen* as walls, they begin to function as such, firmly outlining and guarding the autonomy of the text. In the process, of course, they lose much of the transparency they require in order to transmit their signifieds easily to the intelligence. In devising iconic texts, Blake intends his reader to be impressed by the architecture of the wall and checked by its daunting resistance.[16]

A number of specific devices in Blake's late works contribute to the effect of words as textual walls; let us examine some of the more salient. First, visual illuminations, often occupying a block of half a plate or larger, introduce pictorial signifiers in the midst of alphabetic ones, with the inevitable effect of inducing the eye to pictorialize the verbal portion of the plate. The attention of the reader is thus diverted from a sequential pursuit of words and lines to a visual contemplation of the whole block of text as a

---

[15] Hilton, *Literal Imagination*, 236.

[16] Cf. Wittreich, who speaks similarly of the function of the seven seals in the Book of Revelation and invokes them as Blake's model: "the seals, like the pictures they cover, are there to halt movement, though not to impede progress: they arrest attention, they force the mind into contemplation. . . . John's experience of the Revelation prophecy is like the reader's experience with Blake's illuminated books: he reads them and at the same time beholds" ("Painted Prophecies: The Tradition of Blake's Illuminated Books," in Essick and Pearce, *Blake in His Time*, 106).

single unit, a panel. To look at Blake's text this way—and it is inevitable, once we accept the implications of the notion of composite art as elaborated by W.J.T. Mitchell and others—is to see it as blocks of light space, adorned with little dark figurations, to be played off against blocks of dark space figured with light bounded shapes. Not only do the meanings of the individual words recede in importance in this visual perspective, but so does the continuity of meaning from plate to plate—for the plates become mural panels, moveable units in a hundred-paneled wall. Thus, in the Illuminated Books, the designs exercise an inescapable effect upon the reader of the poetry. The larger designs *block* the progress of the reader's eye from line to line, they look like *chasms* in the field of words, or they *distract* the reader's eye from the text by their *irresistible* magnetism. My lapse into sublime diction will indicate how the designs function as agencies in the sublime effect of the poetry itself. They are mute monuments in the stream of vocality. At the same time, this strong differentiation in itself heightens one's consciousness of the text as text and thus helps to monumentalize the vocal as well, endowing words with the inscrutability and allure of alien being.

But even when one is reading Blake in a letterpress edition without reproductions of the designs, it is difficult to avoid noticing those passages in which the verse seems to be massing itself into a wall of words. Blake often crams his iconic verse with agglomerations of substantives, while minimizing predication and syntactic flow. Plate 16 of *Jerusalem* is a particularly notorious example, crammed as it is with sixty-nine lines of verse, running virtually from one edge of the copperplate to the other, with scarcely more than a squiggle or two of visual decoration (see Figure 1). To compound the impediment to easy reading, the plate is packed with catalogs of proper nouns, 140 of them in the lower half of the plate alone. Although such a crowding of reference and characters inevitably irritates those who come to texts for smooth communication, the effect of this impediment to the reading eye is precisely to reify the signifier and so provoke the tension necessary to the sublime experience. Suddenly, at the turn of a page, row upon row of verses piled high strike the reader's eye, each row composed of discrete horizontal slabs of letters, like so many bricks. It presents itself, in short, as a solid wall of words over which the eye slips, unable to find fastening. A second glance discriminates bristling ranks of capital letters, verse without syntax, nouns without predication, names without context ("Levi. Middlesex Kent Surrey. Judah Somerset Glouster Wiltshire. / Dan. Cornwal Devon Dorset, Napthali" [*J* 16.45–46]). From the start, then, the reader feels fatigue, a vertigo, and even though he may proceed through the text word by word, his ordinary, or Corporeal, understanding never succeeds in amassing or retaining a comprehension of the whole. The reader experiences something like Kant's sublime of mag-

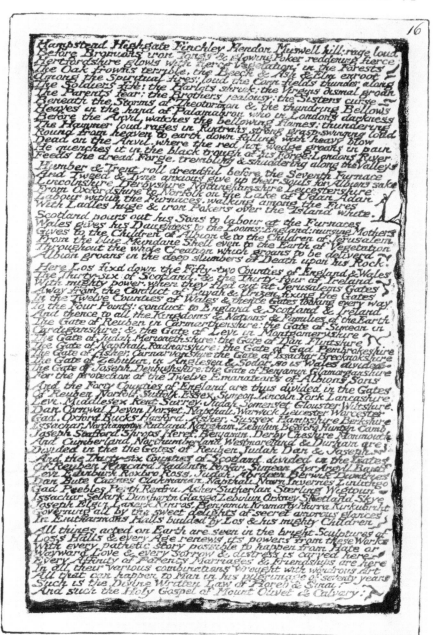

Figure 1. *Jerusalem* (Copy D), plate 16.

nitude, "for there is here a feeling of the inadequacy of his Imagination for presenting the Idea of a whole, wherein the Imagination reaches its maximum, and in striving to surpass it, sinks back into itself."[17]

With less dire effect, Blake enhances the iconicity of his text by favoring regular, periodic repetition of words and phrases, and rectilinear arrangements of these reiterations on the plate:

> And every Month, a silver paved Terrace builded high:
> And every Year, invulnerable Barriers with high Towers.
> And every Age is Moated deep with Bridges of silver & gold.
> And every Seven Ages is Incircled with a Flaming Fire.
>
> (*M* 28.54–57)

> And sixty-four thousand Genii, guard the Eastern Gate:
> And sixty-four thousand Gnomes, guard the Northern Gate:
> And sixty-four thousand Nymphs, guard the Western Gate:
> And sixty-four thousand Fairies, guard the Southern Gate:
>
> (*J* 13.26–29)

> All Human Forms identified even Tree Metal Earth & Stone. all
> Human Forms identified, living going forth & returning wearied
> Into the Planetary lives of Years Months Days & Hours reposing
>
> (*J* 99.1–3)

The perfect vertical alignment of the repeated phrases in the first two passages is immediately apparent to the eye—indeed, more immediately apparent than the meanings of the lines. In the extract from plate 13 of *Jerusalem*, verticality moves into rectangularity as the horizontal structure "And sixty-four thousand . . . guard the . . . Gate" quadruplicates itself in symmetrically spaced columns with a variation in terms filling the lacunae like mortar. The alignments in *Jerusalem* are more complex: the repetition of the word "all" at the beginning and end of the first line squares off the slab of text like a pair of quoins, but the alignments of other repeated terms are not strictly rectilinear. In the paired phrases "Human Forms identified," for example, the lower phrase slips slightly to the left of perfect vertical alignment. The metrically and syntactically congruent phrase "Years Months Days & Hours," in the third line, echoes "Tree Metal Earth & Stone" in the first, but exhibits a similar leftward slippage in its respective position in the line; on the other hand, "reposing" in line 3 moves to the right of a vertical alignment with the congruent "returning" in the preceding line. Here the effect is rather like the crosshatch layering of bricks in a wall: the mortar spaces are always obliquely aligned. More precisely, the interplay of repetition and displaced position creates a kind of visual syn-

---

[17] *Critique of Judgment*, 112.

copation, as well as a misalignment of eye and ear (the former defeated in an expectation of periodic return that is made good for the latter). The effect is a small tension or disequilibrium such as provokes, on a larger scale, the energy of the sublime experience.

When formality in the arrangement of words is made sufficiently conspicuous, it is relatively easy for the poet to create such opportunities for tension: he may establish certain formal expectations for the reader and then manipulate or defeat them; or he may play off the order of the form against the order of the sense:

> The Sons of Albion are Twelve: the Sons of Jerusalem Sixteen
> I tell how Albions Sons by Harmonies of Concords & Discords
> Opposed to Melody, and by Lights & Shades, opposed to Outline
> And by Abstraction opposed to the Visions of Imagination
> By cruel Laws divided Sixteen into Twelve Divisions
>
> *(J 74.23–27)*

This passage is a good example of what Lowth, in his analysis of Hebrew versification, calls "Antithetic parallelism," in which "sentiments are opposed to sentiments, words to words, singulars to singulars, plurals to plurals, &c."[18] Here, not only are the twelve sons of Albion opposed to the sixteen sons of Jerusalem, but the plural antithetical pairs "Concords & Discords" and "Lights & Shades" are opposed, respectively, to the singulars "Melody" and "Outline," while, conversely, the singular "Abstraction" is opposed to the plural "Visions." Such a passage (neatly framed by its opening "Twelve . . . Sixteen" and its closing "Sixteen . . . Twelve") is itself a harmony "of Concords & Discords," a formal, virtually ceremonial, resolution of sharp antitheses, of "Lights & Shades," in the congruences of syntactic parallelism. In short, Blake's verbal arrangement conspicuously promotes and exemplifies an aesthetic of harmonic resolution that the sense of the passage labels as a "cruel law," an offense against the imagination. What is one to believe? The sense rides on the very form that it is concerned with repudiating, and the reader, confronting the two conflicting clarities of sense and form, perceives them condensing into a handsomely impervious textual surface.

Perhaps Blake's use of antithetic parallelism in the passage on the twelve and sixteen sons is a kind of sly irony, a case of the form parodying its own errors. But there is too much evidence in his work of a fascination with numerical concords and oppositions to attribute it all to a parodic impulse. Blake may speak of "Mathematic Proportion" as "subdued by Living Proportion" *(M 5.44)*, but we gain a different impression when confronted in *Milton* and *Jerusalem* with boldly advertised interrelationships of seven and

---

[18] *Sacred Poetry of the Hebrews* vol. 2, 45.

eight, nine and twelve, twelve and sixteen, twenty-four and twenty-eight, twenty-seven and twenty-eight—and, presiding over all, the quaternary, the quintessential form of symmetry, two on two, the double doubled. It is not self-evident that these are "living proportions." Blake's paradoxical attachment to them is explained by the strategies of the sublime mode, which requires for its operation an antithesis of means and ends, like cogs "formd in a wheel to turn the cogs of the adverse wheel" (*M* 27.10)— freedom through impediment, elevation through reduction, transparency of meaning through illegibility, deliverance from system through the imposition of system, and living form through the symmetries of an intellectually detached *discordia concors*. Even so, the "mathematical proportion" that Blake favors has little to do with the unobtrusive proportionings and discreet subordinations that inform, say, the orders of classical architecture, or the narrative of a "well-made" fiction, or the color scheme of a Reynolds oil. All Blake's symmetries are fearful. His numerical schemes crash upon the texts of his work without decorum; their intrusion is arbitrary, abrupt, and unexplained. Like the four equally proportioned subdividings that descend upon the sea of verses that is *Jerusalem*, all such measured orders—numerical sets, parallel lines of words forming visual rows, blocks of texts forming walls—make the form of the poetry in which they intrude more problematic rather than less so. Such orders produce not closure but continued and open-ended speculation.

DIVINE NAMES: ICONIC MICROCOSMS

There are no limits to the scale of an iconic text. Insofar as we can situate ourselves at the proper distance to perceive its form as consolidated and autonomous, a whole poem such as *Milton* or *Jerusalem*—or even an entire canon in illuminated printing—may operate as a magnified word, an iconic center of arrest and release within the midst of the continuities of our ordinary experiences. At the other end of the scale, certain brief and often arbitrary letter-combinations consolidate into irreducible, autonomous, and unchangeable units within the continuities of ordinary language. These are the mythic names. Blake's proper names, particularly those of his own invention, are miniaturizations of those verbal iconic centers of arrest and fascination that are scattered through his work. They are like hard, glittering stones set for ornament within the wall of words. New readers of Blake are struck by their strangeness; later, for more experienced readers, impressions of punning reference, etymological associations, and literary echoes appear to reflect off the surfaces of these names, but the impressions rarely elicit common agreement among critics, or settle steadily into place, and the sense of strangeness remains. Names are intrinsically irreducible;

they are hard givens, unavailable to paraphrase.[19] In those cases where referential connections seem possible, they are often also made to seem difficult. This difficulty may best be seen not in passages where the names are pure inventions, hermetically sealed, but where the names hover at the remote margins of the known:

> A Wine-press of Love & Wrath, double Hermaphroditic
> Twelvefold in Allegoric pomp, in selfish holiness
> The Pharisaion, the Grammateis, the Presbuterion,
> The Archiereus, the Iereus, the Saddusaion, double
> Each withoutside of the other, covering eastern heaven
>
> (*J* 89.4–8)

We know, vaguely, that there are real referents behind these formidable names—or, rather, we are induced to make that assumption about all the names because of the relatively greater familiarity of some of them. Yet even the more familiar are orthographically distorted, estranged, as if read in a dream. Such familiarity as they have is like the faint tracing of an inscription on the wall of their obscurity.

But not all Blake's gatherings of names have even this degree of familiarity. He often introduces unknown proper names before presenting the context that will make these names intelligible, and sometimes no such context ever appears. To cite an extreme instance, in Night VIII of *The Four Zoas*, Los presents the reader with an astonishing list of his progeny:

> And these are the Sons of Los & Enitharmon. Rintrah Palamabron
> Theotormon Bromion Antamon Ananton Ozoth Ohana
> Sotha Mydon Ellayol Natho Gon Harhath Satan
>
> (*FZ* 115.1–3)

This is scarcely the entire list, which continues for another six lines, eliding names of Blake's invention with biblical and historical names before launching into a similar catalog of daughters. The lines quoted, however, are sufficient to provoke some essential observations. Only the first four names refer to characters of importance in Blake's myth; some (Antamon, Sotha, and Ozoth) appear sporadically elsewhere, while the rest (aside from Satan) are apparently summoned into existence for this one occasion, never to appear again. It seems gratuitous to speculate, as some commentators have done, upon the possible symbolic reference of these nonce cre-

---

[19] As the important eighteenth-century grammarian James Harris points out, "one Method of expressing Particulars is that of PROPER NAMES. This is the least artificial, because *proper Names* being in every district arbitrarily applied, may be unknown to those, who know the Language, perfectly well, and can hardly therefore with propriety be considered as parts of it"; see J[ames] H[arris], *Hermes: or a Philosophical Inquiry Concerning Language and Universal Grammar* (London: J. Nourse and P. Vaillant, 1751; Scolar Press Facsimile, 1968), 345–46.

ations, as if characters with a specifiable significance maintained an independent, if shadowy, existence behind them in Blake's imagination.[20] What is more readily apparent is their arbitrary effect, since nothing in the surrounding context of Los's speech serves to identify them further, nor does the elaborate specificity of the roll call contribute to the sense of the context. It seems clear that Blake's preoccupation with naming so far overtakes the claims of narrative continuity that whole blocks of verse comprise nothing but names, a large proportion of them wholly mysterious. The effect is incantatory, a reconstitution of a primitive numinous power inherent in a ritualized utterance of sonorous syllables. Here the invented name, perceived simply as an exotic element within the stream of meaningful words, achieves an iconic status, a status that precedes its possible function as a sign representing conceptual equivalents.

In framing his invented names, Blake rarely, if ever, starts with an abstract concept and then looks for a form to fit it, first finding an appropriate term for the concept in a known lexicon and then disguising the term in a fashion that nonetheless preserves the lexical resemblance. Rather, the name itself, already formed, determines what lexical resemblances are possible and, hence, what abstract concepts may subsequently and fortuitously attach themselves to it.[21] These inventions appear to arise in Blake's mind

---

[20] As Peter Butter has wisely reminded us, some minor characters in Blake's work "are little or nothing more than names. Some commentators seem equally pleased with all these, provided they can scratch together from diverse, sometimes remote and dubious, sources a plausible explanation of what a name stands for. The result is that Blake is both underrated, his best creations being reduced to abstractions, counters in a system of ideas, and overrated, his supposed intentions being accepted for the deed"; see *"Milton*, the Final Plates," in *Interpreting Blake*, ed. Michael Phillips (Cambridge: Cambridge University Press, 1978), 147.

[21] It is important that this point not be misconstrued, as my earlier formulations of it elsewhere sometimes have been. Thus Sheila Spector, for example, believes she has discovered that "despite assertions by V. A. De Luca and Aaron Fogel to the contrary, the meanings of the names apparently are significant" ("The Reasons for 'Urizen'," *Blake/An Illustrated Quarterly* 21 [Spring 1988]: 149). I have in fact never asserted that the names are without significance, or that their forms arise totally ex nihilo. I have thus no wish to deny the probable descent of such names as Oothoon and Urthona from the Oithona and Uthorno of Ossian, or Vala from the Vola of Mallet's *Northern Antiquities*, or Urizen from the Urien of Gray's "The Bard," nor do I mean to slight (even in the present study, as a later section will show) the useful associations that a knowledge of such sources may attach to their Blakean namesakes. I do argue, however, from detailed evidence of letter combinations and the chronology of usages, the high probability that the names arise mostly out of aleatory associations and recombinant letter play, that these forces continue to influence the deployment of the names throughout their history in Blake's works, and that the form of the names empowers the significances that accrete to them, as their potential for lexical resemblances unfolds to the poet over time. Thus when Spector suggests that the fortuituous resemblance of the Hebrew word *razon* to the already invented *Urizen* was "instrumental in shaping Urizen's later characterization" and thus "that even after the names were coined, Blake continued to seek out new meanings to invest his characters with new qualities" (ibid.), she does no more than

nearly spontaneously, through the loosest of associations (usually literary), or else they derive from the letters of names he has already invented. Consider, for example, Enitharmon in her debut appearance in *Europe*, summoning eight of her children before her (*Eur* 14): Ethinthus, Manathu-Vorcyon, Leutha, Antamon, Oothoon, Theotormon, Sotha, and Thirala-tha. The first two, the last two, and the fourth of these names are new inventions, but conceptual rationales for their forms are difficult to find. It is easier to see their connection to the maternal name *Enitharmon*, out of which they derive, anagrammatically or through slight phonetic shifts and condensations, portions of their own literal being; thus from *Enith-* comes *Ethin-* and *Ant-*; from *-ithar-* comes *Thira-*, *-atha*, *-utha*, *-otha*, *Ootho-*, and *Theo-*; from *-tharmon* comes *-tormon*, *-tamon*, *Manath-* (a scrambled *tha-man*), and *-thoon*. Later in *Vala*, Enitharmon appears to produce out of her name those of her own parents, as several critics have observed, for *Enion* and *Tharmas* emerge from *Eni-tharm-on* like a disentwining of the code of her own genetic inheritance. In the same poem, the heat of *Luvah*, earlier the name of a sun god in *Thel* (3.7–8), causes him to melt in the furnaces of affliction, forming perhaps an implicit and subtextual *lava*, and then emanating overtly back into the text as his mirror or "double form," *Vala* (*FZ* 83.14).[22] Only after the letters have performed their recombining operations do associations of conceptual meaning adhere to the newly produced names through perceived punning or etymological connections (for example, Vala is not consistently associated with her "veil" until the period of *Jerusalem*). As with the operations of the divine Tetragrammaton in Kabbalah, these examples indicate that the creative power of Blake's names resides largely in their letters, signifiers that propagate signifieds in our minds.

As semisacred icons, proper names in Blake seem to work like spells—encapsulated portions of imaginative energy that derive from the permanent forms of "Los's Halls," from which "every Age renews its powers" (*J* 16.62). The ancient gods themselves are only "visions of the eternal attributes, or divine names" (*DC*, E 536). This stress on the iconic power of the name helps to explain not only why strange names crop up so abundantly in Blake's writings but also why there is so much attention to listing particular names ("And these their Names & their Places within the Mundane Shell"; "And these the names of the Twenty-seven Heavens & their Churches" [*M* 37.19, 35]); why behind the strange names of certain char-

---

gather new evidence to support my original point. For my earlier arguments, see "Proper Names in the Structural Design of Blake's Myth-Making," *Blake Studies* 8 (1978): 5–22.

   [22] For the derivation of *Tharmas* and *Enion* out of *Enitharmon*, see S. Foster Damon, *A Blake Dictionary: The Ideas and Symbols of William Blake* (Providence: Brown University Press, 1965), 401. For the "lava" suggestion, see David V. Erdman, *Blake: Prophet Against Empire*, rev. ed. (Garden City, N.Y.: Doubleday, 1969), 333.

acters we find the hovering presence of other strange names ("Los was the fourth immortal starry one . . . / . . . Urthona was his name / in Eden" [*FZ* 3.9–4.1]); and why the last line of *Jerusalem* speaks of hearing names. To enforce this emphasis, Blake not only lists names explicitly but frequently ·subjects us to verbatim repetitions of the lists, sometimes in a virtually invariant formulaic order. The arbitrary orderings of such names, their repetitions, and the exotic appearance of the individual names themselves supply their own *raison d'être*. The autonomy of mythic names and their formulaic arrangements imply that they function collectively as a principle of structure in Blake's works, not as a principle of conceptual reference. They serve to separate the world of divine vision from that of space and time, yet to enforce their necessary confrontation. They compose in toto a "stubborn structure," a multi-latticed gate repelling or inviting our entrance into the divine vision, according to the variation of our perceptions. Each separate name, moreover, may be considered as a fragmented individuation of that structure, pointing to the hypothetical existence of some nameless *Ur*-name, the "name" of the divine vision itself.

Iconic Troping: Identification and Catachresis

At first glance, the sublime of the hieroglyphic icon and the bardic sublime of the temporal abyss appear to achieve the same effects: arrest, vertigo, and disorientation. All modes of the sublime, after all, work by violating the norms of the expected, the dependable, and the decorous. Bardic narrative, through its tone, technique, and choice of subjects, offends against decorum by presenting a vision of diffusion, blurred edges, instability of central focus, and forms in excessive flux. The "excess" of iconic vision is, however, of an altogether contrary sort, involving a clearly marked outer form and an astonishingly compressed inclusiveness within. The iconic passages that we have examined display a strongly determinate frame— achieved through the visual shaping of the text, a conspicuous arbitrariness of signifers, numerical exactitude, specifity of detail, and a tone of firm definition—but within this framework there is usually a bewildering array of disparate, even incompatible, elements gathered together. One thinks of the enormous conclave of English places and Hebrew persons gathered together in plate 16 of *Jerusalem*; of the irreconcilable varieties of space and paths inside the vortex in plate 15 of *Milton*; of the men, sprites, animals, minerals, utensils, buildings, facial features, directional points, gates, and worlds huddled in minutely detailed order within the walls of Golgonooza (*J* 12–13). Once a reader gets past feeling lost within such labyrinthine multiplicity, a sense emerges—beyond vertigo and disorientation— that these are structures where all things may be *found*, spaces where they may be harbored and ultimately united. Just as one senses that all the mythic names in Blake's poetry are permutations of one aboriginal name that they may hypothetically reconstitute, so an iconic center such as the vision of Golgonooza comes to seem like an enlarged signifier of that promised final gathering.

This leads one to the notion that the iconic mode in Blake's poetry is the rhetorical arm of his comprehensive scheme to reveal "All Human Forms identified even Tree Metal Earth & Stone" (*J* 99.1). In another well-known passage, Blake writes:

> So Man looks out in tree & herb & fish & bird & beast
> Collecting up the scatterd portions of his immortal body
> Into the Elemental forms of every thing that grows

> (*FZ* 110.6–8)

Behind this myth is the conception that all forms are identified as human when they are seen as the outward manifestations or inscriptions of man's intellect, which is their home. Identification takes place within the reader when all such inscriptions—all forms, images, words—are recognized as an inner possession, part of the human inheritance of the plenitude of language. The icon mirrors this process of recognition by compressing signs so densely and firmly that their contingent signifieds are virtually squeezed out, and all that is left (which is *all*) is a conclave of signifiers, the visible form of intellect mirroring itself.

It appears that the myth of identification is to the iconic mode of the sublime what the fiction of metamorphosis is to the bardic mode. Both processes radically disturb the norms of our ordinary perception of objects and images, and sometimes it is difficult to distinguish the compression of forms from a mere rapid change of forms. But identification is always a process of convergence upon a final point of unity. On the level of the trope, the bardic vision of transformation expresses itself, as we have seen, chiefly in a liberal use of metaphors and similes; in such tropes, the gap between tenor and vehicle intimates a certain supersession of the former by the latter. On the other hand, the trope of identification is closest to what the rhetorical handbooks call *catachresis*, a figure of "violence" or "dissonance" frequently expressing matters under the sign of contraries or incompatibles. Characterized by compression, it involves, in Rosamund Tuve's words, a "relatedness a little difficult to see," a "strangeness, or intellectual high jump."[23] Hence, it is a favorite trope of religious and visionary poets. Another way of describing catachresis is as an expression that

---

[23] Rosamund Tuve, *Elizabethan and Metaphysical Imagery: Renaissance Poetic and Twentieth-Century Critics* (Chicago: University of Chicago Press, 1947), 130–31.

brings things together within a single conceptual space that they cannot logically share. For example, we recall that in Golgonooza

> the Eyes are the South, and the Nostrils are the East.
> And the Tongue is the West, and the Ear is the North.
>
> (*J* 12.59–60)

This presents us either with a face that only Picasso could paint, or else with directional points that no terrestrial compass could hope to find. The ordinary referentiality of one set of terms wars against the ordinary referentiality of the other. We cannot speak easily of vehicle and tenor here, for the facial images and the geographical regions rob each other of their vehicular power. Ordinary troping allows a certain transmission of signification—although at the expense of some effacement of the signified. But in a case such as this, we must admit either a complete breakdown of signification or force our imagination to an altogether new third construct, in which the human senses and the points of the universe will be integrated and co-identified.

Catachresis is always a dangerous trope for poets, for it shares common aesthetic ground with the grotesque and thus risks provoking the disgust or crude embarassment that grotesque forms often produce. Many readers who can willingly entertain the multiple overlays of schematic orders in passages canonically sanctioned, such as the visions of Ezekiel and Revelation (and a taste for such visions is scarcely universal), will nonetheless balk, or worse, smile condescendingly at such bald, unrefined modes of asserting identification as the exhaustive assignment of British counties to Hebrew tribes in plate 16 of *Jerusalem*, to take a salient example.[24] The only way to admire a conceit of this kind is to make a leap of identification even more profound than that asserted in the text itself—an identification with the mind of the poet in the act of composition. The eccentric catalog of tribes and counties then begins to radiate with a new kind of richness as we enter what we imagine to be Blake's own motives and mood in its execution. We soon become aware of an exuberant, even playful inventiveness, for surely the specifics of his groupings in the catalog are largely nonce improvisations. We begin to detect a scrupulous respect for the reader—who, if told that Albion and Israel are in fact one, is owed no less than a complete and exact accounting of particulars. We take note of the craftsman's patience in executing this long catalog through all the laborious stages to the final printed form. Above all, we come to admire the daring that Blake must have needed in order to offer to his hypothetical public a

---

[24] It is easy to respond by laughing; graduate students of mine in the past have had some fun with this distribution of counties, claiming that Levi, for example, "lucked out" by drawing the prosperous home counties of Middlesex, Kent, and Surrey, whereas poor Zebulun had to content himself with the bleak wastes of Orkney, Shetland, and Skye.

sequence that he surely must have known utterly violated every existing standard of poetic decorum—and hence we are moved by the faith in the reader's good will that this daring must have implied.

This study has commented on Blake's manipulation of the reader's response, on his magisterial erection of barriers and curbs, his compelling wizardry of verbal bedazzlement, his program for our eternal salvation. Although there is plentiful evidence for these strategies and goals, they present an overly imperial conception of his poetic role and hence require qualification. We need to recognize also how vulnerable to the reader's judgment he is willing to make himself; how, more than any other major poet, he is prepared to forego self-protective concessions to conventionality and to risk exposing the most experimental and unsettling reaches of his poetic conception to possible embarrassment and scorn. The confrontation of text and reader is designed, as I have argued, to produce an annihilation of self, but it is not the reader's self alone that is affected here. If "The most sublime act is to set another before you" (*MHH* 7.17), then Blake exemplifies his own principle, setting the reader before him, in an act of faith and trust, first as a brother, then as another self. The sublime is never achieved in the aggrandizement of the defensive, imperial self, but rather in the uncovering and identification of the intellectual self—and this is accomplished by risky leaps of desire or love on both sides of the reader-text divide. Nowhere is the potential for such identifications more momentous than in catachretic embarrassments of the iconic mode.

All modes of the sublime are risky, of course, and court embarrassment, as Pope brilliantly demonstrates in *Peri Bathous*. The bardic sublime, however, risks less than the iconic, even though the Bard often presents himself in a posture of loss. Since bardic vision renders corporeal space and time, even if in attenuated, magnified, or accelerated guises, it detaches the reader less radically from the familiar and the expected. Second, because bardic vision presents the vast, the dark, the changing, and the dire mainly as the *content* of the text, as an affair of the hypothetical or fictional signified, it allows the reader safe disturbances, frissons at one remove from actual reality. The iconic style, on the other hand, shifts the source of disturbance chiefly to the signifier, so that the reader is accosted and shaken in the immediate reality of the encounter with the text. As willing as Blake is to produce such disturbances, he is nonetheless not so daring as to permit himself a purely hieratic mode of writing at any point in his career—not even in *Jerusalem*, which approaches the mode most closely. His works never read like the gnomic *Sefer Yezirah* of Jewish mysticism, or, to refer to his own time, like that most vulnerable and nakedly iconic of all sublime poems, Smart's *Jubilate Agno*. Rather, like the "Human Forms" at the end of *Jerusalem*, temporarily wearied of Eternity and reentering "the Planetary lives of Years Months Days & Hours" (*J* 99.3), Blake's poetry continually reenters the abyss of the bardic sublime. Hence, a vision out of the Burkean sensibility, a world of metamorphosis, swathed in the mists of the North, of measureless times and spaces, indistinct forms, loss, and obscurity surrounds and adjoins another vision—one that brings to mind sacred sculptures standing in the solar clarity of the ancient East, a vision determinate and singular, measured and finite, a miraculous (or astonishing) compression of all contingent forms into one intellectual identity—the living Word of Eternity. How these visions adjoin in particular texts becomes our next focus of inquiry.

Chapter IV

NARRATIVE SEQUENCES

MODES OF ORGANIZATION

T HE BARDIC and iconic styles not only supply Blake with different kinds of local sublime effects, but they also function as structuring elements in his organization of whole poems. This is particularly so when both styles are juxtaposed in the same work. Blake's longer poems—those with aspirations beyond the purely lyrical, and especially those that seek to mobilize complex narrative sequences—are cunningly but by no means conventionally organized, and the unconventionality is inevitably directed toward enhancing the sublime effect. This enhancement depends, in various ways, on how he plays off discontinuities against expectations of continuity, and how he situates, concentrates, or juxtaposes the stylistic units that form parts of the longer sequence. (By "unit" I mean sequence of verse that is internally homogeneous—in tone, verbal style, argument and authorial attitude, setting, continuity of narrative action—and capable of being differentiated by these criteria from adjacent units, as "bardic" verse, say, is differentiated from "iconic.") In some instances, for example, interruptions of narrative flow (often accompanied by stylistic shifts) defeat linearity and render the text a mosaic of differentiated blocks. In other instances, obvious interpolations and revisions import the history of the text into the surface of the text, thus provoking the impression of different depths juxtaposed, of early and late strata of meaning. In yet other instances, medleys of visions and vignettes, each internally perfected, may jostle one another like the textual variants in a myth cycle that awaits a harmonizing redactor—and, in the case of *Jerusalem*, they may surge restlessly against the confines of a rigidly symmetrical superimposed macrostructure. By such various strategies of organization, often in combination with one another, Blake is able to achieve the effect of sublime moments on the large scale of entire works at the same time that he obtains the effect of sublime grandeur, of multitudinousness and depth, on an economical scale not paralleled by other poets in the epic tradition.

SUDDEN CENTERS: OPENINGS AND LIMINAL EFFECTS

The episode of psychic indeterminacy that marks the central phase of the sublime moment has its equivalent in poetic sequences when a new subject, or new tone, or new mood intervenes in the general flow of discourse and halts it, arrests it, or raises its intensity of pitch. The most familiar examples of this episodic discontinuity in the poetry of the sublime are Words-worth's "spots of time," which give us, in Geoffrey Hartman's words, "a moment of arrest, the ordinary vital continuum being interrupted; a sepa-ration of the traveler-poet from familiar nature; . . . a feeling of solitude or loss or separation."[1] Blake's poetry, too, is filled with such interruptive ep-isodes, although they have received less attention from critics—perhaps because, unlike Wordsworth, he does not accompany them with built-in explanations of their significance. Both poets are partly indebted to the epic tradition for precedents, for this tradition strongly authorizes inter-ruptions in the line of poetic action. Homer, Virgil, and Milton, tradition-ally the supreme exemplars of the sublime style, all provide interruptions, ranging in scale from the self-contained epic simile, such as the vignettes of peacetime inserted into the battle narratives of the *Iliad*, to much longer passages of static description or interpolated narrative that detain the prog-ress of the main action (for example, the shield of Achilles or the creation of the world in *Paradise Lost*). In the eighteenth century, this mode of nar-rative organization is revived in the Ossianic poems; the six relatively brief books of *Fingal*, for example, contain no fewer than nine interruptive tales, all devoted to events that have preceded the main action and are generally quite unrelated to it. Macpherson's misfortune as an aspiring sublime poet, however, is his inability to find the stylistic markers or idiom that would forcefully differentiate his interruptions from the principal action. Sublim-ity requires such differentiations, especially those that produce astonish-ment, curiosity, an initial sense of difficulty, and an ultimate attraction. Blake is a master of these requirements.

Breaks in the narrative continuum are particularly apt to produce such impressions when the newly introduced elements bring to the scene an unexpectedly enlarged dimensionality, as if veils were parting to reveal un-suspected, abyssal vistas of time and space, or the workings of vast, un-known powers. The several retellings of the fall in *Vala*[2] are a case in point.

---

[1] Geoffrey Hartman, *Wordsworth's Poetry 1787–1814* (New Haven: Yale University Press, 1964), pp. 17–18.

[2] In this study, I prefer to use the title *Vala* when referring to the poem as a work of imagination, a narrative construct, reserving the more conventional *Four Zoas* designation for the manuscript as a material document with all its fragmentary appendages and editorial cruxes. From the probably early inscription of the title page to the undoubtedly late transcrip-tion of Night VIII, Blake always knew this poem as *Vala*, and he never repudiated this title in any of the internal headings of the nine Nights. The lightly penciled-in replacement *The Four Zoas* (not especially appropriate to a poem that nowhere mentions the phrase), eventu-ally inscribed on the title page, may have only been intended as a provisional tryout; Blake usually inked over those pencil tryouts he wanted to endorse. In any case, my use of *Vala* for the poem as a poem is meant to respect the diachronically staged nature of Blake's achieve-

Interrupting his narrative with retrospective accounts of warring in heaven and falling gods, Blake is heavily indebted to *Paradise Lost*—but where Milton is laboriously detailed and circumstantial in his retrospective accounts, Blake is reserved and elusive in the extreme. This elusiveness is largely responsible for the uneasy sense of wonderment, dread, and disequilibrium that these passages often produce in sensitive readers. In the accounts of the fall, we are usually left uncertain about the precise nature of the events described, the motives of the participants, the relation of causes to effects, and the distance of these primordial events from the narrative present. Even in those accounts where relatively more information is presented, this information is frequently contradicted by that given in other accounts, for, notoriously, none of the interposed versions of the fall tell precisely the same story, and they each select different points of origin for the start of the catastrophe. Each retelling of this event thus makes the past more, rather than less, shadowy and creates an effect of receding depths within depths.[3] We emerge from these plunges into *Ur*-time back into a narrative present that has acquired enlarged implications as a result of the interruption, even if it remains difficult for us to say precisely where we have been or what we have seen.

In *Vala*, these interruptions in the narrative continuum are sporadically distributed—but in some poems, Blake embodies the narrative break in passages that are pivotally situated within the work as a whole. The effect is to turn such a pivotal passage into a center that simultaneously organizes the rest of the work about it and gives it the character of an opening into a hitherto unrealized dimension of existence. *America* provides a clear-cut example of this effect that is worth looking at in some detail. For the most part, this poem displays a particularly animated or "terrific" version of the bardic style; its quasi-mythicized reenactment of the American Revolution is linear in narration (a tumble of events) and highly agitated in its imagery and exclamatory, paratactic phrasing. At the virtual center of the poem (just before the exact midpoint of the "Prophecy" proper if one counts by lines, or just after it if one counts by plates), on plate 10, a very different setting and idiom temporarily intrude. At that crucial point in the narrative when the King summons the thirteen colonies to his defense, there is a pause, followed by a strange and unexpected excursus:

---

ment, most evident in this work, and to discourage the long-standing convention in Blake studies of recognizing only "final" intentions as real, even when that recognition means the critical obliteration of the genuine integrity of supposedly superseded creative gestures.

[3] The variant versions of the fall in this poem are clearly laid out in Brian Wilkie and Mary Lynn Johnson, *Blake's "Four Zoas": The Design of a Dream* (Cambridge: Harvard University Press, 1978), 255–60. See also Leslie Brisman's extended critical analyses of these versions of "origins" in *Romantic Origins* (Ithaca: Cornell University Press, 1978), 227–75.

Silent the Colonies remain and refuse the loud alarm.

On those vast shady hills between America & Albions shore;
Now barrd out by the Atlantic sea: call'd Atlantean hills:
Because from their bright summits you may pass to the Golden world
An ancient palace, archetype of mighty Emperies,
Rears its immortal pinnacles, built in the forest of God
By Ariston the king of beauty for his stolen bride,

Here on their magic seats the thirteen Angels sat perturb'd
For clouds from the Atlantic hover o'er the solemn roof.

(*Am* 10.4–12)

In this passage, the hectic swirl of blood, clouds, and high-pitched clamor typical of the poem up to this point disappears. In its place, there is a grandly mysterious setting, couched in an elaborate and stately syntactical construction that virtually brings the narrative to a stop. A serene sublimity pervades the imagery, at once suggesting magnitude ("vast"), height ("hills," "summits," "pinnacles"), power and majesty ("palace," "mighty Emperies," "king," "God"), the uncanny or numinous ("magic"), the recuperation of time and origins ("ancient," "archetype"), and ultimate transcendence ("[where] you may pass to the Golden world"). In this setting, furthermore, chronological time is collapsed or reversed; no map in 1775 will show the Atlantean hills, drowned according to tradition since the early ages of the world, and yet the contemporary colonial leaders find themselves in their midst. Even the traditional separation of the reader from the dramatic characters of epic narrative collapses in this context, for "you" are unexpectedly included among them and granted their visionary privileges.

All this is impressive and arresting, yet we are left wondering what this passage, so coded with the marks of charged significance, really has to do with the American Revolution or the progress of the narrative. We seem to have been delivered into a domain of myth left tantalizingly inexplicit and kept largely inaccessible even as we probe it. Who, after all, is Ariston, and what is he doing here? Blake's two other references to the name, equally laconic, and a possible source in Herodotus prove of little help.[4] What and where is "the forest of God"? No sources can help at all here. What is the moral or political import of the symbols presented—prorevolutionary or counterrevolutionary? References to shady hills, forests, stolen brides, palaces, Emperies, and kings carry pejorative associations (particu-

---

[4] For the source in Herodotus, see Damon, *Blake Dictionary*, 27. The other references to Ariston in Blake are in *Song of Los* 3.4 and *Four Zoas* 141.6 (ms. frag., E 845).

larly in a poem celebrating the birth of republicanism).[5] On the other hand, they are inextricably linked to bright summits, beauty, immortality, and the Golden world, all positive images for Blake. Even God remains equivocal; is he the tyrannical figure who elsewhere in the poem "writes laws of peace, & clothes him in a tempest" (11.12), or is he the God whose image Orc is said to embody (2.8)? In short, the passage evades moral categories and resists a settled interpretation, even though the style and lustrous imagery seem designed to command the reader's special attention.

In this respect, the reader's situation is not substantially different from that of the thirteen Angels themselves. The unequivocal call levied on them by the Guardian Prince for the maintenance of a fixed order forces them into a moment of arrest and crisis in which all categories become equivocal. They are poised at the brink of revolution, at the meeting point between old and newer worlds, between limiting certainties and unlimited unknowns, full of sinister dangers and expansive gratifications. While they remain in this crisis state of "perturb'd" concentration, they no longer dwell in historical time or geographical space, for these are realms of categorical limitation that belong more properly to the Guardian Prince. The outcome is inevitable, for once the vision of a liberation from fixed order is glimpsed, it is immediately recognized as the program of the revolution itself, and the thirteen Angels emerge from the timeless moment back into contemporary history, from a perturbed state of arrest into new resolution, all "indignant burning with the fires of Orc" (11.2).

Readers of the first section of this study will recognize that the thirteen Angels have passed through a classically orchestrated Sublime Moment, complete with a dread blocking agent (the Guardian Prince) and an initial astonishment (silence and immobility), followed by arousals of attraction and repulsion, a polarization of faculties, and a final transcendence that liberates the subject from the initial block. What makes this rendering of the sublime moment particularly noteworthy is that the poetical surface of the passage demands the same response from the reader that the historical crisis demands of the incipient colonial rebels. The reader, too, is dislocated from the stream of stylistically impassioned narrative continuity, held by a new majesty of idiom, baffled by imponderables and the coexistence of paradoxes, exposed to "worlds not realised"—and if the effect is successful, he emerges as no longer a colonial in the empire of adherence to linear conceptions and unequivocal categories of meaning. The Atlantean passage in *America* clearly marks an intervention of the iconic mode, a text like the account of the vortex in *Milton*, whose semantic equivocations and stylistic enchantments the reader must "pass" in order to come out on the

[5] The pejorative side of this vision is explored in Deborah Dorfman, " 'King of Beauty' and 'Golden World' in Blake's *America*," *ELH* 46 (Spring 1979), 122–35.

other side with heightened consciousness. It thus provides a proleptic experience of the great liberation toward which the revolutionary polemic of the narrative thrusts.

After the sublime interruption of Atlantean myth, *America* returns to the same style of bardic narrative with which it began, as if the interruption had never taken place. Yet the Atlantean passage transforms our sense of the narrative so that it seems no longer a linear sequence of events but rather a space organized about a deep center. A more patently concentric pattern of narrative organization appears in *America*'s sister poem *Europe*, in which Blake seems self-consciously intent on enhancing the centering effect. The "Prophecy" section of the poem consists of two sharply differentiated and discontinuous narratives, one embedded entirely within the other, and a nonnarrative excursus, like the Atlantean passage in *America*, which is further embedded within the interior portion. The first narrative, set in a night of festivity in Enitharmon's "crystal house," is virtually devoid of action. The bulk of it consists of Enitharmon's long invocation to her children, a slow, ceremonial roll call, florid, stilted, and unctuous in its rhetoric ("Who shall I call? Who shall I send? / That Woman, lovely Woman! may have dominion?" "My weary eyelids draw towards the evening, my bliss is yet but new" [5.2–3,10]). Its dainty artificiality mirrors the smug hypocrisy and falsity of her attitudes and the brittle fragility of her nocturnal crystal world (the rococo trills of that similar and nearly contemporaneous creation, Mozart's Queen of the Night, present a striking and apt parallel).

As if to underscore the brittleness of this scene, Blake snaps it exactly in two by sending Enitharmon into a dreamy sleep in the middle of her speech (the "crystal house" scene consists of precisely fifty-nine lines before the break, and fifty-nine lines after it resumes) and inserting a new line of narrative. This new narrative is everything that Enitharmon's discourse was not; in place of a time-suspended, highly ceremonial soirée, we are given the thick of real contemporary history, the movement of men and nations; in place of false fancy, there is harsh fact (albeit quasi-allegorized); in place of a courtly, florid rhetoric, there is a fast-paced style ("Shadows of men in fleeting bands upon the winds: / Divide the heavens of Europe" [9.6–7]), closely resembling the hectic bardic idiom of the historical narrative in *America*; in place of action unfolding in almost frozen slow motion (until the last plate of the poem), there is a packed series of events—plagues and counterplagues, collapsing palaces, disgraced Ministers, fettered citizens, the final sounding of the revolutionary trump. Then, just as suddenly as it began, the scene ends, and Enitharmon's blandly oblivious discourse resumes where it had left off—although with a new shock to the reader, who is likely to realize the falsity of that discourse with a force not possible before its interruption. Enitharmon's world is now seen as a mere painted veil that parts to reveal a more trenchant reality.

Yet even the turbulent historical movement that occupies the middle section of *Europe* is subject to a pause. Amid the chaos of ruined halls and fleeing councillors, a more solemn narrative voice emerges, retarding the flow of events with eighteen lines of rich, lambent description and condensed cosmogonic exposition (10.6–23). The lines beginning with "Thought chang'd the infinite to a serpent" (10.16–23) are rightly considered one of the most powerfully direct and economical explanations of the nature of the fall in Blake's whole corpus, but the earlier part of the passage is more interesting for the present discussion, because it is more enigmatic and more focused on a single elaborated emblem, a cynosure of our attention:

> There stand the venerable porches that high-towering rear
> Their oak-surrounded pillars, form'd of massy stones, uncut
> With tool; stones precious; such eternal in the heavens,
> Of colours twelve, few known on earth, give light in the opake,
> Plac'd in the order of the stars, when the five senses whelm'd
> In deluge o'er the earth-born man

> (*Eur* 10.6–11)

This description of a mysterious ancient temple reveals a clear kinship with the passage on Ariston's palace in *America,* for it maintains much the same ambiguous combination of awesomeness, allure, and potential dread. Commentaries on it are usually content to refer the reader to Druidism as the archetype of all repression and to interpret the Guardian Prince's visit to the temple as an attempt to reinvigorate his own tyranny.[6] Such readings are not necessarily incorrect, but they are incomplete. They do not account for the elaboration of detail, or for the grave dignity of the verse movement with its slow accumulation of phrasal modifiers, or for the positive, even redemptive resonances of much of the imagery ("venerable," "precious," "eternal," "give light").[7] If the great pillars are "uncut with tool," have they then been formed by the Divine Hand? It will not do to brush aside suggestiveness of this sort for the sake of a formulaic negative reading. At the same time, one cannot ignore the hints that these shining pillars are somehow connected to an abstracted zodiacal determinism and the overwhelming of corporeal man. These ambiguities are built into the passage and are not to be resolved in any one-sided reading; the diction and the shaping of the verse endow with dignity and beauty what the prose sense of the pas-

---

[6] See, e.g., Bloom, *Blake's Apocalypse,* 164–65.

[7] Cf. Revelation 21.11 and 19 on the New Jerusalem: "and her light was like unto a stone most precious, even like a jasper stone, clear as crystal"; "And the foundations of the wall of the city were garnished with all manner of precious stones."

sage renders as dire. We are, after all, brought in this passage to a glimpse of the dimly remote past, close to the origins of things—that is, close to the period when the primordial sources of good and evil, beauty and terror, were not yet fully disentwined. What the passage achieves for us, then, is a deliverance into the realm of the sublime, which is a state cultivated precisely for the recovery of the deepest origins and for the attainment of a vision capacious enough to include all contraries of moral categorization.

This achievement is a matter of orchestrated poetic effects and is lost in discursive paraphrase. But these effects are themselves heavily dependent for their force by their situation in the midst of a different kind of poetry that surrounds the central passage—the bardic narrative of contemporary historical events, couched in a heated rhetoric in which polemical categories (conservative-radical, oppression-liberty) are easily discerned and partisan sympathies easily aroused. To read the "Prophecy" section of *Europe*, then, is to pass through a series of concentric stylistic and narrative frames into a deep center of speculative awareness, and then back out again. Enitharmon's artificially timeless world, which fears and seeks to retard history, is exposed by the strife of contemporary politics that occupies her intervening, if unremembered, dream. Likewise, this historical passage is placed in its own somewhat limiting perspective by the glimpse afforded into a deeper gulf of time—one that, indeed, takes us virtually to the threshold of time's beginnings and the workings of vast powers, both beautiful and strange.

Blake's most ambitious attempt to build a poem on a structure of concentrically embeddded frames is to be found in *Milton*.[8] The major interposed tale within a tale, the Bard's Song, defers the principal narrative, but even the Song's own central story is deferred by four plates (3–6) probably inserted late in the sequence, which take us back to shadowy and catastrophic origins, "when Albion was slain upon his Mountains" (*M* 3.1) and Urizen's seven ages of confinement into material form ensued (3.6–27). These ancient events, along with the tale of Palamabron and Satan (itself retold indirectly to a "Great Solemn Assembly"), are told to Milton as a member of an audience in Eternity, intuited by Blake in Lambeth when Milton's spirit entered him, understood in Felpham, written down and engraved presumably in South Molton Street, and now read by us. This structure of concentric framing plunges us, as it were, through a kind of shaft back to the primordial past and then retrieves us again. But the jour-

---

[8] Susan Fox is one of the few critics who has recognized *Europe* as a "prototype" to the concentric structure of *Milton*, although she does not observe the extent of the involuted layering in *Europe* itself and is silent on the pattern's first manifestation in *America* (see *Poetic Form in Blake's "Milton,"* 10–12).

ney into the deep past is one designed to remake the present, and it thus suggests that the reading of *Milton* is intended as a transformational act, aided and organized by the poem's narrative structure.

When Blake offers to Butts his famous definition of "the Most Sublime Poetry" as that which divides the Corporeal Understanding from the Intellectual Powers and cites, to prove it, a "now perfectly completed . . . Grand Poem" of his own composition, a "Memento" of "three years trouble" in Felpham (E 730), in all probability it is *Milton* that he has in mind. Whether the writing of *Milton* crystallized for Blake his discursive understanding of the sublime moment as a point at which the faculties radically divide, or whether the poem was written as a large illustration of the doctrine itself, it would be impossible to say. In either case, it is significant that no other poem in the Blakean canon is so pervasively structured about a series of crisis points or flash recognitions in which falsely joined forces are disengaged and polarized, with the figure of error repudiated (for example, Palamabron and Satan, Pity and Wrath, Milton and his Selfhood). And, concomitantly, no other poem lays such stress on the providential moment, the Moment in each day that Satan cannot find (35.42), the Moment in which the Poet's Work is done (29.1), or the closely linked moments when first Milton and then Los assimilate their powers with Blake.

This absorbing fascination with moments, with points of crisis out of which vision precipitates, helps to explain the massive retardation of *Milton*'s story line, for when narrative time within a poem stops, the moment in which it is suspended is held frozen and expands before our gaze. The long description of the World of Los that occupies the center of the poem (25.66–29.65) provides the most conspicuous example. It is the "Vegetable World" that appeared on the poet's left foot when Milton entered it (21.12) and that the poet views in detail from Los's "supreme abode" (22.26)—hence, it represents both an outwardly projected image of the greatness that the poet has attained, the "all" to which he has access, and the objective content of his comprehensive vision. The World of Los is the anatomy of a sublime moment reconstructed as a spatial survey, and, like the mythic descriptions at the center of *America* and *Europe* (which it resembles on a much grander scale), it is morally and intellectually ambiguous. The World of Los encompasses in its inclusiveness both the paradisal "Vision of beatitude" (25.70) and the demonic "pits & dens & shades of death" (27.33), and a great deal of mythmaking and visionary description that evade discursive paraphrase (see, for example, the extraordinary description of linear time as a magnificent, three-dimensional circular city [28.44–59]). The value of the World of Los passage is not to be found in the lessons of its cosmography, but rather in the exuberance of its invention and the multitudinous variety of its scope. The responsive reader passes through it and returns to the narrative, and to Milton's ultimate confrontation with Satan, with an enhanced sense of how crucial it is to overcome Satanic one-dimensionality.

These passages in which the narrative gives way to another mode of presentation are notable, then, not for the meanings they communicate but rather for the way in which they modulate the apprehension of meaning as the reader moves through the text. They are passages in the primary sense of the word, modes of transit from one state of the reading experience to another. Such passages are analogous to the "liminal" structures examined in anthropological studies of tribal rituals of passage. Liminality represents an aspect of the ritual that, by presenting the neophyte with strange iconic representations of central mysteries, is designed to dissociate him from his old structures of custom and then return him to the social structure with a renewed sense of its values.[9] It is noteworthy that these liminal episodes are generally absent from such narrative works as *Tiriel, The Book of Urizen, The Book of Ahania*, and *The Book of Los*, which are concerned with tracing the bondage to time and space, the narrowing of perceptions, and the establishment of unequivocal moral law (a poem such as the linear *Visions of the Daughters of Albion*, which strains against this bondage, also strains toward liminality in the passionate questionings of Oothoon's speeches). These works tend to be stylistically uniform, affording little in the way of textual breaks or openings that the reader can enter for transformations of consciousness. Concomitantly, we find little discontinuity in the line of narrative in these works. Their actions, to be sure, often seem repetitive or unmotivated by the standard rules of cause and effect, but generally one action follows another. There are no conspicuous pauses in the action during which the poet transfers the reader to a different plane of discourse.

The vision of unmitigated continuity, then, is a vision of bondage. But even in *Milton* and *Jerusalem*, certain gestures toward continuity are necessary to the design of the whole. Milton must journey from his state of celestial unhappiness at the beginning of the poem to his union with his Emanation at the end; Los labors continuously in *Jerusalem* and sometimes journeys, in order to "search the interiors of Albions Bosom" (*J* 45.3–4); the reader's eye must journey from the first plate to the last; and all of us must return, after closing Blake's works, to the continuities of our "Planetary lives of Years Months Days & Hours" (*J* 99.3). Such continuities become redeemed, like the politics of the thirteen Angels, when they are penetrated by liminal openings.

---

[9] For a useful account of these liminal structures, see Victor Turner, *The Forest of Symbols: Aspects of Ndembu Ritual* (Ithaca: Cornell University Press, 1967), 93–110.

INTERPOLATION, OR THE TEXT AS PALIMPSEST:
THE EXAMPLE OF *VALA*

In making the distinction here between those poems in which Blake organizes the narrative around a central interruption and those in which the action proceeds in a continuous line, one must consider *The Four Zoas* as a special case. Here, we are given a visionary ending that delivers the characters and the readers from time's bondage, attached to an unbroken linear account of successive temporal ages, a problematic combination that Blake's many labored revisions of the manuscript, most of them disruptive of smooth narrative continuity, may have been designed to address. These revisions introduce *real*, not metaphoric, openings into the text at the same time that they introduce disruptive content—for with the insertion of new leaves, they pry apart pages formerly contiguous, or they cram in writing where there once was space, or they force the reader's eye to leave its conventional vertical descent of the lines on the page in order to move laterally to outcroppings in the margins. It is essential, when dealing with the *Zoas* manuscript as a total work of art, to understand that the fact of interpolation is itself as significant as the content that is interpolated.

Night I provides three illustrative examples. First, the dire song of the Demons of the Deep intrudes a vision of strife and horror into the nuptial feast of Los and Enitharmon, an account that is altogether celebratory in tone in the earliest surviving continuous stratum of text, just as the leaf on which the song is written breaks into a series of pages previously numbered and stitched together (*FZ* 15–16).[10] Second, Eno stretches out a moment of time and opens a center in an atom of space—providential acts described in a marginal insert that itself opens a space within the continuity of the adjacent lines of the text inscribed earlier (*FZ* 9.9–18). Third, at the end of the Night, an added leaf (21–22) retells the story of the fall, a retelling that not only supplements but also at many points severely contradicts Enitharmon's earlier version (*FZ* 10.9–25) inscribed in the substrate text. The first of these examples *cancels* the tone of the earlier, interrupted continuum; the second *adds* a supplement of providential purpose to a darkening narrative; the third *revises* a previous understanding of a past event, render-

---

[10] G. E. Bentley, Jr., correctly notes in his edition of the poem that all overt evidence of violence and strife in the Nuptial Feast section of the First Night derives from lines either inserted into the substrate text or inscribed over erasures; see *Vala or The Four Zoas: A Facsimile of the Manuscript, a Transcript of the Poem and a Study of Its Growth and Significance* (Oxford: Clarendon Press, 1963), 168. Bibliographical information used in the present study comes from this edition, unless noted otherwise, and from my own examination of the manuscript in the British Library.

ing it less determinate, and more complex, than we had thought. These vexations to the narrative and thematic continuity of the poem are mimed by the physical appearance of the text itself, with its cancellations, super-impositions, and erasures. Revision and interpolation are rarely neutral elements in the Blakean text, rarely data of bibliographical interest only. They are part of its system of signification, like the pictorial designs.[11] Indeed, in a text such as *The Four Zoas*, where their presence is immediately obvious to the eye, they are a part of the visual design itself.

All writers, it may be argued, insert and cancel passages in their manu-scripts, and, furthermore, a manuscript such as *The Four Zoas*, presumably unfinished and left in a state not intended for public presentation, would seem inhospitable territory for discovering planned aesthetic effects in its overall graphic appearance. But most writers also labor assiduously to make their graftings and second thoughts undetectable in the finished work, whereas Blake is content to allow his revisions to retain a superim-posed appearance even to the last. One reason why reading the *Zoas* is such a choppy experience, even in a "clean text" edition in which all the vicissi-tudes of the manuscript have been relegated to the notes, is that Blake has taken so few pains to harmonize his newer material with the earlier layers that he has retained. Interpolation, moreover, is nearly as evident in "fin-ished" works such as *Milton* and *Jerusalem* as it is in a working manuscript such as *The Four Zoas*. For example, the narrative digression about Albion's fall and the binding of Urizen that retards the progress of the Bard's Song in plates 3–6 of *Milton* is the product of repeated interpolations, with one plate inserted before the assembling of the first extant copy, and three more introduced in later copies. Together, they open a wide space within an earlier perfect continuity of subject and syntax between the last line of plate

---

[11] Donald Ault has offered perhaps the most uncompromisingly radical interpretation of what Blake's revisionary impulse signifies:

> How the poem was transformed from its *Vala* state into *The Four Zoas* suggests that revi-sion takes on a double significance: it is both something that Blake did to the text and something that the text does, through the agency of narrative, not only to the reader but to itself. Indeed, Blake's whole enterprise constitutes the irreducible presence of multiple interfering and incommensurable structures that operate (1) to rule out a pre-existent un-derlying world that surface events (i.e., those narrated by the linear text) partially rearrange and partially distort, and (2) to generate a narrative field in which the past is not closed and complete but open—unfinished and revisable.

See "Re-visioning *The Four Zoas*" in *Unnam'd Forms: Blake and Textuality*, ed. Nelson Hilton and Thomas A. Vogler (Berkeley and Los Angeles: University of California Press, 1986), 107–8. These views are massively elaborated in Ault's impressive study *Narrative Unbound: Re-Visioning William Blake's "The Four Zoas"* (Barrytown, N.Y.: Station Hill Press, 1987); it should be noted that Ault's conception of the poem as a synchronic structure of narrative interferences differs radically from the view of the poem presented here, a view that stresses its time-generated nature and the adventitious character of its revisions and interpolations.

2 and the first line of plate 7.[12] A number of similar examples may be gleaned from *Jerusalem*. For example, from their interruptions of continuous sense and their anomalous script, plates 31, 37–39 (in the earlier ordering), 56, and 61 all appear to be late insertions in their respective sequences before the assembling of the first extant copy.[13] Were they to be removed, continuities of subject matter and even syntactical connections between the preceding and succeeding plates would become immediately evident, and they are not much concealed as the text now stands. It is useless to argue that Blake did not expect his readers to notice these palpable interruptions to sequential continuity, for the text preserves their evidence as unmistakably as lunar craters preserve the evidence of early meteoric impact. Moreover, it would be a disservice to Blake's artistic intelligence to imagine that he did not notice these discontinuities himself. If we notice interpolation in Blake, it is perhaps because he happily permits it, or even encourages it.

Nowhere in Blake's work is interpolation more noticeable than in the *Zoas* manuscript, and the poet may well have been content with the look of the text precisely as he left it to posterity. For most of Blake's revisions are indeed re-*visions*; they register the eruption of new or deeper conceptions of a subject already rendered, and the fact of the re-seeing may form as much an element of what Blake wishes to impart as the conception seen anew. We become aware of differentiated levels of seeing when the new emerges in the midst of the old and the disjunctions between them are clearly marked. Interpolation and revision introduce a sense of geological depth to the unrolling linear surface of the narrative, a depth in which we glimpse the successive strata in the growth of the poet's mind. The text not only encompasses traditional fictive time, the diachronic story line, but also recuperates the author's time, making the history of the poet's creative acts an integral part of the created work. The text becomes an autobiographical palimpsest, in which old and perhaps superseded labors are nonetheless kept, like the acts of Los, "Permanent, & not lost not lost nor vanishd" (*J* 13.60). The more palpably the revisions interrupt or intrude, the more they endorse the possibility of fresh vision and providential opportunity.

At the same time, this newness of vision is always presented as a recovery of an elder reality. The poet's repeated returns to his own narrative are attempts to refocus, through revision, his understanding of characters and episodes, as if to see farther and more sharply into the already established

---

[12] For details, see Erdman's textual note to *M* 2.26 (E 807).

[13] For discussions of inserted plates in *Jerusalem*, see David V. Erdman, "The Suppressed and Altered Passages of Blake's *Jerusalem*," *Studies in Bibliography* 17 (1964): 21ff.; G. E. Bentley, Jr., *Blake Books* (Oxford: Clarendon Press, 1977), 225 and 228; and my essay "The Changing Order of Plates in *Jerusalem*, Chapter II," *Blake/An Illustrated Quarterly* 16 (Spring 1983): 192–205.

givens of his mythic history (thus, for example, in Night VIII, the Christian episodes are a late superimposition on a pagan narrative of warring Zoas, but conceptually the textual *superimposition* is a revelation of an *underlying depth*—the redemptive sacrifice of Jesus situates all the willful struggles of the Zoas in an a priori providential context). Thus, conspicuous textual revision is the material substrate in the *Zoas* manuscript for the heightened sense of time rendered in its embedded narrative, the poem *Vala*. In *Vala*, time forces itself on us in unsettling ways, taking the form either as an abyss of regressions or as an onward flow of changes and successions. Within the comprehensive frame of a fall and revival of the Eternal Man, ages, structures, and the personal fortunes of characters rise and fall, then rise and fall again, like the to-and-fro of waves in the oceans of Tharmas.[14] In the midst of this forward momentum, there are repeated moves to catapult the imagination back into the past. This is seen particularly in the characters' obsessive quest for origins, their attempts to recover the events of the fall, of the time before the fall, and even of earlier falls in shadowier times before that.[15]

This ambience of time in flux, time as a series of catastrophes, time as a boundless depth or an adventitious growth, imports us into the milieu of the Burkean sublime, the milieu of presences and absences, of chaotic energies, abyssal recesses, and blurred boundaries. It is fitting, therefore, that as a chronicle of origins and changes, *Vala* is materially incarnated in a text that curiously mimics the impression of a Burkean landscape. Geological metaphors are again fitting: whether we look at the ruins of ages heaped upon ages accumulating within the story itself or at the revisions piled on revisions in the actual writing of the text, the overwhelming impression is one of successive strata.[16] The text resembles an aerial contour map, mostly

[14] In her essay "Vala's Garden in Night the Ninth: Paradise Regained or Woman Bound," Catherine Haigney speaks of "eruptions and subsidings [that] compose so relentless a rhythm of alternation that one loses all ordered sense of narrative past/future timing," and even the Last Judgment is "something cataclysmic that rolls on and on in a never-ending present" (*Blake/An Illustrated Quarterly* 20 [Spring 1987]: 123). The loss of an "ordered sense" of time in *Vala* does not, of course, deliver us from the oppressive sense of time as a limitless abyss; it is not so much the present but rather the onward roll that is "never ending," for all the presents of *Vala* are, in fact, fragile and evanescent.

[15] Noting that "getting to a beginning point behind a given beginning point is as much Blake's technique as his theme" in *Vala*, Leslie Brisman observes (paraphrasing an insight drawn from Foucault) that "origin, for Blake, is much more the way in which man in general—Albion—articulates himself upon the already-begun" (*Romantic Origins*, 227–28).

[16] Just as the content of the poem invites and yet frustrates attempts to pin down the "true" circumstances and the precise beginning of the events that constitute the fall, so the autograph text often yields evidence itself of earlier irrecoverable strata that call into question the absolute authority of the extant lines. To observe, for example, that the first seven pages of the manuscript are unmistakably inscribed over heavy erasures, is to perceive the very notion of a

dominated by a somewhat uneven plateau (the idiom and conceptions prevalent in Nights II–VII), but often crossed by scarred outcroppings (most of Night I, for example), or by deep mysterious fissures (the juncture, say, of the two Nights VII). Editions that offer an "ideal" *Four Zoas* compounded of the latest available readings, all outfitted in a neat uniform typeface, and commentaries that assume a consistent and uniform authorial intention effectively flatten out these contours and thereby deprive the reader of one of the most immediately powerful effects that acquaintance with the manuscript can give, its layered turbulence: the agon of Blake, wrestling with a tale that he cannot seem to get to the bottom or to the end of, superimposed upon the agon of his obstreperous Giants in their unsettled cosmos.[17]

The disturbances that make the *Zoas* manuscript a history of its own process of evolution, analogous to the geological evidences of creation, are by no means simply a matter of local cancellations and interpolations. At least two major catastrophes (in the neutral sense of sudden, massive, and pervasive change) leave their bibliographical evidence in the manuscript precisely at those points at which the story or theme is itself undergoing some sort of decisive shift. Critics have long been aware of one of these— namely, the perturbations that take over the manuscript in Night VII as soon as Blake runs out of the plot material gleaned from the earlier Lambeth Books that has sustained him since Night IV. But a much greater disturbance, from the bibliographical perspective, has received less critical attention, and that is the change that comes over the whole poem at the exact point at which the ornate (or "copperplate") transcription on plain paper ends, and a new, less elegant transcription[18] takes over throughout the remainder of the work, on proofsheets of Blake's *Night Thoughts* designs. It is worth examining this transition in some detail. The copperplate text ends on page 42.18 with the words "She ended," as Ahania completes her admonition to Urizen, and the harsher script inscribes the harsh transformation of the narrative as Urizen "burst[s] forth the black hail." A few more lines of added script bring us over to page 43, to the sudden and

---

"real" beginning to this poem as problematic, for any *new* beginning, clearly seen as new, cannot be *the* beginning.

[17] In its review of David Erdman's 1982 edition of *The Complete Poetry and Prose of William Blake*, the Santa Cruz Blake Study Group makes a similar and telling point about *The Four Zoas:* "the very strangeness of the manuscript fascinates us: its surface chaos, its false starts, its palimpsestuous revisions and deletions are invitations to a kind of labor which is itself deleted from the print edition. . . . To correct the graphic traces of a struggle for resurrection to unity is to assume that they are irrelevant to the reader's experience of the text as a struggle *in writing*" (*Blake/An Illustrated Quarterly* 18 [Summer 1984]: 15).

[18] The lines inscribed on the *Night Thoughts* proofsheets are evidently a transcription of earlier material—i.e., a fair copy, and not a first-draft invention. For evidence, see the Textual Notes in E for *FZ* 51.23 and 53.15 (E 832–33).

striking presence of the *Night Thoughts* proofsheets, where the poetry matches the astonishments of the new textual matrix: "Then thunders rolld around & lightnings darted to & fro" (43.1). Within the first page and a half of this new transcription, the entire cosmos built up in the preceding forty-two pages collapses, and a new setting, new characters, and a new tone are introduced that prevail throughout most of the remainder of the poem.

To move from the base-layer copperplate transcription to the *Night Thoughts* transcription is to move from a kind of Homeric clarity of tone and atmosphere to a seemingly unending *Sturm und Drang* that persists well into the apocalyptic *peripeteia* of Night IX itself, deferring closure for as long as possible. Not even the Christianizing impulse that sets in around the time of the transcription of Night VII and VIII and leads to the second major wave of disruptive rethinking in the poem can quite manage to prevail over the atmosphere that the *Night Thoughts* pages have introduced. Compared to the world of the copperplate substrate, what succeeds it is a world of strife, darkness, wild settings, and stormy climes. In the copperplate substrate, for example, there are no contentious exchanges between any of the characters (all overt strife in these early Nights is to be found exclusively in overwrites and interpolations), whereas the *Night Thoughts* section begins in an explosion of angry contention, and this becomes the norm for interpersonal relations thereafter in the base transcription of this section virtually up to Night IX. In terms of setting, moreover, the characteristic imagery of the copperplate verses suggests an ordered world of early human advancement, from the pastoralism of Night I, with its "towns & villages and temples, tents sheep-folds and pastures," its "joyful Earth & Sea," and its "Bright Souls of vegetative life" (13.14, 21, 24), to the organized agriculture, the "barns and garners" (30.7), and technological advances of Night II ("Some fix'd the anvil, some the loom erected, some the plow /And harrow formd & framd the harness" [24.10–11]), culminating in the "wondrous building" (30.16) of Urizen's architectural masterwork. Once having crossed into the *Night Thoughts* sequence, however, one enters a barely habitable universe of alien powers, a world of flux without progress, captured in such characteristic imagery as the "heaving deluge" and "broken rocks" of Night IV (47.2; 52.13), the "Grim frost beneath & terrible snow," (58.13), the "dismal vales" and "iron mountains top" (62.17) of Night V, the "burning wastes / Of Sand" and the "horrid bottomless vacuity" of Night VI (70.21–22; 71.23), the "forests of affliction," "dark caves," and "dim air" of Night VII (77.10, 20; 79.27), and the "Scaly monsters of the restless deep," the "sullen north wind," and the "clouds & flaming fires" of Night VIII (108.27; 110.9, 24). One quickly recognizes here the quintessential idiom of the dark or terrific sublime promoted by Burke, and it is a strong indication of the aesthetic direction that the poem suddenly begins to take from page 43 of the manuscript onward.

Given this new direction, it is fitting that the first character to emerge from the cataclysm of Urizen's fall is Tharmas, a figure habitually associated with raw, chaotic physical power. As a mythic being, Tharmas inflicts trauma on the cosmos by destroying the foundations of the "sweet world / Built by the Architect divine" (48.27–28); as a poetic invention, he is perhaps the emblem of a trauma that the poet has himself imposed on his own developing text. Tharmas is notably absent from earliest extant layer of copperplate transcription found on pages 7–42, except for two fleeting allusions where he seems "little more than a name"[19] or personification of the sea. As a substantial character, Tharmas appears in the base layer of text only in the *Night Thoughts* proofsheets (pp. 43ff.); his important actions at the beginning of Night I are, by contrast, entirely confined to lines inscribed over several layers of eradicated earlier text.[20] One begins to suspect that Blake had composed *and* transcribed the text of the copperplate pages before he had even fully worked out the conceptions and character relationships that were to occupy the remaining two-thirds of the poem. If this is the case, then the radical discontinuity in the material format of the manuscript that occurs on pages 42–43 is the powerful visual correlative not only of a cataclysm in the world of the characters but also of a crisis in the composition of the poem, the outward marker of a substantial rethinking.

Were the absence of Tharmas from the earliest extant stratum of text the only evidence of this compositional gap, it might be attributed to coincidence, but there are many other evidences of rethinking. For example, there is no actual indication in the surviving lines of the copperplate stratum that Tharmas and Enion are the parents of Los and Enitharmon (and, in fact, even some residual signs of a rather different assignment of parentage[21]); it is not even certain that Tharmas and Enion have any con-

---

[19] As my former student John B. Pierce has pointed out, in "The Shifting Characterization of Tharmas and Enion in Pages 3–7 of Blake's *Vala* or *The Four Zoas*," *Blake/An Illustrated Quarterly* 22 (Winter 1988/89): 94.

[20] These superimposed lines are, as Pierce suggests (ibid.), probably later in composition than the text of pp. 43ff. since they contain concepts and terminology generally absent from the substrate transcript of *Vala* but common in *Milton* and *Jerusalem*.

[21] I suspect that the original parents of Los and Enitharmon were Luvah and Vala. Not enough has been made of H. M. Margoliouth's important observation that Vala "must be [originally] identifiable with the Woman-Serpent" of 7.10ff. who gives birth to Los and Enitharmon, as the description there matches Luvah's later description of Vala as a Dragonwoman (26.7–13); see *William Blake's "Vala:" Blake's Numbered Text* (Oxford: Clarendon Press, 1956), xx. In addition, Enitharmon's comment on her (unnamed) parents, "To make us happy let them weary their immortal powers / While we draw in their sweet delights" (10.3–4), seems connected to a later scene in which "Los joyd & Enitharmon laughd, saying Let us go down / And see this labour & sorrow; They went down to see the woes / Of Vala & the woes of Luvah, to draw in their delights" (30.53–55). Whereas there is no textual

nection to one another. These relationships are all firmly established, how-ever, within the first half-dozen or so pages of the *Night Thoughts* tran-script. In these same pages, the figure of Urthona (altogether absent from the preceding copperplate transcription) first appears in the base text of the poem, and his identification with Los—crucial to the whole future devel-opment of Blake's myth—is here first asserted. In short, it is in the opening of the *Night Thoughts* pages, not in anything that we can detect from the copperplate stratum of pages 7–42, that the entire dramatis personae of what we have come to regard as the *Zoa* myth—the four principal powers, their loves, their genealogies—are for the first time assembled. From the standpoint of the myth's cohesiveness as a narrative, the first three Nights in their earliest surviving form are rendered virtually superfluous.

It is indeed as if the world of the first three Nights has been superseded. After the fall of Urizen's cosmos on the verso of the first leaf of the *Night Thoughts* transcription, no character in the poem alludes to or appears ca-pable of recollecting any of the major incidents described in pages 1–42—neither Los and Enitharmon's youthful Rousseau-flavored days of wander-ing in noble savagery in Night I (9.19ff.), nor their great nuptial feast, nor the subsequent building of Urizen's extravagant Golden Hall.[22] Instead, their memories seem to conflate the most recent catastrophe of collapse, described at the end of Night III, with the primordial catastrophe never actually shown in the poem, the "day of terror & abhorrence" (50.2) when Luvah took the Horses of Light, and chaos ensued. Thus in Night IV the Spectre of Urthona greets Tharmas as if he were seeing him in his ruin for the first time: "Tharmas I know thee. how are we alterd our beauty decayd / But still I know thee tho in this horrible ruin whelmd" (49.27–28), and he then proceeds to a recollection of the primordial "day of terror" as if that event and their present plight were two contiguous moments (see 50.1–27). The Spectre betrays no sense that there may have been two ca-

---

evidence anywhere in the first three Nights of Tharmas or Enion wearying their powers on behalf of their offspring, the power-exhausting labors of Luvah and Vala are a major theme of Night II. Los and Enitharmon are the beneficiaries of these labors: the work goes into the building of Urizen's Golden World, which Los has called "this bright world of all our joy" (11.16–17). Los and Enitharmon's rather heartless interest in the woes of Vala and Luvah makes more cogent plot-sense if we postulate an original scheme in which the youngsters considered the tribulations of their elders as nothing more than services due to superseding inheritors.

[22] Helen T. McNeil has observed that "the Zoas themselves posit radically different pasts according to the emotions of the present. Indeed, time recalled from the perspective of a distinct present . . . can hardly be said to exist in *The Four Zoas*" ("The Formal Art of *The Four Zoas*," 385). McNeil does not consider to what extent this situation is a product of textual revision; this consideration allows us to see that recollections of the characters are not totally incoherent, but rather are warped in certain uniform ways by the textual matrix; these recol-lections cohere well enough *so long as they all arise in the same layer of transcription.*

tastrophes, and that the more recent, although the immediate cause of his horror, has been given different causal antecedents in the preceding narrative from those he recollects. Likewise, in Night V, when Urizen finally wakes up from the coma induced by his fall two Nights earlier, he remembers nothing of the events of Nights I-III, recalling only how he "fell from [his] throne sublime" (65.8) in the crisis of Luvah and the horses. The copperplate narrative of the early Nights presents a very different story, showing Urizen acquiring rather than losing the trappings of monarchy as a consequence of the crisis ("Take thou possession! take this Scepter! go forth in my might," the deteriorating Eternal Man tells him [23.5]), and he is in fact first seen occupying a "starry throne" (37.1) only at the beginning of Night III as Ahania begins her fateful entreaty. It is as if on awakening, Urizen has backdated his own fall to the time of the Eternal Man's crisis, a crisis that the copperplate narrative shows as actually tending to Urizen's political advantage. He is indeed correct in recollecting a fall from a throne but appears unable to distinguish a belated and recent event from a primordial event. Like other characters from Night IV onward, he regards the catastrophe described at the critical juncture of the two transcriptions as a site of true origins.

I have been suggesting that this criticial juncture indicates a newly conceived starting point for Blake the poet, as well. The end of the copperplate transcription at page 42.18 marks what was probably a considerable pause in the composition and transcription of *Vala*, and when composition resumed, it produced a story that is, to all intents, complete in itself, an unbroken sequence from a catastrophic fall to a final apocalypse. This story contains, either through direct reference or retrospective allusion, all that is essential for one to know about the dramatis personae, their histories, and their relationships. It is, of course, possible that this pattern of forgotten origins and new beginnings was part of Blake's earliest conception of *Vala*, that it was deliberately built into the poem's composition from the start, and that the shift to transcription on the *Night Thoughts* proofsheets signifies nothing more than an exhaustion of his supply of blank paper. A great deal of manuscript evidence has to be dismissed as coincidence in order to make this alternative plausible,[23] but even if it is so dismissed, the

---

[23] Coincidence would also have to explain why the leaves of pp. 1–42 of the ms. were once stitched together separately from pp. 43–84, which display a different pattern of stitch holes. Blake's stitches, like modern paper clips, were presumably intended to keep batches of leaves together for setting aside (evidence of some kind of a pause in composition or transcription), but it is odd that Blake would not want to keep all of Night III together when he set it aside—unless the latter half of the Night (pp. 43–46) did not yet exist when he stitched the first half with the rest of the copperplate pages. There is also the matter of dating: the title page of the ms. asserts a date of "1797," which probably reflects an early compositional stage preserved at least in part in the extant copperplate substratum—but one is scarcely four leaves into the *Night Thoughts* proofsheets before encountering unmistakable evidence of late transcription;

disjunction of crossing from Night III to IV, from the copperplate pages to the proofsheets, is *experienced* in the reading as a kind of temporal gap, a distancing hiatus that gives to the early Nights the feeling of a dimly receding era and to the authorial conception a feeling of interruption. It is also significant that Blake chooses to emphasize rather than conceal this sense of disjunction by using the new paper. And it is of more than casual importance that it should be *this* paper, rather than any other supply he might have used. Critics have long suggested that in *Vala* Blake was attempting to vie with and supersede Young's *Night Thoughts*. Nothing illustrates the attempt with more striking visual force than the inscription of Blake's original poetry in a space designed to hold the lines of Young—a space, moreover, that breaks into the forms of the surrounding designs, which are the product of an earlier Blake half in contractual bondage to the conceptions of a dead poet and half his own man. And if the argument offered here is valid, there is yet one more level of supersession; the narrative that occupies that proofsheet portion of the *Zoas* manuscript overrides Blake's own earlier conception of this poem's beginnings. A whole history of displacements, then, is encoded in the material substrate, the new paper supply, and this code is subtly employed to direct our reading of the poet's latest thematic intentions.

Of course, in revising the earlier framework of *Vala*, Blake, typically, makes no attempt to discard it. On the contrary, he takes deliberate pains to bind the copperplate sequence to the *Night Thoughts* sequence. For example, he starts the new transcription at the very point at which the copperplate lines end, rather than beginning on a new sheet; he inserts anticipatory asides in Ahania's speech that help to make Urizen's explosive response less of a surprise;[24] and, most significantly, he rewrites the first six

---

the sheet for pp. 48–49 had been previously used as a backing sheet for the printing of one of Hayley's *Ballads* in May 1802, as Bentley was the first to observe, and he plausibly argues that the whole project of the *Night Thoughts* transcription probably could not have begun much before that date (see the *Vala* facsimile, pp. 161–62); Erdman's counterargument to Bentley—that pp. 48–49 could have been inserted late [see E 817, Textual Notes]—is based on conjectural inferences rather than material evidence, and in the absence of telltale signs of Blakean interpolation—disjunctive narrative, anomalous script styles, doctrinal self-contradiction—should probably carry less weight. It is, of course, true that the copperplate section could have been *composed* a good deal later than 1797, and the *Night Thoughts* group a good deal earlier than 1802, but in any case the gap between the two dates at least supports rather than detracts from the notion of a gap in composition, especially in the light of other pieces of evidence that point independently in the same direction.

[24] See, e.g., 41.18 and 42.7–8, where Ahania's inserted references to Urizen frowning or turning pale as she speaks create a sense of a dramatic confrontation building up to a crisis, whereas no such sense emerges from the copperplate substrate. Indeed, in the first stratum of text, Ahania's speech provides no direct indication of being addressed to Urizen at all (for example, the "thee" and "thy" of the line "He looked up & saw thee Prince of Light thy splendor faded" [39.17] were originally "the" and "with," respectively, in the first stratum).

and a half pages of the poem in order to entrench from the start the probably new concept of Tharmas and Enion as the parents of Los and Enitharmon. In this fashion, Blake secures a certain narrative continuity while doing little to conceal—indeed, even advertising—the presence of massive narrative disjunction. This paradoxical procedure is an artistic masterstroke, and confers on the poem much of its uncanny grandeur. Had Blake in fact dropped the first three Nights from the manuscript, a conceptually and narratively coherent tale of great power would remain, but it would be essentially a linear sequence like the *Book of Urizen*, on which its plot is based, and what would be lost (aside from numerous poetic felicities) is the impression rendered of chronological depth—the idea not merely of events in succession, but of ages in succession, the earlier seen through the later.

The paradox of a poem that maintains a surface continuity (at least for seven Nights), while thoroughly revising its world a third of the way through, duplicates the paradox of our general apprehension of time past: that it is and must be both an unbroken continuum of undifferentiated moments and also a thing periodized into a palimpsest of discrete epochs, forming a series of receding frames into which we peer with ever-increasing difficulty and awe, as in an abyss of infinite regress. This second kind of apprehension brings temporality into the gravitational field of the sublime and Burke's "artificial infinite." Thus David Hume, attempting to explain why the contemplation of remote antiquity inspires awe, states that "to our senses, time or succession is always broken and divided. . . . The mind elevated by the vastness of its object, is still farther elevated by the difficulty of the conception, and being obliged every moment to renew its efforts in the transition from one part of time to another, feels a more vigorous and sublime disposition."[25] Hume's conceptions of the sublime closely resemble Burke's, and we recognize in the serial regress of ages described here the familiar indefinite sublime object—which, like all sublime agencies of blockage or difficulty, characteristically provokes in the observer an upsurge of transcendent vigor. As part of an epic dealing with transformations in time, the onset of the *Night Thoughts* transcription in *Vala* also renders a transformation *of* time in the direction of the Burkean sublime. This onset makes the past problematic by instituting a new point of origins that seems sufficient for all that follows; at the same time, however, the poem taken as a whole shows this point to be clearly false as an

---

These are good examples of the adventitious stitching that enables Blake to recycle old material into new and often disjunctive contexts. It also succinctly demonstrates that anything in the copperplate pages that specifically looks forward to or anticipates material in the *Night Thoughts* proofsheet pages is found only in added or substituted text.

[25] David Hume, *A Treatise on Human Nature*, 3 vols. (London: John Noon, Thomas Longman, 1739–1740), vol. 3, 286.

origin, for behind it lurks that stretch of anteriority (the copperplate pages), hard to recollect or keep in focus (since even the characters themselves cannot do it) and obscurely connected, at best, to more recent events, yet always *there*, a perpetual reminder of receding depths.

Both as an epic tale and as a manuscript, a bibliographical document, *Vala* or *The Four Zoas* testifies to the hold of the Burkean imagination on Blake even as he engages in one of his most ambitious poetic achievements, and it is a force that increases rather than diminishes as the poem moves onward from its early phases. The strenuous contentions of the dramatis personae and the waste grandeur of their settings are reinforced by a matching vastness in the temporal frame, with its receding indefiniteness and its unstable points of departure. These qualities, moreover, inhere not only in the subject matter of the poem, but are intrinsic to the physical matrix that conditions the way readers process that subject matter. If, as suggested earlier, the visible record of interpolation and revision gives to the manuscript the appearance of a sublime wilderness, full of slippery continuities and abrupt discontinuities, it also congeals on its two-dimensional surface a sense of the labor of ages, epitomized in the successive periods of a poet's creative life. Finally, it inscribes clearly the essential qualities of Blake's sensibility that are closest to Burke's—namely, an affinity for ongoing struggle, for contentions against blocking obstacles (even of the poet's own former making), and a delight in displaying such struggle in all its phases.[26] Unlike *Milton*, the Blakean work that enshrines par excellence the power of the concentrated moment, *Vala* or *The Four Zoas* stakes as its territory the vast progress of time's extended developments, the borderlessness of existence, the successive superventions of power and strength. It is the most impressive example in Blake's canon, and perhaps in major poetry of the age, of the art of the Burkean or bardic sublime.

MEDLEY, OR THE TEXT AS COMPILATION: THE EXAMPLE OF *JERUSALEM*

Blake's two longest poems, *Vala* and *Jerusalem*, form a pair of opposed counterparts, as do their eponymous heroines in the myth of Albion itself. The first presents itself in a disorderly manuscript, containing a wilderness of graphic styles, differing paper stocks, and palpable waves of revision. The second is an exquisitely finished etched book, physically uniform

---

[26] Even the late Christian interpolations in *The Four Zoas*, which seek to replace a sensibility fascinated by contention with one based on mutual yielding and reconciliation, do not on the textual level pose an exception to this statement, for they too must attempt to contend with and prevail against earlier material of a quite different character, which is uncomfortably left surrounding them.

(aside from some variation in script styles), and tailored to a plan of pronounced regularity, symmetry, and numerical precision (one hundred plates divided into four chapters of equal length, with a framing of full-page designs at the beginning, the end, and the medial interstices). If *Vala* epitomizes the bardic style, then *Jerusalem* enshrines the iconic; whereas *Vala* is relentlessly linear and temporal, with its overt time-measuring divisions (successive "Nights"), its sequential narrative, and its open display of its own compositional development, *Jerusalem* is much more a spatial construct. One first perceives the regularity of its periodic divisions, the mirroring of its opening and closing devices, and, of course, the overpowering presence of two-dimensional fields of representation—the multitude of designs. The text too, as every reader discovers, is nonsequential, with episodes arranged to form a contiguous collocation rather than a continuous line.

The puzzle of *Jerusalem*'s poetic structure has engaged the attention of a good many critics, and there is a growing consensus regarding the nature of the problem, if not of its ultimate solution.[27] The problem is that variations on a relatively small set of mythic and thematic motifs are replicated and distributed like well-shuffled cards to all four chapters of the poem, so that each chapter becomes a medley of the entire set of motifs; as a result of this comprehensiveness, the chapters are not so clearly differentiated from one another as to make the purpose of the divisions self-evident. Moreover, if there is not enough differentiation in the progress from chapter to chapter, there is too much in the relation of each individual passage to the next; the same process of shuffling and distribution that homogenizes the whole fragmentizes the parts. The features that give rise to these problems do not readily disclose their rationale, and it is not my aim here to propose a definitive explanation of them. Rather, it is to suggest how we might view the problematic features—the repeated local discontinuities, the nonprogressive nature of the whole, the disparity between the formal regularity of the large divisions and the looseness of the arrangements contained inside them—as vehicles of a sublime sensibility and producers of sublime effects. As the most ambitious of all Blake's poetic achieve-

---

[27] For surveys and summaries of the most important critical literature on *Jerusalem*'s structure, see Easson, "William Blake and His Reader in *Jerusalem*" and Stuart Curran, "The Structures of *Jerusalem*," both in *Blake's Sublime Allegory*, 316–17n and 329–31, respectively; Mitchell, *Blake's Composite Art*, 171–72; Minna Doskow, *William Blake's "Jerusalem": Structure and Meaning in Poetry and Picture* (Rutherford, N.J.: Fairleigh Dickinson University Press, 1982), 13–14; and Paley, *The Continuing City*, 278–83. Most of these critics properly take to task the attempts of their predecessors to superimpose a coherent thematic progression upon the poem's four-part organization, although not all proceed in their commentaries to follow their own strictures.

ments, *Jerusalem* presumably should exemplify in the greatest degree the requirements of "the Most Sublime Poetry."

One does not proceed far in such an inquiry before discovering that the macrostructure of the work, the sequence of four chapters, is the wrong place to start. As the poem itself asserts in one of its most famous lines, "he who wishes to see a Vision; a perfect Whole / Must see it in its Minute Particulars" (91.20–21), and in this case, the Particulars consist of those many verse sequences, varying in length from a paragraph to several plates, that seem individually discrete and indivisible. The boundaries of these sequences are often hard to detect, for they are not always coterminous with the beginning or ending of plates—and Blake, furthermore, is adept at starting new sequences with "Ands" and "Thens" to create a factitious continuity. Once they are isolated, however, it becomes possible to determine what kind of poetic form these sequences possess in themselves, and hence toward what form they build in the aggregate. Blake gives us some help in this matter when, for example, he rearranges the order of sequences in Chapter 2 of the poem in certain copies (D and E), thereby exposing the faultlines within the chapter's surface continuity, the boundaries of tectonic units that remain indivisible. It will be helpful to our understanding of *Jerusalem*'s general construction if we pause over this section of the poem. In the rearrangement of Chapter 2, plates 29–41, 43–46, and 47–50, as numbered in Copies A, C, and F, emerge as observable blocks (the first two are transposed in the second ordering, with a probably later readjustment to the position of plate 42). Once we become sensitized to the existence of such blocks, it then becomes easier to notice divisions within these units even where the sequence has remained intact in all copies. Thus, the thirteen-plate block 29–41 is easily observed to fall into two divisions that differ markedly in subject matter, lettering style, and patterning of the designs—plates 29–32, dominated by the story of Los and Reuben, and plates 33–41, the account of the conclave of cathedral cities gathered to save Albion. I have elsewhere analyzed in some detail the formal properties of this second sequence and how they relate to the issue of the chapter's reordering;[28] it will suffice here to summarize the information most relevant to the present context.

Briefly, the "cathedral cities" sequence manifests a striking artistic unity in terms of tonal consistency, narrative cohesion and scope, and design arrangement. Particularly in its likely original form, before the evident interpolation of several plates (37–40) into what is now the received text, the sequence encapsulates a narrative displaying in condensed form the

---

[28] See "The Changing Order of Plates in *Jerusalem*, Chapter II," 192–205. The thrust of my argument is that Blake's motivation in rearranging the order of the chapter in later copies may have been to achieve a more pleasing and balanced distribution of visual designs.

whole sweep of mythic history—from the shock of Albion "turning from Universal Love" (34.7), through collective attempts to deal with the crisis (34.14ff.), to the verge of apocalyptic possibilities (whose fulfillment is hinted at in the concluding design on plate 41 of what appears to be "The Bride and Wife of the Lamb" [41.28] riding with her Savior in a divine chariot). At the same time, the accompanying designs display not only a coherent thematic progression but also an extraordinary regularity of distribution through the sequence, which becomes ornamented and framed by an array of visual symmetries. Had Blake chosen to issue this sequence as a separate illuminated poem, we would find it a self-sustaining work of art, an internally perfected miniature epic, and we should scarcely need the remaining mass of *Jerusalem* in order to comprehend it. From observing the aesthetic autonomy of the sequence, it is a quick step to wondering how these conditions came about. It then becomes difficult to avoid making the inference that the text, the accompanying designs, their patterned distribution, and perhaps even the etching process all belonged to a single creative stretch of inspiration and execution. And if this is the case with the "cathedral cities" sequence, why should it not be the case with the many other sequences that together make up the poem as a whole? From such a perspective, *Jerusalem* might most plausibly be characterized as a congeries of originally separate "poems," each internally self-sufficient, but all related to the same body of doctrine and mythic material, gathered perhaps over the years into the compilation that constitutes the present text.[29]

To test this notion of the autonomy of the separate sequences, we might briefly examine the other narrative blocks in Chapter 2 that have been exposed to view by the reordering of the plates. While plates 29–32, 43–46, and 47–50 do not display the extraordinary regularity of design distribution that we observe in 33–41, they show no lack of narrative comprehensiveness and poetic self-sufficiency. Thus, all the sequences start at the same originating point of mythic history, with Albion "turning his back to the Divine Vision" (29.1) or from "Universal Love" (34.7), or with the same

[29] This position represents a return in part to one of the oldest views in twentieth-century *Jerusalem* criticism—that of the early editors D. J. Sloss and J.P.R. Wallis, who see the poem "not as an ordered whole, nor even as a series of visions, but as a congeries of episodes"; see *The Prophetic Writings of William Blake*, 2 vols. (Oxford: Clarendon Press, 1926), vol. 1, 439. The view of Sloss and Wallis that Blake attended poetically only to "the vision that possessed him at the moment" (ibid.) is a crude approximation of a more complex truth. It is true that what always matters most to Blake as a writer is the piece of writing directly before him, that he throws his energies into the present center, the "now," and pays little attention to lubricating the reader's exit routes from that center to textual befores and afters; at the same time, I would maintain that Blake never loses sight of a comprehensive framework for these autonomous creative episodes, such as the literary tradition of compiled cycles of myth and legend affords, in which the local autonomy of each episode is preserved within the interrelatedness of the whole.

event told from the prelapsarian perspective of the Divine Vision itself ("I elected Albion for my glory" [43.6]), or else presented as a bodily rupture and rebellion ("Luvah tore forth from Albions Loins" [47.4]). And after exploring various permutations of the fallen state, three of the four sequences conclude on a tremulous note of expectancy, of hovering redemptive possibilities: "the Divine Mercy / . . . Redeems Man in the Body of Jesus Amen / And Length Bredth Highth again Obey the Divine Vision Hallelujah" (32.54–56); "O God thou art Not an Avenger!" (41.28); "Come then O Lamb of God and take away the remembrance of Sin" (50.30). The one sequence that fails to conform to this pattern, plates 43– 46, nonetheless proves to offer the most sweeping survey of Blake's basic myth in a condensed or synoptic form. It begins, as we have seen, with a reminiscence of the prelapsarian state, moves on to Albion's dispossession and his "darkning rocks" (43.28), then performs a selective scan of the history elaborately presented in *Vala*, pausing to repeat at length the account of the strife between Albion and Luvah from Night III of the former poem and then collapsing the action of the next four Nights with references to the escape of Enitharmon and the Spectre of Urthona from the wreckage of the fall (*J* 44.1–4; derived from Night IV of *Vala*) and their almost immediate assimilation in the bosom of Los (*J* 44.16–17; from Night VII of *Vala*, pp. 87–90). The sequence then quickly moves into the present, as Los explores contemporary London in search of lost Minute Particulars (45.2–38) while a European (and presumably Napoleonic) war rages ("the strife of Albion & Luvah Is great in the east" [45.55–56]); finally, the aggregation of Albion's Sons into Druidic powers brings the cycle back to where it started: "All things begin & end, in Albions Ancient Druid Rocky Shore" (46.15). The sequence is thus the vehicle of an entire epic cycle, radically condensed into four plates.

Such severe condensations of a cyclic narrative are also evident in the remaining sequences of Chapter 2. Thus, the final plate sequence 47–50 not only surveys the fall, its ensuing effects, and possibilities of redemption, but it repeats the survey three times (with varying details), in a fluctuation between despair and hope that starts in the third person narrative, continues through Erin's long speech, and proceeds beyond it in the response of the Daughters of Beulah.[30] In contrast, the first main sequence

---

[30] Luvah's bloody separation from Albion (47.3) opens the first downward cycle, which reaches its nadir in Albion's last words "Hope is banish'd from me" (47.18), and the ascension begins in the first line of the next plate with the appearance of the "merciful Saviour" and continues with the redemptive manifestation of Erin (48.1–52). Erin's speech, however, plunges us back into a catalog of deep gloom until a sudden turn at (49.52) again raises providential hopes. These, however, gradually deteriorate as the speech progresses, and she closes with ominous reflections on "Albions curse" (50.17). A brief and inconclusive rising

in Chapter 2, plates 29–32, has a thematic rather than a rhetorical unity, based on the perils of natural sexual attraction, but its most interesting poetic feat is to play off an elaborately told "local" narrative against a radically pared down narrative of the most sweeping cosmic events. The tale of Los sending Reuben over Jordan, busy with detail, suddenly opens into the foundational myth of Blake's imaginative world, retold in a few lines:

> And the Four Zoa's clouded rage East & West & North & South
> They change their situations, in the Universal Man.
> Albion groans, he sees the Elements divide before his face.
> And England who is Britannia divided into Jerusalem & Vala
> And Urizen assumes the East, Luvah assumes the South
> In his dark Spectre ravening from his open Sepulcher
>
> And the Four Zoa's who are the Four Eternal Senses of Man
> Became Four Elements separating from the Limbs of Albion
>
> . . . .
>
> The Atlantic Continent sunk round Albions cliffy shore
> And the Sea poured in amain upon the Giants of Albion
>
> (*J* 32.25–32, 39–40)

The passage takes to an extreme the tendency we have observed in *Jerusalem* of squeezing epic cycles into condensed synopses. Here the mythopoeia of half a lifetime's elaboration is beheld as in a globe-shaped mirror; everything is there, but in drastically contracted form. And as with actions beheld in such mirrors, the reduction of the grand myth to a *précis* has the effect of distancing us from the events described. In so doing, it enhances our sense of the passage as a text—that is, as a retelling or recycling of some other, primal telling, one that matched the grandeur of its subject in full.

Chapter 2 of *Jerusalem* reveals features of narrative structuring that are in fact widespread throughout the work as a whole. An exhaustive chapter-by-chapter demonstration of the point may be spared here, for once one is alerted to the characteristics that typify the individual subunits—such as their tendency toward synoptic inclusiveness[31] as narrative sequences, and their self-sufficiency as artistic wholes—these features leap easily into prominence wherever one peruses the work. Our main concern here is with

---

movement, embodied in the "sweet response" of the Daughters of Beulah, "Expanding on wing" (50.23) brings us to the end of the chapter.

[31] The term "synoptic" is used here in its sense of "constituting a synopsis" or summary, not in its New Testament sense of a story harmonizable with other versions of the same events—the sense intended, for example, by Joanne Witke in "*Jerualem*: A Synoptic Poem," *Comparative Literature* 22 (Summer 1970): 265–78. In the case of *Jerusalem*, of course, the two senses cannot be entirely divorced. If each sequence in the poem tends toward internal comprehensiveness (synopsis in the first sense), different sequences are virtually certain to repeat much of the same material, as one finds in the Synoptic Gospels.

their contribution to *Jerusalem*'s efficacy as a sublime poem. With that concern in mind, it might be useful to think of the whole work as a compilation or medley of texts jostling for attention and space within the strict confines of the twenty-five-plate chapter divisions. Although the medley form is not unprecedented in Blake's earlier work (notably in *The Marriage of Heaven and Hell*, with its rich mix of didactic exposition, visions, "voices," and "texts," and even earlier, in the discontinuous vignettes, non sequitur conversations, and song sprees of *An Island in the Moon*), critics of *Jerusalem* have tended, with reasonable plausibility, to suggest more ambitious models farther afield, such as Ezekiel, Revelation, and the four Gospels. None of these works, however—even Revelation, with its famous "synchronic" visions,[32]—poses the problems of discontinuity and repetition on the scale found in *Jerusalem*.

Morton Paley's more recent suggestion of Handel's *Messiah* as a possible model has the advantage of offering a sublime work from the poet's own century, one whose musical form sanctions those absolute repetitions usually forbidden to poetic continuity. A "song for many voices," in Paley's phrase, *Jerusalem* is indeed an oratorio of solos and massed choruses,[33] but its resemblance to the *Messiah* also extends to matters of textual form; the oratorio's libretto is in fact what *Jerusalem*'s text seems to be—a selection and compilation of prior discrete texts, borrowed in redistributed order from a single cycle of sacred stories. To regard *Jerusalem* in this light, as a gathering of texts out of a cycle, leads us, finally, to models more poetic than musical, models more closely connected to literary trends of Blake's own historical moment, including the vogue of a primitivist sublime. Gatherings and redactions of bardic remains and ancient mythic cycles, real or feigned, were prominent features of the literary scene of the day and could provide Blake, who clearly felt their appeal, with ample precedents for producing his own version of such forms. The result would be a work that resembles a compilation of brief epic lays, all derived from and reflecting a never fully stated, prior body of cyclic myth, with the inevitable variations, truncations, overlaps, and repetitions that such compilations typically display.

Macpherson's Ossianic lays, Chatterton's Rowleian and Saxon poems, the Icelandic Eddas as popularized by Gray and Bishop Percy, the Welsh

---

[32] As various commentators have noted, Blake's synchronicities in *Jerusalem* may be indebted to Joseph Mede's theory of synchronic prophecy in Revelation. According to Mede, "the whole Revelation from the fourth chapter . . . is distributed into two principall prophesies, either of which proceedeth from the same time, and endeth in the same period"; thus, "they labor in vain, that so go about to interpret the Revelation, as if the events every where should succeed one after another, in the same order and course, as the visions are revealed" (*The Key of the Revelation*, trans. Richard More [London: J. L. for Phil. Stephens, 1650], 12 and 27).

[33] See *The Continuing City*, 293.

bardic material published in William Owen Pughe's *Myvyrian Archailogy,* to cite some of the compilations that Blake found valuable, all constitute sequences of short forms (aside from the Ossianic epics *Fingal* and *Temora*) that are self-contained selections from a larger cycle of legendary or mythic material. In Blake's time, even the Bible could be enlisted into this genre of bardic compilation, as its composite and multitextual nature became better understood.[34] While the component units of these cyclic gatherings are all related to the same anterior body of myth or legend, they are sufficiently independent of one another to make its retelling often a competitive rather than a collaborative venture. In the Eddas, for example, the outer narrative frames of the individual lays often consist of dramatic exchanges between characters in conflict, but these exchanges are usually mere pretexts for long expository accounts chronicling divine history and eschatology, cataloging mythic names, and mapping out supernatural geography.[35] One might be describing typical features of *Jerusalem* itself, and, as in *Jerusalem*, the various accounts are sufficiently comprehensive as to overlap one another, repeating with variations certain salient points.

Macpherson's Ossianic cycle achieves something of the same effect without the overt repetition of specific incidents. Instead, it recreates in each new lay the same hallucinatory landscape, the same atmosphere, much the same returning cast of characters (for example, Fingal, Swaran, Oscar, Ossian, the spirit of Loda), and many of the same place names. The result is to establish the constants of the Ossianic world as an overwhelming psychic presence, like the imagery of a haunting recurrent dream, while subordinating the importance of linear narrative development. Although each

---

[34] Thus the antiquary Edward Davies, whose influence has been seen in *Jerusalem*, thought that Genesis itself might be regarded as a "collection of documents" (with Moses as a redactor), especially the first few chapters with their overlapping considerations of the same events and introductory tags that "point out the beginnings of detached compilations"; see *Celtic Researches on the Origin, Traditions & Languages of the Ancient Britons* (London: J. Booth, 1804), 40. More recently, Jerome J. McGann has argued the case for Blake's awareness (through the mediation of the English biblical scholar Alexander Geddes) of the contemporary German Higher Criticism and its understanding of the Bible as a composite text redacted from many sources. See "The Idea of an Indeterminate Text: Blake's Bible of Hell and Dr. Alexander Geddes," *Studies in Romanticism* 25 (Fall 1986): 303–24.

[35] Although Blake presumably would not have had access to such poems of the Elder Edda as the *Hávamál* ("Sayings of the High One"), *The Lay of Grimnir*, or *The Lay of Vafthrudnir*, which all display to a high degree the encyclopedic tendency (with much inevitable overlap) at the expense of local incident and drama, many of these characteristics survive in the lays of the Prose Edda, available to Blake in the version presented in Percy's translation of Mallet's *Northern Antiquities*. Blake could have acquired a sense of the repetitive element in this myth cycle by comparing the end of the Prose Edda with those portions of the apocalyptic *Völuspá* or "Song of the Prophetess" presented in Mallet; likewise, he could have noted overlapping similarities between the latter lay and another Eddaic poem, "Baldur's Dreams," made famous in Gray's version, "The Descent of Odin." For a good modern translation of the complete Poetic Edda, see *Poems of the Vikings: The Elder Edda*, trans. Patricia Terry (Indianapolis: Bobbs Merrill, 1969).

Ossianic poem has an ostensible forward-moving plot, these inevitably prove in retrospect to be quite unmemorable, and it is the visionary setting, the characters forever fixed in postures heroic or pathetic, that stays in the mind. Indeed, unless one is making special efforts to keep track of the plots, reading all the Ossianic poems in a stretch *seriatim* is not unlike the experience of reading *Jerusalem* in the same fashion; soon the lack of a developmental progression from section to section is noted, and one gets the feeling of running in place. The sense of an overarching unity to the whole cycle is perpetually suggested (since at every individual point the fundamental elements of the Ossianic cosmos are reproduced), but this unity never quite comes into sharp focus.

The appeal of this sort of work to devotees of the eighteenth-century sublime should be fairly obvious, and it is not simply a matter of the oracular tone of such poetry, or its content of "terrific" settings and action. Compiled texts such as the Ossianic cycle, the redactions of Icelandic poetry, or even the Bible, as the Higher Criticism conceived it, presume the existence of a primordial core of mythic "truth," and then proceed both to provoke a supercharged fascination with this core and to interfere with our access to it. They are like a much-fractured mirror, whose individual facets discontinuously repeat the reflected image again and again, but with subtle variations and discernible gaps. In this respect, they function like the characteristic sublime object of eighteenth-century aesthetics, offering an image of greatness or numinous power, a power that the spectator yearns to appropriate even as opacities and indeterminacies built into the image make that appropriation difficult. The spectator must surmount the discontinuities and intimidations of the image in order to become one with the anterior power that it screens. In the case of bardic or primitivist collections, then, one must distinguish between the sublimity of the content and the sublimity of the form. The content may indeed include many sublime moments of astonishment and wonder, but it is the form that provokes the quest for lost origins, for recovery of the heyday of the gods; it is precisely because the vision of that state is multiplied in so many flashing and epitomizing glimpses that we become acutely aware of our removal from it. Simultaneously, our awareness of the textual vehicle *as* a body of texts, as an arrangement, a redaction, a compilation of versions, comes to the fore. The sublimity of the reading experience becomes inseparable from the opacity suggested by that phrase *body of texts*; we are consciously in the presence of belated "remains," to use a popular eighteenth-century term for these primitivist collections, and the sublimity evoked is akin to that attendant on physical ruins of the ancient past, which always stimulate an effort of intellectual restoration.

In Number V of his *Descriptive Catalogue*, Blake tells us that "The British Antiquities are now in the Artist's hands," and everything that follows regarding the content of these "poems of the highest antiquity" (Druidism,

Arthurian lore, starry figurations, British geography, Hebrew patriarchs) suggests that he has *Jerusalem* in mind, and perhaps in hand (E 542). The collective status of these "poems" hovers between that of a plurality of texts and a single encyclopedic text, and their attributed authorship similarly slides in an ambiguous fashion between inventions of "the highest antiquity" and the poet's own: "All these things are written in Eden. The artist is an inhabitant of that happy country; . . . The Artist has written it under inspiration, and will, if God please, publish it; it is voluminous, and contains the ancient history of Britain, and the world of Satan and of Adam" (E 543). Here, then, is more evidence to support the idea that Blake conceived of *Jerusalem* as a composite or unifying cycle of "poems" that presume to a status of antiquity as they themselves transmit an even elder sacred lore. (An idea of textual plurality is perhaps encoded surreptitiously in the last line of the work: "*they* are named Jerusalem" [99.5; my emphasis].) To model his most ambitious work on those compilations of myth and legend popular in his time helps to secure for Blake's own myth an aura of ancient provenance, enabling it to rival other myth cycles of known antiquity, such as the biblical and the Nordic, on their own terms of presentation. In fabricating one's major work out of small, self-sufficient episodes and epitomes, all pointing to a prior central myth from different directions, there are strategic advantages that an unfolding of the myth in a single, grand consecutive story does not afford. The latter is the method of fiction, with its illusionistic effects of immediate mimesis and its factitious completeness of beginnings, middles, and ends; the former is the method of documentary witness, and the more the documents multiply and variants abound, the more persuasively they argue for the substantive truth of the anterior lore, although that is never glimpsed whole at any length.[36]

Jerusalem's form of aggregated multiple perspectives seems designed, then, to secure conviction of the truth of an underlying revelation, but only at the price of a partial screening and distortion of that revelation by the very texts that are its witnesses. This is perhaps another way of suggesting that *Jerusalem* as a whole functions as a sublime object, a striking exemplar of the sublime as text. We have already observed in previous chapters how a text can substitute for a material phenomenon in evoking that sublime moment of division between the Corporeal Understanding and the Intellectual Powers; we have also observed, particularly in *Jerusalem*, some of the stylistic devices that facilitate this process by inducing in the verbal medium an iconic density approaching materiality. It is worth adding that

---

[36] This is essentially the premise on which the antiquaries who influenced Blake, such as Jacob Bryant, Edward Davies, and others, usually operated. Thus, for example, the greater the number of variant references to Noah that Bryant thought he could discover in Greek and Celtic mythology, and the more distorted and farfetched they appeared, the more they confirmed, in his opinion, the historical veracity of the biblical account of the Flood.

by giving *Jerusalem* the appearance of an antiquarian collection, Blake enhances the solidification of the whole into a material artifact, making it seem not a text mimetic of a mythic action, but rather a text mimetic of other texts (not unlike Chatterton's Rowleian forgeries), as if it were pretending to be, like them, a relic retrieved from a remote and heroic past. In this way, *Jerusalem* represents Blake's tribute to the bardic sublime, which always seeks to generate awe and astonishment out of contemplations of the abyss of temporality.

But this tribute proves equivocal; to solidify the bardic voice into a visible text is to subject bardic power to the principles of iconicity. Ultimately the iconic sublime is never a matter of turning texts into material objects so that they can compete with cliffs, ruined palaces, and memorials of old battles as agents of astonishment. Rather, it is a matter of permitting the intellect to find itself within the play of textuality, attended by an utter subjugation of material concerns. Hence, Blake's technique of rearranging bardic chronicles into radically condensed vignettes, gathered into a discontinuous compilation, works on two conflicting levels: for devotees of antiquities, it creates a thirst to recover the whole myth, *how things really were*, in order to repair the fracturing wrought in this telling. But for those who find wholeness only in an atemporal order, in the reification of intellect in Words of Eternity, the reduction and distancing of the chronicles serves to put them in their place, small and far away. In this perspective, their terrors, based on evocations of the ruins of time, are not the terrors that should provoke the true sublime.

Blake, of course, would not be the complex poet that he is if he were not attracted to both perspectives. The action of *Jerusalem*, such as it is, offers a cornucopia of effects drawn from the dark, Gothic storehouse of the antiquarian and Northern sublime of eighteenth-century literature, with more than enough terrors to satisfy Burke himself—fallen kings turning to stone, Thor-like heroes at the forge contending with batlike apparitions, continents rolling apart, dire Druidical circles and human sacrifice, wars across Europe, ancient British queens weaving entrails like Gray's Fatal Sisters. Once we have registered the symbolic significance of these images, their contribution to the discursive framework of the poem, we are still left with the surplus reflections they cast, as images, on the poet's tastes. Blake would not repair to these figures so obsessively if they did not retain some excitement for him. He will not allow them, however, to coalesce into a single, continuous epic, in which their terrors would be magnified. They are to be forced, instead, into a structural framework that advertises their status as texts rather than terrors. In struggling thus with bardic narrative, Blake struggles with an impulse strong in himself, but his victory serves him well, for it enables him to move more decisively in the poem toward his own countersublime, the reification of a visionary textuality.

We understand *Jerusalem* better if we distinguish textuality as an ideal from texts as artifacts or documentary remains, for the interplay of the ideal and the artifact is a crucial determinant of the poem's total form. Texts can be opaque, shapeless, open-ended, competitively proliferating, mutually conflicting, or redundant. Textuality as an ideal, however, refers to the sum of the resources of language available to make the operations of intellect visible and determinate. From its perspective, writing is revealed as "wond'rous," books as the gift of God (*J* 3.3–5), and "every Word & Every Character" as "Human" in its power to be "clearly seen / . . . according to fitness & order" (*J* 98.35, 39–40). Texts are belated and dependent, forever referring back to a body of meaning that they partly reveal and partly obscure; textuality is a priori and autonomous, not a vehicle of meaning but the sum of the conditions of ordering that make meaning possible. Hence, the appropriate symbols of textuality can never be located in any specific word or letter, but rather must be sought in such forms that make the principle of determinate order visibly conspicuous—in short, whatever is capable of displaying symmetry, closure, inclusiveness, numerical exactitude, and all the other resources of the iconic style. It follows that all such ordering operations in *Jerusalem*—the limitation of the poem to a hundred plates, the symmetrically disposed distribution of the designs, and, most obvious of all, the division of the work into four equal chapters—are the nonreferential ambassadors of ideal textuality into the disorderly domain of bardic texts.

This intervention of pattern has a crucial role in modulating one's experience of reading the poem, and, in the short run, it creates an impression of more disorder rather than less. If, as has been argued here, *Jerusalem* originally took shape as a medley of poetic texts or a collection of shifting versions of a cyclic myth, then its ultimate "official" organization into sequentially numbered chapters, its consecutive pagination from 1 to 100, and its fixed order of plates (except for the anomalous Chapter 2) not only belie the poem's origins but also set up expectations of continuity and progression that the internal ordering of the episodes fails to satisfy. As Morton Paley has put it, "the organizational container reinforces the expectation of a strong narrative line, an expectation which is subverted time after time in the work itself."[37] On closer inspection, it appears that the subversion of expectations is performed by the organizational frame itself. Discontinuity is never a problem in extended poetic sequences so long as the discontinuity advertises itself as such; *Songs of Experience* as a totality is discontinuous, but not confusing, because the generic indicators signifying "collection" are so clearly marked. Likewise, a long "discontinuous" poem such as Whitman's *Song of Myself*, to take a work in some ways similar to *Jerusalem* in subject, theme, and form, is generally unproblematic because the relative autonomy of its component units are marked rather than con-

---

[37] *The Continuing City*, 303.

cealed. But if the fifty-two numbered sections of this poem in its final version were run together in one continuous sequence, with all numerical and other indications of separation removed, or if all the lines were simply divided into four equal batches, its readers would likely find the work much more confusing than they do now—perhaps as confusing as some readers find Blake's "Song" of *Jerusalem*.

But in the case of *Jerusalem*, the problem posed by the disguise of the work's generic affinities is more complex than in the example just given. Bibliographical evidence strongly suggests that the scheme of four equal divisions was, in fact, one of the last structural ideas to be incorporated into *Jerusalem*, and Blake's execution of this scheme must necessarily have involved considerable tinkering with the sequences already compiled and etched, so that their own individual cohesion and autonomy became effaced.[38] To balance the designs symmetrically,[39] to reach an even hundred

[38] Faintly legible traces of deleted etching in finished copies, as well as clearly surviving evidence from certain proofsheets, make a strong case for this point: thus the designation "In XXVIII Chapters" scratched off the title page (plate 2), but detectable in black and white copies such as A and D, hints at an early scheme that could scarcely have accommodated itself to one hundred plates (unless the individual chapters were mere atomies)—and, even were it to do so, it could not have resulted in divisions of equal length, as in the final scheme. On the other hand, a deleted "End of the 1st Chap" on plate 14 is suggestive of a second scheme that easily accommodates itself both to one hundred plates and to equal chapter divisions, a seven-part scheme of fourteen plates each, with two extra plates to make the full complement of a hundred. In evidence of yet another organizational scheme temporarily entertained, an unmistakable page number "12" (visible in an intermediate-state proofsheet of plate 28 in the Pierpont Morgan Library, but masked in all finished copies of the poem), engraved on a plate clearly designated as the beginning of Chapter 2, strongly indicates a projected format of ten chapters of ten plates each (if Chapter 2 began at "12," then its introduction "To the Jews" would have been "11"—which leaves ten plates for Chapter 1). Other such early and superseded engraved page numbers give one reason to believe that material now found in Chapter 2 once formed part of Chapter 1. Thus, a "6" clearly visible on one of two proofsheets of plate 34 in the Rosenwald Collection, Library of Congress, and faintly visible in extant finished copies, as well as a "9" faintly detectable on plate 40, suggests that the highly wrought and homogeneous "cathedral city" sequence, plates 33–41, was once, before the interpolation of the manifestly late plates 37–39, the centerpiece of a ten-plate Chapter 1. If what is now "34" was once "6," then the present "33" would have been "5," and it is a fact that plate 33 forms a much stronger narrative link with the present plate 4 than it does with the present plate 32. Moreover, plate 41 (which would have been "10") provides a strong poetic terminus and conforms in its visual layout to one that Blake employs at the conclusion of all the extant chapters (an upper half-page of text followed by a half-page design). On the other hand, there is no clear break in the text at plate 10 of the present Chapter 1—further evidence that this chapter must have been a very different affair when Chapter 2 started at "12." One can only speculate how many more substantial shifts of this kind, before *Jerusalem* acquired its extant ordering, lie forever buried from view, as they would be wherever Blake's masking of etched clues to his early intentions managed to be fully successful. For further details on the early and superseded engraved numbers, see Erdman, "Suppressed and Altered Passages," 48–49, and my "Changing Order of Plates in *Jerusalem*, Chapter II," 204 n. 20.

[39] It is a curious fact that large block-designs in *Jerusalem* cluster in Chapter 1 toward the

plates, and to consolidate a sprawling collection of etched sequences of undoubtedly varying lengths into uniform sets of twenty-five would require at some points the abridgment of certain sequences and at other points stretching sequences out with added or interpolated plates. In the process, many plates would inevitably become dislodged from their original sites and dispersed to widely separated parts of the work, and finally, a good deal of textual mortar would be required to connect and cover over the joints. There is no lack of bibliographical evidence in the work for such modifications, but the modifications never succeed in utterly transforming a poem that is exuberantly wayward and multifocused into one that is, in theme and narrative, coherently fourfold. *Jerusalem* remains a work strangely frozen in a process of transition, looking in one direction to the disordered compilations of bardic texts, each with its own retrospective agenda of recovering lost mythic origins, and in the other direction, to the promise afforded by the symbols of textuality, the recovery of the fitness and order of the Intellectual Powers.

This position of equivocation between awesome alternatives appears strikingly like that displayed in the classic liminal structure of the sublime moment, so that *Jerusalem* as a whole could be characterized as a sublime moment spatially stretched over one hundred plates, with the equivocations of that state inscribed in the indeterminacies and tensions of its textual makeup. As observed at the outset of this study, these equivocations always involve issues of blockage and access, of an opacity augmented and a radiance gained, of heightened pain and perfected delight. How the first half of these sets of terms applies in the present context should not be difficult to see. By effacing the boundaries of the discontinuous set pieces of the poem, by compacting these pieces into artificial and arbitrary divisions, and by inserting markers of continuity, Blake increases the density of the work's texture, rolls it up, as it were, into a conglomerate mass, and induces in the text's heterogeneity a dire connectedness, rendering that labyrinthine effect noted by several critics.[40] These offerings to opacity would have little to do with the sublime were it not for the conspicuous accompanying presence of the symmetrical fourfold order that overarches them. For those who wander inside the textual labyrinth, this presence offers the tormenting hope that the labyrinth can be made meaningful—as many critics, who have tried to apply this or that fourfold set of significations to bring order to the internal workings of the poem, have found at their cost. This hope belongs to the dynamics of the corporeal sublime,

---

beginning of the chapter, in Chapter 4 toward the end, and appear more or less medially distributed in Chapters 2 and 3. For a table showing the distribution of large designs in the work, see Bentley, *Blake Books*, 231.

[40] See, e.g., Easson, "William Blake and His Reader in *Jerusalem*," 314; Curran, "The Structures of *Jerusalem*," 340; and Mitchell, *Blake's Composite Art*, 170.

which is always an affair of alluring objects that coyly withdraw as we approach them, because they have no outline we can grasp. It is only when we begin with the notion that the fourfold divisions of *Jerusalem* are without meaning (in the sense of some particular set of referential terms constituting their sole key) that the symmetry imposed on the poem becomes not a reinforcement of the labyrinth but a source of liberation from it. The symmetrical impositions then prove instead to be the a priori generators of meaning, inviting and capaciously hosting all the possible fourfold schemes that critics may care to apply. And just as there is an order but no necessary meaning to the four major divisions of the work, there are meanings but no necessary order to its internal sequences.[41] This is another way of expressing the idea that *Jerusalem* displays a structure of frozen transitions; the meanings are reaching out for the organizing forms, the forms for embodiment in signification, often coming tantalizingly close to an embrace at many points—yet nonetheless providing scope, to borrow a Wordsworthian phrase, for something ever more about to be.

Near the center of *Jerusalem*, on plate 48, there is a scene in which a figure out of the narrative is received into the embrace of a text. When Albion dies,

> the merciful Saviour in his arms
> Reciev'd him, in the arms of tender mercy and repos'd
> The pale limbs of his Eternal Individuality
> Upon the Rock of Ages. Then, surrounded with a Cloud:
> In silence the Divine Lord builded with immortal labour,
> Of gold & jewels a sublime Ornament, a Couch of repose,
> With Sixteen pillars: canopied with emblems & written verse.
> Spiritual Verse, order'd & measur'd, from whence, time shall reveal.
> The Five books of the Decalogue, the books of Joshua & Judges,
> Samuel, a double book & Kings, a double book, the Psalms & Prophets
> The Four-fold Gospel, and the Revelations everlasting

(*J* 48.1–11)

[41] This is not to deny the possible presence of overlapping structures of meaning such as Stuart Curran has posited in his groundbreaking essay "The Structures of *Jerusalem*," based on discernment of periodically distributed thematic echoes. My point is that such patterns are likely to arise not from some all-determining *Ur*-plan, deeply lodged in the original compositional impulse, but rather from opportunities perceived and exploited by the poet in the process of his late tinkerings, as many passages are shifting about. One must also allow for the possibility that the discerning eye will inevitably discover periodic patterns in a work that is synoptic—or, better, hologrammatic—in its texture (in a hologram, light waves from every part of the whole image are captured on each local part of the plate, so that different aspects of the image will yield themselves to different angles of perception, while always maintaining the appearance of a coherent whole).

A discursive translation of this scene would probably run as follows: that Albion's actual history is "buried" in the surface narratives of the Bible (a notion encouraged by certain antiquarian speculations), which serves therefore as its repository and the site of its possible restoration to light. But this discursive translation misses an important element of the passage, which is that the providential character of the textual repository appears to be here entirely a function of its character as an icon or spatialized form, a three-dimensional field of centers and bounding perimeters, of numerical precisions and finely crafted organizations, as the imagery clearly suggests ("surrounded," "builded," "canopied," "pillars," "order'd & measur'd," "*written* verse" [my emphasis]).[42] The Scriptural repository of Albion's remains is indeed "a sublime Ornament," and its sublimity inheres in the intellectual orderings that, at their purest, most minute, and most particular, only textuality provides.

The scene of Albion's reception into the repository of a text may be taken as an emblem of the relation of the disordered components of narrative in *Jerusalem* to the rigorous symmetry of its ultimate form. To put it more precisely, this relation may be expressed as a ratio: Albion's acts and passions are to his dead body as the complete cycle of myth underlying the poem is to the compilation of discontinuous texts that are the myth's "remains"; and Albion's body is to its Scriptural repository as the body of component texts is to the ideal of textuality enshrined in *Jerusalem*'s symmetrical envelope. The relation of the exterior envelope to *Jerusalem*'s internal narrative parts is, then, not so much one of "tension," as Morton Paley has suggested,[43] but rather one of providential reception and enclosure. In finally imposing this exterior form on the body of narrative materials in *Jerusalem*, Blake's aim seems directed not at casting off this body as an embarrassing excrescence but rather at enshrining it—that is, at housing it in a structure that, like many reliquaries, is more beautiful than the remains contained in it. The beauty of the containing form is as much a matter of the promise that it holds as it is an aesthetic pleasure for its own sake, for this form is an image of the mansion of intellectual humanity that the sleeping remains shall inherit when the final awakening takes place.

But there is another pleasure to be gleaned from the preserved remains themselves: they perpetuate the excitement rendered by old tales of the fall, tales of struggle and momentous confrontations, rendered in a cacophony of uninhibited competing tellings, for these are generators of passion and, on that account, not to be scorned. Thus in Los's Halls, "every pathetic

---

[42] Note, incidentally, how Blake, through opportunistic manipulations, manages to compact the Bible into sixteen books, thus bestowing on that sprawling compilation of sacred texts the same dose of fourfold order—here squared—that he imposes on his own aggregated text *Jerusalem*.

[43] *The Continuing City*, 307.

story possible to happen from Hate or / Wayward Love & every sorrow & distress is carved" (*J* 16.63–64). Where Los leads, Blake must follow, and he thus builds the memorial texts of the bardic sublime into *Jerusalem*'s wall of words, thereby acknowledging its genuine powers to stir passions and communicate intensity. As Jesus is merciful to Albion, Blake is merciful to himself—or at least to impulses within himself that repeatedly draw him to modes of the terrific sublime that have always provided him with occasions of renewed inspiration; poetic impulses of any sort may be forgiven, but they are not to be cast out.

At the same time, Blake is also careful to furnish *Jerusalem* at various points with passages that, in the midst of all the narrative lays, compete with them to attract the reader to a rival kind of poetic intensity. These passages tend to be descriptive rather than narrative—albeit descriptive in the specially conditioned fashion that, in the previous chapter, we saw as characteristic of iconic verse. The objects of description tend to be constructs capable of receiving a spatial survey but not of being localized; their ordering displays features of correspondence and symmetry, and their limits are clearly established, often with a numerical specificity—yet they evade encompassment by the mundane reason; their details are cataloged abundantly, even exhaustively, but they never settle into any visualizable shape in the ordinary sense; they package a due amount of translatable symbolism along with a great deal of surplus strangeness that cannot be accommodated to a discursive reduction. Among such passages, we may include the concentrically expanding geographical survey of Albion's Gates, Ireland's counties, the nations of the world, and the perimeters of the Vegetable Universe (plate 72); the dark anatomization of the Covering Cherub (89.9–51); the corresponding anatomy of Jerusalem's beauty (85.22–86.32); and, most famous of all, the great fabrication out of words of the city of Golgonooza (12.25–13.29), a passage that, in parts, skirts the bizarre in testing the limits of possible mergers between particular details and abstract visionary schemata:

> And every part of the City is fourfold; & every inhabitant, fourfold.
> And every pot & vessel & garment & utensil of the houses,
> And every house, fourfold
>
> (13.20–22)

In relation to the narrative sequences that surround them, such passages function in the liminal mode described earlier in this chapter, taking the reader temporarily out of the continuities of cause-and-effect action, linear narrative, and consecutive moral argument by concentrating the mind on the stasis of form while dissociating it from the expectations of the reason. Yet in relation to *Jerusalem* as a whole, these iconic passages have a somewhat different importance, for no portion of the poem—not even the narrative sections—offers continuity at any lengthy stretch, and there is no crucial need to arrest the tumble of continuous narrative such as Blake may have felt was required in *America* or in *Milton* after the Bard's Song. Even the iconic sequences in *Jerusalem* have the character of autonomous poetic texts, scattered among texts of other kinds. The juxtaposition of these different kinds of texts mirrors, on the particular level, the general medley of impulses that combine to determine the poem's overall complexity of form.

That play of impulses produces a work whose final form seems caught, as we have seen, in a transition between opposing allegiances: on one hand, the recovery of a domain of original and ultimate truth, the myth as a total continuous cycle; on the other, the ideal of textuality, the ordered play of signifying forms, independent of time, place, and action. These poles have, in themselves, only an ideational reality; there is no continuous cycle of myth in Blake's work, no manifest total presence, but only the sum of the myth's variants. Likewise, textuality is an abstraction that can only find embodiment for its play of orderings in particular language and writing. Between these ideational poles is the body of texts itself—the composite of sequences that, in the aggregate, are named *Jerusalem*. Some of these sequences attempt, as we have seen, to synopsize or miniaturize the unavailable totality of the mythic cycle; they reproduce comprehensive continuous action as delimited text. It follows, then, that the antinarrative sequences of the poem, the iconic nodes of formal concentration, are attempts to image the opposite pole, to synopsize the ideal set of principles that constitute textuality and reproduce these also as delimited text. The textual matrix of *Jerusalem* thus becomes the material arena for the interpenetrating disport of rival sublimes that have haunted Blake's imagination since he began his enterprise as a major poet—the bardic vision of receding vistas, dark powers, and surging action on one hand, the iconic vision of concentrated presence, radiant formal clarity, and ineffable autonomy on the other. Although all parts of *Jerusalem* display a kind of redshift toward the pole of iconicity, the bardic impulse is never excluded. The text locks both visions perpetually in a contentious but not unforgiving embrace and makes of *Jerusalem* (on one level at least) not only a sublime poem but a kind of discourse on the sublime, enacted as a debate of the two sublime modes.

That the margin of victory must go to the forces of textuality is guaranteed by the symmetrical macrostructure imposed on the work as a whole. But Blake has no more intention of making it seem like an easy or complacent victory than the outer symmetries of the fourfold city of Golgonooza display an easy or complacent relation to the plethora of details vibrating within them. This comparison leads to a final speculative analogy: that *Jerusalem* is to the canon of Blake's major sublime works what the vision of Golgonooza and other iconic topoi within the poem are to the surrounding medleys of bardic narration. In that case, all the major long works are organized to contribute to an ongoing discourse on the sublime. Thus, to continue the speculation, *Vala* or *The Four Zoas* is the quintessential expression of bardic grandeur, the sublime of indefinite vistas, while the medial epic *Milton* concentrates appropriately on plenary possibilities of the medial sublime moment. That leaves to *Jerusalem* the sovereign and embracing final word, as the fully articulated embodiment of the sublime of the text.

PART THREE

WORLDVIEW: IMAGERY OF SUBLIME SETTINGS

Chapter V

THE SETTING OF NATURE AND
THE RUINS OF TIME

T
HE SETTINGS of Blake's narratives—the spatial and temporal
contexts in which they unfold—have received little critical attention, perhaps because they are so elusive. By "setting," I refer here
not to the quasi-official districts of poetic space belonging to the more
programmatic side of his mythology—Eden, Beulah, Ulro, the Lake of
Udan Adan, the forests of Entuthon Benython, and the like—which often
appear as no more than names attached to varied assortments of concepts.
Rather, I propose to draw attention to the irridescently shifting backdrops,
the continuous passing imagistic display of terrains, weathers, human
monuments, stretches of space, and mementos of time that, without entering the mythic action in any overtly determining way, eloquently enhance
its atmosphere and underline its significance.

Blake's settings, of course, never take the form of invariant fictive givens,
like Hardy's Wessex or Faulkner's Yoknapatawpha County; indeed their
presence is often manifested only in passing similitudes and metaphors,
and hence it is seldom easy to discuss setting in Blake without verging on
a consideration of his myth on one hand (the various actions of named
characters) and his themes (his "ideas" discursively rendered) on the other.
Nor is it at all desirable to preclude such a consideration, for the play of
images that constitutes these settings provides a natural, almost instinctive
obbligato to the formal workings of myth and theme, all the more revealing in its lack of a palpable programmatic design. An approach to Blake's
poetry via its settings also has this advantage (apart from avoiding the too-
heavily traveled mythic and thematic routes): it grounds the discussion
more thoroughly in the discourse of the sublime—which, in its eighteenth-
century versions, is heavily saturated in a sense of place and time, of subjects confronting objects and of moments that stand out against time like
a figure in a ground. Having observed the extent of Blake's conversance
with the theoretical issues of sublime aesthetics, we should not be surprised
to discover in his work a ready familiarity with its characteristic literary
effects, especially its deployment of imagery that expresses a heightened
sensitivity to temporal and spatial surroundings, in sum, to the greater configurations of the world.

Apart from recurrent, if unsustained, upsurges of a pastoral mode in his work early and late, Blake's imagistic settings are typically sublime, in the sense made conventional by his age. In his *Lectures on Oratory and Criticism* (1777), for example, Joseph Priestley lists "large rivers, high mountains, and extensive plains; the ocean, the clouds, the heavens, and infinite space; and storms, thunder, lightning, volcanos, and earthquakes, in nature; and palaces, temples, pyramids, cities"[1] as images productive of the sublime; and any reader can readily locate in Blake's poetry instances of every item from this thoroughly conventional list. Some of them, like clouds and thunder, are obsessively ubiquitous, and some—temples and cities, for example—are clearly central to the structure of his imagery and symbolism. Indeed, our point is not to show that the typical locales and surroundings found in so much of his poetry present features conventionally regarded as sublime. It is more the point to inquire why Blake is so insistent on these settings and what their various features have to do with one another. In particular, this inquiry should lead to a sense of the connections between the imagery of settings and Blake's encompassing enterprise of creating a "Most Sublime Poetry." We may thus learn how Blake's settings enlist the world of space and time to serve as a dramatic projection of the inner dynamics of the sublime experience, including its psychology of astonishment and all the discontinuity, bafflement, losses suffered, and heights attained that are involved in that experience.

THE SUBLIME SCENE AND THE SEARCH FOR ORIGINS

If we recall the myth of the Ancient Britons discussed in the first chapter, we note that the "human sublime" (the Strong man) is the belated manifestation of a catastrophe (he emerges when the Britons "were overwhelmed by brutal arms") and that before the catastrophe, the sublime as we know it did not present itself as a distinctive entity, for it was incorporated in what was "originally one man, who was . . . self-divided" (E 542–43). The sublime, then, is apparently not a primary state of being; it is an experience of an elevation that can come only at the expense of and as the token of some prior loss. All particular forms of sublimity are belated, the product of some previous disaster, itself sublime. Some memorable lines from *Europe* illustrate the point:

> Thought chang'd the infinite to a serpent; that which pitieth:
> To a devouring flame; and man fled from its face and hid
> In forests of night; then all the eternal forests were divided

---

[1] Joseph Priestley, *A Course of Lectures on Oratory and Criticism* (London: J. Johnson, 1777), 154.

Into earths rolling in circles of space, that like an ocean rush'd
And overwhelmed all except this finite wall of flesh.

(Eur 10.16–20)

Before we get to the fateful confrontation of the ocean of space with the frail barrier of the human senses, the kind of moment that Kant or Burke or Wordsworth would regard as quintessential of the sublime encounter (one thinks of the famous Dream of the Arab in Book V of The Prelude), we are given a whole series of prior disasters. Before the ocean of space could exercise its dread power against finite flesh, the infinite unitary forests were themselves divided in order to produce this grandeur. Moreover, the same "eternal forests" that seemed unitary when compared with the succeeding interplanetary spaces appear no better than a chaotic wilderness of obscurity ("forests of night") to the diminutive man who had earlier hidden within them, there to meet, as we know from elsewhere in Blake, sublimely fearful terrors. And even this encounter is the outcome of previously terrifying encounters with sublime objects, "serpent" and "flame." What we seem to have here is an indefinite regress of sublimes, each catastrophic—and each catastrophe is the external equivalent of an "astonishment" that leaves the human subject reduced and bereft of unity. From a Blakean perspective, much of the trauma that the connoisseur of the material sublime experiences in his encounter with the overwhelming object comes from reliving this catastrophic diminishment.

If the sublime experience speaks of its own belatedness, then how do we recover the "infinite" that was first "chang'd"—an absolutely prior, unitary "all"? "One cannot approach the sublime," Leslie Brisman has said, "without enquiry into, or shocked recognition of, origins."[2] But we must also recognize that these origins are perpetually receding as we approach them. Each of them provides the vestigial memory of an even superior greatness, earlier still, a lost "all" that was compacted into a unitary state of plenitude before a splitting that produced the material sublime. The sequential structure of the latest sublime moment, then, is identical to that of any earlier catastrophe that preceded it: a unitary state of being > a point of discontinuity > a splitting of the unity > a transfer of power > a new mode of the sublime. How do we know where we are in this repetition of losses and recoveries?

Perhaps the answer lies beyond the threshold of time and space as we know it—that is to say, the pattern of the sublime moment may have preceded the beginnings of the outward creation that it would eventually come to inhabit. In Boehme, whom Blake studied well enough to pick up a number of useful conceptual paradigms, there is an account of the origins of the material creation that can serve equally as a myth of the birth of the

---

[2] Brisman, Romantic Origins, 19.

sublime. In this account, God's Unity is sundered by his own Will or Desire for variation, and this event manifests itself in a series of Properties from which all particular forms derive:

> The First Property is the Desire which causes and makes harshness, sharpness, hardness, cold, and substance. . . . The Second Property is the stirring, or Attraction, of the Desire; it makes stinging, breaking, and dividing of the hardness; it cuts asunder the attracted desire, and brings it into multiplicity and variety; it is the ground of bitter pain, and also the true Root of Life; it is the *Vulcan* that strikes fire.[3]

In this account, there is a striking approximation of the two modes of astonishment discussed earlier in this study—one producing a stony stupor and a harsh, wintry sublime; the other, the thunderbolt that, as it disquiets and terrifies, cracks open gates to new forms of plenitude ("the ground of bitter pain, and also the true Root of Life"). In order to stimulate the liberating expansiveness necessary for the infinitude of creation, even in the divine Mind there must be a blocking agent, a cold hardness that resembles the impervious, obstructive, forbidding mountainous mass of the Burkean sublime (it is the "wide world of solid obstruction" that Urizen, in what may be a parody of Boehme, compacts out of the void as the first of his makings [*BU* 4.23]). But the splitting of this mass is only the echo or repetition of an earlier catastrophe, a sundering of the divine unity out of an aboriginal restlessness, an unappeasable appetite for consolidating the "great": "the will desires to be something . . . and compresses itself to something, . . . a harshness, like a hardness."[4] Any quest for a pure point of departure, an absolutely prior state of infinitude at rest, gets lost in the divine Abyss. Boehme's account provides Blake with something more than a few motifs for *The Book of Urizen*, *The Book of Los*, and various related texts; it links the sublime (the propagation of new forms of greatness) to catastrophe and sundering on the level of pure paradigm, prior to all material incarnation, and it invests all material sublimes with a melancholy born of the sense that the true origins of their greatness lie in an unfathomable recess.

If the taste for the sublime reveals itself ultimately as a quest for origins, it is a quest marked by both the extraordinary ambitiousness of its aims and the extraordinary difficulties that attend its means. "The more that one inquires into the eighteenth-century sublime," Wallace Jackson has remarked, "the more it reveals an oddity at its center: the attempt to repair, at one leap, a sundered spiritual unity and to restore directly and immedi-

---

[3] [Jacob Boehme], *The Clavis, The Works of Jacob Behmen, With Figures illustrating his Principles*, ed. William Law (London: M. Richardson, 1764–1781); vol. 2 (1764), 9–10.

[4] Ibid., 11.

ately the ideal that the soul seeks."[5] Yet it so often turns out that the "great" object needed to provide the stimulus for this restorative leap is itself a sundered thing, unworthy of rendering the ideal sought and finally capable only of stirring memories of still earlier sunderings in an infinitely regressive chain. Kant believed that the inadequacy of the material sublime would give rise in the mind to immediate ideas of a totality possessed within, but this dialectic leap required the sublime object to possess at least some deceptive pretensions to totality. For Blake, however, there can be no deception and hence no stimulating moment of astonishment; the scars of the catastrophes that have deformed these objects are engraved too plainly on their surfaces. The works of nature, the constructions of human civilization, and the gulf of time in which these things arise and undergo change are all filled with seductive traces of an originating power or plenitude, but one finds that one cannot make an immediate leap back to the origin but only to other traces of it—or, to put it more grimly, to its ruins.

Blake's works are full of catastrophes: overwhelming floods, precipitous falls, chasms suddenly yawning, toppling buildings, howling storms, fierce battles, vast conflagrations. These momentous events may be seen as a parody or even as an allegory of the sublime experience. Viewed as parody, the scenes of catastrophe show the splitting of a unitary subject that yields up its greatness to something alien and forbidding (we recall from the first chapter that astonishment too often "astonishes" those whom it overcomes—that is, it turns them to stone). As allegory, the division of unitary objects into greater and lesser forms may serve as a material or prefigurative representation of the fundamental sublime event, the division of the mind into thwarted corporeal and liberated intellectual faculties. Or, to put it another way, every sublime event may be seen as a redemptive and homeopathic reenactment of a prior catastrophe.

As the settings of Blake's poetry are often scenes of either catastrophe in progress or sites that memorialize catastrophic effects, they are hence continually signifying the deformation or the recovery of the sublime. We must come to see these settings, therefore, not merely as extravagant yet basically ornamental accompaniments of narrative, or as symbolic vehicles for particular extrinsic "meanings," but as essential elements in a discourse about sublimity itself. For Blake, all history and geography encode a myth about the *formation* of the sublime. Properly studied, they tell us why we recognize the sublime as sublime, and how we reexperience what is "Most Sublime" by learning to recognize its fallen versions, strewn about the natural and temporal world. Their images, moreover, provide a coherent view of this world—a coherence that differs from those offered by the scientist

---

[5] Wallace Jackson, *The Probable and the Marvelous: Blake, Wordsworth, and the Eighteenth-Century Critical Tradition* (Athens, University of Georgia Press, 1978), 172.

and the empirical historian, but one that brings it into congruence with the workings of the human mind, as Blake sees it. For world and mind image one another, each with its flash-exchanges of power, its momentous turns that narrow the gap between catastrophe and enlightenment, its aggrandizements founded on depletion, and its true grandeurs recovered out of the depths of loss.

Blake's characteristic settings bring with them shadings of the large contexts of eighteenth-century discourse from which they mainly derive. The natural settings are inextricably related to theories of cosmogony and geological catastrophism widely known in his time; the backdrop of stone circles and fallen temples to the popular cult of ruins and Druidic antiquities; the coordination or interfusion of Anglo-Celtic and Hebraic places to the pursuit by contemporary syncretic mythographers of universal cultural origins; the visionary locales of symmetrically disposed, numerologically precise, and abstractly diagrammatic settings to theosophical and pseudo-Kabbalistic interests in the autonomous power of signs. The theory of the sublime is useful in integrating these disparate though sometimes overlapping interests, by uniting them under its own common denominators, manifested inwardly as a psychology of desire and outwardly as an episode of catastrophe.

As Blake understands them, theories of the sublime in the period converge with meditations on the ruins of time, with investigations of the wonders of nature, and finally with antiquarian and occult strands of thought in a common program of attaining or recovering a lost power. As in the sublime experience, where the will is first baffled and reduced, then driven to nullify the gap between these limitations and the highest aspirations, so in the domain of natural religion, the vestiges of creation hide God and reveal him, measuring the vast gap between the present and the day of creation, while sculpturing the energies of that day in lasting stone. The cult of ruins depends for its pleasures on a similar recognition of a glory lost and revealed. Likewise, the endeavors of the syncretic mythographers to discover common origins of dispersed cultures aims at nullifying the widening chasms of history and geography by hypothesizing some aboriginal point at which a single human culture directly knew God's presence. Finally, all interests that focus on hieratic signs, on names and numbers that encapsulate power, on the studied letter of the text, on incantatory formulas and iconic visions, take to a rarified degree of paradigmatic abstraction a similar preoccupation with alienating, "altogether hidden" potencies that are altogether desired. Blake would see all these domains as essentially the same domain, or at least understand them to be nestled within one another. In this understanding, he not only presents his own vision of things but also scrutinizes much of the scientific and speculative thought of his time, unifying these ideas as tropes of the sublime. In each of these domains, a negative "great"—too much time, too much space, too much change, too much opacity—is conjured out of the loss of a prior plenitude, yet stimulates the desire for a reversion to what was originally great—precisely the pattern of the sublime experience, as we have observed it. A closer look at these domains is now in order.

NATURAL CATASTROPHE AND THE BIRTH OF CORPOREAL MAGNITUDES

The sublime in nature, as typically understood in the eighteenth century, resides in heights, depths, rifts, fluidities, voids, looming barriers, and violent energies that measure the exceeding greatness of the external world against man's incapacity and diminishment. Blake himself sometimes seems to share this understanding. In the Proverbs of Hell, we are advised that "The roaring of lions, the howling of wolves, the raging of the stormy sea, and the destructive sword are portions of eternity too great for the eye of man" (*MHH* 8.27). As Morton Paley has pointed out, the items that compose this series represent standard terrors of the Burkean sublime,[6] and all but the "destructive sword" belong to the world of nature. At first glance, the Proverb seems to praise nature's terrifying excess—but on closer inspection, the assertion becomes less clear. In the first place, what is the antecedent of "too great"? Is it "portions" or "eternity"? If the former, the "eye of man" is overwhelmed by a threatening excess in the visible world, but with the possibility that some other faculty or higher sense remains serene. This would be a sublime tailored to the specifications of Burke and Kant; we recall Kant's dictum: "that magnitude of a natural object, on which the Imagination fruitlessly spends its whole faculty of comprehension, must carry our concept of nature to a supersensible substrate" (see Chapter I, note 18). If, on the other hand, the antecedent of "too great" is "eternity," then the sense of the Proverb becomes quite different: the eye of man is able to apprehend clearly the threatening forms of nature, but his vision cannot grasp the "too great" transcendent form of which they are the outward manifestation. The second reading is more dire than the first, since it suggests an eternity "altogether hidden" to an eye bound to corporeality, but neither reading credits man with a greatness equal from the outset to the vision he beholds.

These ambiguities are compounded by the problem of natural terrors as "portions of eternity." In what sense are they portions? Are they partial selections from a more comprehensive "eternity" that contains their contraries, such as reason to their energy, love to their hate, attraction to their

---

[6] *Energy and the Imagination*, 24.

repulsion? Or are they portions in the sense of synecdochal representations of the whole? In the first case, they imply a divided eternity, in which "greatness" has become lodged in the agents of catastrophe; in the second, their palpable destructiveness implies an eternity that is itself deformed. To read such equivocations in this Proverb of Hell is not to deny that it functions at one level as part of a rhetorical strategy to praise excess. But the reading also points to the darker implications that must accompany any move to render the alien and the dangerous as sublime. The "eye of man" must first postulate its own deficiency, either failing to apprehend the object or failing to apprehend eternity, or both; and the object that poses as "too great" is either only a part of a whole or else mirrors a whole that is itself deficient to human need. Or, to put it succinctly in its bleakest perspective, the object appears "great" only if the subject shrinks; otherwise the object must appear either as a fragment or as a ruin.

The Proverb about the howling of wolves scarcely offers such a bleak perspective on natural terrors overtly. One quickly observes, however, that as Blake's poetic landscapes become more elaborate in their array of sublime effects, the perspective tends to darken accordingly, and imagery of diminishment, fragmentation, and ruin comes to the foreground. As in Boehme's myth of creation, the process of diminishment typically takes the form of a condensation into a formidable compact body (a sublime of mass), which in turn gives way to a catastrophic splitting of the mass and the creation of an abyss yawning between the fragmented parts (a sublime of vacancy). Blake's later Lambeth books are filled with scenarios of this sort:

> And self balanc'd stretch'd o'er the void
> I alone, even I! the winds merciless
> Bound; but condensing, in torrents
> They fall & fall; strong I repell'd
> The vast waves, & arose on the waters
> A wide world of solid obstruction
>
> (*BU* 4.18–23)

> Sund'ring, dark'ning, thund'ring!
> Rent away with a terrible crash
> Eternity roll'd wide apart
> Wide asunder rolling
> Mountainous all around
> Departing; departing; departing:
> Leaving ruinous fragments of life
> Hanging frowning cliffs & all between
> An ocean of voidness unfathomable
>
> (*BU* 5.3–11)

Coldness, darkness, obstruction, a Solid
Without fluctuation, hard as adamant
Black as marble of Egypt; impenetrable
Bound in the fierce raging Immortal.
And the seperated fires froze in
A vast solid without fluctuation,
Bound in his expanding clear senses

. . . .

Till impatience no longer could bear
The hard bondage, rent: rent, the vast solid
With a crash from immense to immense
Crack'd across into numberless fragments

. . . .

. . . the innumerable fragments away
Fell asunder; and horrible vacuum
Beneath him & all sides round.

(BL 4.4–10, 15–18, 24–26)

In these passages, the turbulent imagery of sundering and condensation, solidity and void, obstruction and flux, immensity, strength, thunder, collapse, and ruin somewhat conceals a simple underlying pattern of binary opposition: void and solid alternate with one another in a continually repeating series; the sublime of mass and the sublime of vacancy are the products of mutually engendering catastrophes. The two passages quoted from *The Book of Urizen* show this clearly enough, for the "rock of eternity" (*BU* 4.43) that is seen "wide asunder rolling" into "an ocean of voidness" in the second passage is the same "wide world of solid obstruction" that Urizen condensed out of "the void" in the first. But even earlier, we are told, he had "form'd this abominable void / This soul-shudd'ring vacuum" (*BU* 3.4–5). Likewise, in *The Book of Los*, the adamantine mass that Los shatters is one that he had earlier shaped by stamping back the "flames of desire" (*BL* 3.27). This mirror regression of alternating states merely projects in temporal terms the fact that the vacuous abyss and the obstructive mass are the perpetual measures of each other's greatness. Only when eternity splits asunder do its ruinous fragments begin to loom "mountainous," towering as "hanging frowning cliffs" along the fault lines of the fissure. To cite another text, this is the "abyss of the five senses, where a flat sided steep frowns over the present world" (*MHH* 6). Alternatively, these rocky verticalities demarcate the borders of the abyss and therefore outline its breadth, as the eye estimates the vast distance yawning "from immense to immense." The steep sides of the abyss produce the grandeur of height, its breadth the grandeur of space, and the sensation of falling the grandeur of depth and the irresistible power of gravitation.

It would be wrong to regard the terrifying landscapes found in the later

Lambeth Books, *Vala*, and elsewhere in Blake's work, including *Jerusalem*, merely as symbols of psychological or moral states, disconnected from any real interest in nature per se. Nor should we imagine that the idiom of the natural sublime used in these works owes its presence simply to the prevalence of a period style, perhaps reproduced out of half-conscious habit. Blake shows everywhere an abiding fascination with theories of the origins and changes of nature, and he is well aware of why these origins and changes produce a pattern that conforms, in a peculiar, dark, and terrifying way, to his own conception of the sublime. For Blake, natural history itself encodes the sublime dynamic, and he would regard his images as reflecting accurate science as much as they emblemize concepts outside their own realm. In those theories of origins that stressed the drastic interventions of earthquakes, floods, vulcanism, and solar eruption, Blake would see a perfect corroboration of the patterns of discontinuity, astonishment, and power-transfer that make up the sublime experience. Indeed, in the great controversy between the uniformitarians and the catastrophists that raged in natural philosophy from the late seventeenth century onward, Blake stands squarely in the catastrophist camp.[7]

In postulating the formation of the abyss out of the splitting of a uniform solid, Blake follows the most famous of the catastrophist thinkers, Thomas Burnet, who in his *Sacred Theory of the Earth* attributed the present state of nature to a series of stupendous sudden upheavals.[8] Burnet's work is less science than it is a vast epic phantasmagoria of the material sublime from creation to apocalypse (rather like the Nine Nights of Blake's *Vala*), and nowhere is his imagination more extravagant than in his account of

---

[7] One reason that Blake may have so strenuously opposed Newton and the Deists may lie in their insistence on a uniform and unchanging cosmic history and their resistance to accounts of natural history that depended on catastrophe. The catastrophists were frequently linked with antinomian principles in theology and politics as well as with an excessive attachment to imagination and the aesthetic sublime. For a comprehensive and highly instructive treatment of these issues, see Paolo Rossi, *The Dark Abyss of Time: The History of the Earth and the History of Nations from Hooke to Vico*, trans. Lydia G. Cochrane (Chicago: University of Chicago Press, 1984), esp. 33–49 and 69–107.

[8] Burnet's possible influence on Blake has received little study. Apart from the resemblances cited in the present text, the strongest evidence for Burnet's direct influence appears in his discussion of the "Mundane Egg": "We have show'd . . . that the figure of [the Earth], when finisht, was Oval, and the inward form of it was a frame of four Regions encompassing one another, where that of Fire lay in the middle like the Yolk, and a shell of Earth inclos'd them all" (*The [Sacred] Theory of the Earth*, 3d ed., 2 vols. [London: R. Norton, 1697], vol. 1, 184). While Blake could have found his Mundane Egg or Shell in many sources, this one is close enough to the famous diagram of *Milton* plate 33, with its fire and four overlapping regions, to suggest a direct connection (although Blake characteristically applies his revisionary touches—for example, placing the shell at the center of the scheme and the fire at the circumference).

that most awesome of ancient catastrophes, the Deluge.[9] In Burnet's opinion, the incremental rainfall described in Genesis cannot account for the magnitude of the event, and he stresses instead the opening of chasms: "*Moses* tells us, that the Fountains of the great Abysse were broke open, or *clove asunder*."[10] In brief, Burnet postulates an antediluvian earth that possessed an unbroken, uniform, level, and entirely solid surface (cf. *M* 15.32: "Thus is the earth one infinite plane"). In the catastrophe of the Deluge, this solid crust collapsed inward to create an abyss and release a flood of subterranean waters, with a host of dreadful attendant consequences:

> . . . for the sinking of the Earth would make an extraordinary convulsion of the Regions of the Air, and that crack and noise that must be in the falling World, and in the collision of the Earth and the Abyss, would make a great and universal Concussion above, which things together, must needs so shake, or so squeeze the Atmosphere, as to bring down all the remaining Vapours.[11]

In this cataclysmic description, one hears anticipations of the drastic events that afflict Urizen and Los in the passages quoted earlier: Burnet's squeezing of the atmosphere to bring on precipitation resembles Urizen's binding of the winds so that "condensing, in torrents / They fall & fall"; the "crack and noise" of the "falling World" is heard again in the cracking of Los's impacted confines and their "crash from immense to immense"; the up-ended fragments of the caved-in earth assimilate themselves to the "hanging frowning cliffs" that remain when Eternity rolls wide apart. Perhaps more telling than these instances of similarity is Blake's habit of introducing oceanic imagery to describe the abyss of space that yawns between the fragments of the shattered world. Thus, between the "frowning cliffs" just cited, "an ocean of voidness unfathomable" emerges; elsewhere, we note that the division of the eternal forests in *Europe* produces spaces "that like an ocean rush'd" (10.19); accompanying the segregation of "the pendulous earth" at the end of *Urizen*, "the salt ocean rolled englob'd"; most dramatically of all, when Urizen's solidly constructed world cracks and collapses into the "nether Abyss" at the end of the Third Night of *Vala*, it is the surging sea of Tharmas that wells up amid the fragmented ruins.

Natural catastrophism thus supplies Blake with corroborative images for the sublime dynamics of partition, with its corollaries of height (faultline precipices), depth (the abyss), and a space for flux (the inrushing ocean). But a dynamics of compression emerges as well from the same catastrophic scene. The two dynamic systems are intricately related and often difficult

---

[9] See Morton D. Paley, *The Apocalyptic Sublime* (New Haven: Yale University Press, 1986), 8–16, for a useful account of the importance of the Deluge as a subject in the visual art of the Burkean sublime.

[10] *Theory of the Earth* vol. 1, 10.

[11] Ibid., 67.

to distinguish. Fissure and separation ordinarily produce a void and the influx of chaotic fluidities, but an excess of compression may produce fissure of the primary substance and the emergence of a denser mass. One writer who made natural cataclysm the occasion of sublime poetry provides just such an arrangement. In his *Botanic Garden*, Erasmus Darwin thus describes the creation of the Earth:

> From the deep craters of his realms of fire,
> The whirling Sun this ponderous planet hurl'd,
> And gave the astonish'd void another world.
> When from it's [*sic*] vaporous air, condensed by cold,
> Descending torrents into oceans roll'd;
> And fierce attraction with relentless force
> Bent the reluctant wanderer to it's course.[12]

As David Worrall has pointed out, Blake echoes this passage in *The Book of Urizen* (4.14–23) in his description, cited earlier, of Urizen's world-making acts, involving first a combat with fire (4.14), then a condensing of the winds into torrents, then the formation of the ocean.[13] Blake makes no use here of Darwin's notion of the sun as a sort of vast volcano ("deep craters"). Yet these processes, particularly vulcanism, greatly attract Blake's interest elsewhere. The volcanic process combines the sublime of sundering (a rift opens in a solid, forming a chasm in which fluid wells up) and the sublime of concentration or mass (the rift is the product of inwardly directed pressures and the fluid that issues forth turns into mountain-building stone).

In the latter context, vulcanism can suggest the birth process, the creation of new forms of greatness. As Burnet describes it,

> The Mountain begins to roar and bellow in its hollow caverns; cries out, as it were, in pain to be deliver'd of some burthen, too heavy to be born, and too big to be easily discharg'd. The Earth shakes and trembles, in apprehension of the pangs and convulsions that are coming upon her; And the Sun often hides his head, or appears with a discolour'd face, pale, or dusky, bloudy, as all Nature was to suffer in this Agony.[14]

A passage such as the preceding allows us to see clearly the underlying volcanic reference in, say, the lament of the Shadowy Female, pregnant by Orc, in the Preludium to *Europe*:

---

[12] Erasmus Darwin, *The Botanic Garden*, 2 vols. (London: J. Johnson, 1791 and 1794), I.ii.14–20.

[13] See, for this and other Blakean echoes of Darwin, David Worrall, "William Blake and Erasmus Darwin's *Botanic Garden*," *Bulletin of the New York Public Library* 78 (Summer 1975): 397–417.

[14] *Theory of the Earth* vol. 2, 38.

I wrap my turban of thick clouds around my lab'ring head;
And fold the sheety waters as a mantle round my limbs.
Yet the red sun and moon,
And all the overflowing stars rain down prolific pains.

(*Eur* 1.12–15)

The image of a laboring head fits an active volcanic crater better than it does a pregnant woman, and the "turban of thick clouds" or shroud of smoke and vapor that habitually clings to the tops of volcanos seems to corroborate the figure, as do the red sun and moon (cf. Burnet's "dusky, bloudy" sun). This is not to claim that the Shadowy Female is a volcano, but to indicate how the figure of the volcano attaches the imagery of natural catastrophe to the production of new, compact, and separated forms out of the old. The figure is thus available for other partitive and ejaculatory events. Thus we read of "the burning fires / Of lust, that belch incessant from the summits of the earth" (*VDA* 2.9–10), and elsewhere Orc himself assumes the form of a volcano in eruption:

As when the Earthquake rouzes from his den his shoulders huge
Appear above the crumb[l]ing Mountain. Silence waits around him
A moment then astounding horror belches from the Center
The fiery dogs arise the shoulders huge appear
So Orc rolld round his clouds upon the deeps of dark Urthona

(*FZ* 91.6–10)

If the cataclysms described in *Urizen* and *Los* consist essentially of falling movements, then here we have a process of elevation, a transfer of mass from the depths below to the heights above. The sublime of the abyss and the volcanic sublime are thus reciprocal types; each offers a catastrophic discontinuity, but while the discontinuity of fissure produces precipitous depth, vacancy, and oceanic flux, the discontinuity of eruption produces mountainous height and concentrated mass. Volcanic catastrophe would seem, for a variety of reasons, to be more easily available as a trope for renewal, triumph, and recovery of the buried fires of life. But as we have already seen, in the domain of the natural sublime, forms that are structurally reciprocal are also temporally reversible—and indeed, as we observe in the passage from *Vala* above, old mountains are already crumbling as Orc's rising shoulders form new ones.[15]

The reciprocity and reversibility of sublime patterns, as Blake sees them,

[15] Blake's ambivalence about mountains is usefully discussed in Nelson Hilton, "Blake and the Mountains of the Mind," *Blake/An Illustrated Quarterly* 14 (Spring 1981): 196–204. Blake's desire for the sun of imagination to rise above the mountains (see *J* 95.11–12) is, Hilton says, "a struggle perhaps, because mountains are the 'risings' of the earth, the objects of increasing Romantic adoration" (203).

is closely connected to his sense that the sublime experience is reflexive, that whenever one views a form of opposing greatness, there is always a shadowy image of oneself (as one was or might yet be) lurking behind it. Here the speculations and evidences of the catastrophists, while useful in grounding his readings of natural history in something more than arbitrary poetic fancy, are not entirely sufficient to Blake's purpose. For, whether they posit a divine cause for catastrophe, as Burnet did, or suggest materialist origins, as in Darwin's account, these natural philosophers firmly separate the author of sublime effects from their passive subject. But in idealist theories of the sublime, as we have seen, this separation tends to get blurred: the greatness that we see "out there" turns out to have resided within all along, but we need to see it out there first in order to see it at all. Blake participates in this perspective but he is deeply skeptical of nature's capacity to provide an adequate mirror; there are too many receding mirrors within that mirror, each bringing its own incremental distortion and deformation. Hence he tends, in his poetry, to accommodate the catastrophists' vision to the idealist position—but in so doing, he subjects the latter to parody.

The arch-protagonist of this parody is Urizen. While it is a commonplace to regard Urizen as a parody of the creator-God of Milton and Genesis, it is less common to view him as an almost frantic factotum of the Burkean sublime, by turns performing all its parts—producer, product, and perceiver. This versatility substantially reflects the convergence in eighteenth-century thought of theology, natural philosophy, and psychology. Burke tells us that "in the scripture, wherever God is represented as appearing or speaking, every thing terrible in nature is called up to heighten the awe and solemnnity of the divine presence."[16] "Every thing terrible in nature" is certainly assembled as Urizen prepares for his first public manifestation:

His cold horrors silent, dark Urizen
Prepar'd: his ten thousands of thunders
Rang'd in gloom'd array stretch out across
The dread world, & the rolling of wheels
As of swelling seas, sound in his clouds
In his hills of stor'd snows, in his mountains
Of hail & ice; voices of terror

[16] *Philosophical Enquiry*, 69. For a poetical example of this Burkean dictum (although predating Burke's treatise), one may turn to Smart's Seatonian Prize poems, which interwove representations of the Miltonic Deity with images drawn from eighteenth-century natural history, e.g.: "But not alone in the aërial vault / Does he the dread theocracy maintain; For oft, enrag'd with his intestine thunders, / He harrows up the bowels of the earth" ("The Power of the Supreme Being," lines 30–33; *Collected Poems of Christopher Smart*, ed. Norman Callan, 2 vols. (London: Routledge and Kegan Paul, 1949).

Are heard, like thunders of autumn,
When the cloud blazes over the harvests

(*BU* 3.27–35)

Here Blake rings most of the changes of the terrible sublime—its darkness, obscurity, and terror, its grim topography of stormy heights and deeps— in order to invest Urizen with associations of unfettered disruptive power. But this investiture is granted only so that it may be all the more thoroughly taken away. Urizen's grandeurs succeed finally in astonishing no one more strongly than himself, and within a few dozen lines he is transformed from a force producing the sublime into its product. The active, strong-willed maker and disrupter of landscapes becomes a passive, disrupted landscape himself, the site of catastrophic fissure and eruption:

In stony sleep ages roll'd over him!
Like a dark waste stretching chang'able
By earthquakes riv'n, belching sullen fires

(*BU* 10.2–4)

Here the only "greatness" that Urizen manifests is a quantitative magnitude of vacancies, the abyss of waste space and of past ages made measurable by a kind of fossil record of natural catastrophes.

By identifying both the terrible power and the terrible product of the natural sublime with the figure of Urizen, Blake is suggesting that these two states are allotropic versions of one another (in Kantian terms, they are equivalent, respectively, to the dynamical and the mathematical sublimes). But he is not content to let the equation rest there; he insists, rather, on incorporating into it the perceiver of the sublime as well—that diminutive, overawed, baffled, thwarted, yet ever-intrepid figure who appears so prominently in eighteenth-century aesthetics. For if Urizen starts out as a generator of the sublime experience and then serves as its petrified object, he eventually goes on to become an individualized seeker of such objects, as if they were entirely external to himself. *The Book of Urizen* touches on this search, but the richest account of it occurs in the extraordinary description of Urizen's journey in Night VI of *Vala*:

For infinite the distance & obscurd by Combustions dire
By rocky masses frowning in the abysses revolving erratic
Round Lakes of fire in the dark deep the ruins of Urizens world
Oft would he sit in a dark rift & regulate his books
Or sleep such sleep as spirits eternal wearied in his dark
Tearful & sorrowful state. then rise look out & ponder
His dismal voyage eyeing the next sphere tho far remote
Then darting into the Abyss of night his venturous limbs
Thro lightnings thunders earthquakes & concussions fires & floods

Stemming his downward fall labouring up against futurity
Creating many a Vortex fixing many a Science in the deep
And thence throwing his venturous limbs into the Vast unknown
Swift Swift from Chaos to chaos from void to void a road immense

$$(FZ\ 72.3–15)$$

In this grimly impressive passage, the abyss has expanded beyond anything presented in previous accounts of the Urizenic adventures. In what is now clearly a setting of interplanetary space without center or bounds, the "hanging frowning cliffs" of *The Book of Urizen* reappear as "rocky masses frowning," but the cliffs have swollen into whole worlds in orbit, and the volcanic lava pools ("Lakes of fire") are now their suns.[17] At the same time, every possible natural shock or cataclysm is compounded (all massed together in the single line 75.11 to amplify the stunning, concussive effect). But if the terrors of the natural sublime are here expanded to their utmost, the journeying human figure who becomes their subject is correspondingly diminished. Once, Urizen presented himself as a vast force that *moved* nature, as a spirit within it (cf. *BU* 3.30–32: "the rolling of wheels . . . sound in his clouds / In his hills . . . in his mountains"). Then, he became nature's inert body, and now he is simply a figure moving through a nature wholly alien, scarcely recognized in its unmanageable vastness as the fossil of his former self. The individual and the world are separated, indifferent forces here; Urizen is largely ineffectual in his repeated attempts to give this order to this world, and, despite its obstructive sublimity, it is finally ineffectual in stopping his course.

Ironically, the vast enlargement of space and Urizen's diminishment into the form of a solitary voyager restores to him that freedom of movement he once enjoyed when he first appeared on the scene as an awesome wintry deity. Although Urizen has little taste for the Burkean sublimities that he is forced to encounter on his voyage, these encounters stimulate him to an energetic countersublime. Whatever orderly regulations he enters into his books, he scarcely regulates his own behavior by them. His survey of the abyss prompts him to move impulsively; "darting" and "swift," he becomes a risk-taker on a grand scale, "throwing his venturous limbs into the Vast unknown"; he struggles hard, "labouring up against futurity." Even his weary pauses serve finally to measure the strength of his determination to go on. In short, Urizen becomes another exemplar of the intrepid, individ-

[17] In his treatise on the *Construction of the Heavens* (1784), William Herschel, who contributed heavily to the theory of a decentered cosmos, promotes an analogy between the astronomical heavens and the disorganized, much-altered topography of the earth; he would have us regard the heavens as "a naturalist regards a . . . chain of mountains, containing strata variously inclined and directed, as well as consisting of different materials"; quoted in Rossi, *The Dark Abyss of Time*, 113.

ualistic Romantic quester, one who wrests awe away from the sublime objects he encounters and attaches it to the magnitude of his own passion and struggle. *Mutatis mutandis*, he joins a company of travelers that includes the Romantic version of Milton's Satan, the night-wandering boy of the early books of *The Prelude*, Childe Harold, and the Poet-visionary of *Alastor*, to name only a few of the most conspicuous, all of whom make the sublime setting an occasion for their own grand manifestations of soul, strength, or persistence. In taking Urizen's career to this stage, Blake thus completes the dialectic of the eighteenth-century sublime experience, having first lodged power in a nature-producing deity, then manifesting it in the grandeur of creation itself, and finally transferring it to an isolated individual who sets his face against this creation in order to assert his own grandeur.

The joke in all this, one that constitutes an implicit critique of all such Romantic questers, is that Urizen wrests his grandeur merely from his former self, as all his earlier selves did also in their turn, in the indefinite regress of sublime origins. For, to put it plainly, Urizen is not really a "person" but rather the name for a catastrophic continuum, a series of splittings, compressions, inflations, diminishments, reapportionments, and individuations, which at any point along the line may localize itself in an isolated perceiver of the world or else spread itself throughout an object perceived. There is no final recovery of grandeur in this continuum, because there is no stable self to recover it. Whatever stability was once possessed fled when the self parted from a unity that was "all," leaving only the fluxes of nature as its residue. "The ruins of Urizens world," then, are more than the fragmented parts of his former giant body, now projected in space—for even that former body was itself a ruin, and the ruin of a ruin. Indeed, Urizen's world was, almost by definition, a ruin from the start, if we can speak of "starts" in such an affair.

The notion of sublime nature as a body of ruin is by no means original to Blake, and indeed he uses its common currency to give weight to the personifications of his own bardic chronicles. Years earlier, Macpherson's Ossian relied on the catastrophic metamorphoses of nature to generate a pleasing melancholy out of a sense of loss and desolation:

> The oaks of the mountains fall: the mountains themselves decay with years; the ocean shrinks and grows again: the moon herself is lost in heaven; but thou [the sun] art for ever the same; rejoicing in the brightness of thy course! When the world is dark with tempests; when thunder rolls, and lightning flies; thou lookest in thy beauty, from the clouds, and laughest at the storm. . . . But thou art perhaps, like me, for a season, thy years will have an end.[18]

---

[18] "Carthon," *Poems of Ossian* vol. 1, 95.

This passage gets its force by momentarily elevating the natural sun above the tempests and darkness of the lower world (like the transcendent mind rising above its engagement with the sublime of terror and obscurity), only to cancel that elevation and consign it after all to the darkness of passing things. In what is perhaps the best-known passage in his *Theory of the Earth*, Burnet rhetorically achieves a similar effect:

> The greatest objects of Nature are, methinks, the most pleasing to behold; and next to the great Concave of the Heavens, and those boundless Regions where the Stars inhabit, there is nothing that I look upon with more plaesure [*sic*] than the wide Sea and the Mountains of the Earth. There is something august and stately in the Air of these things, that inspires the mind with great thoughts and passions; We do naturally, upon such occasions, think of God and his greatness: and whatsoever hath but the shadow and appearance of INFINITE, as all these things have that are too big for our comprehension, they fill and over-bear the mind with their Excess, and cast it into a pleasing kind of stupor and admiration.

> And yet these Mountains we are speaking of, to confess the truth, are nothing but great ruins; but such as show a certain Magnificence in Nature; as from old temples and broken Amphitheatres of the *Romans* we collect the greatness of that people.[19]

The first of these paragraphs manages to pack itself with virtually the whole of the ensuing century's way of talking about the natural sublime—mountains, sea, and heavens, inspirational thoughts and passions, simulacra of the infinite, reflections on the greatness of God, baffled comprehension, the mind filled and overborne by excess, pleasing stupor—a manner that should be now thoroughly familiar to us.[20] The second paragraph, however, qualifies all this with an ominous "and yet." If the whole machinery of the sublime response is dependent on ruined forms, then sublimity can only be a second-best delight, flourishing, as it were, in exile from the satisfaction of recovered origins. Nor is it a matter of recapturing from these ruined forms remembrances of better mountains, better seas, that existed before the catastrophe; in this respect, the analogy of "old temples and broken Amphitheatres" is misleading, for Burnet's geology stipulates that mountains and seas came into being for the first time *as* ruins, deforming an originally smooth earth that knew nothing of such forms. The sublime, then, turns out to be a totally ex post facto phenomenon, a catastrophe of

---

[19] *Theory of the Earth* vol. 1, 94–95.

[20] The standard account of the eighteenth-century cult of mountains as sublime objects, and particularly Burnet's role in its development, remains Marjorie Hope Nicolson, *Mountain Gloom and Mountain Glory: The Development of the Aesthetics of the Infinite* (New York: Norton Library, 1959); see also Basil Willey, *The Eighteenth Century Background: Studies on the Idea of Nature in the Thought of the Period* (London: Chatto and Windus, 1940), esp. 27–34.

the beautiful (the paradisally smooth, green, shoreless antediluvian earth), and all its ecstasies are the mark of our disinheritance.

Burnet himself might respond to this interpretation by pointing out that the ruins of the planet are but the negative measure of a positive power (namely, the wrath of God) that continues to exist undiminished in its plenitude and that will show itself once again at the end. Such a view certainly becomes common in the eighteenth century as a way of preserving the idea of nature's grandeur while reconciling it to the scientific evidences of catastrophe and deformation. Thus the aesthetician Usher, probably with Burnet in mind, tells us how "the pensive eye traces the rugged precipice down to the bottom, and surveys there the mighty ruins that time has mouldered and tumbled below. It is easy in this instance to discover that we are terrified and silenced into awe, at the *vestiges* we see of immense power; and the more manifest are the appearances of disorder, and the neglect of contrivance, the more plainly we feel the boundless might these rude monuments are owing to."[21] Here, it is not the height of the precipice that terrifies but rather the traces that it incorporates of what has gone before, a power no longer visible in its proper self, yet leaving the mark of its passing in "ruins," "vestiges," and "monuments." We are not so far from Blake here as it may first appear. Usher's "immense power" (not explicitly named as God) betrays a tendency toward disorganization and chaos from the start. It manifests itself in "disorder" and "neglect," and its monuments are "rude"—and these forms cannot have appeared as less rude and more ordered on that terrible day when the precipice was split than they do after ages have rolled over them. It is always difficult to extract the glory of God out of earthquakes and avalanches without reducing God, to some degree, to little more than an earthquake or avalanche.

It remains to Blake to take these suggested coalescences of creator and creation to their ultimate stage. The notion that the earth's craggy surface is God's dead or comatose body (expressed in the figure of Urizen, and, later, in Albion's "stony sleep") is neither a theological conundrum nor a private poetic extravagance. To arrive at the notion, Blake had available to him the mechanist philosophers' widely held view that God, in Ernest Tuveson's words, "coincides with rather than transcends His universe" and that nature is "the very image, so far as we can comprehend it, of God Himself, in his extended omnipresence."[22] Blake needed only to combine this view with the position of the catastrophists that nature's body is a ruinous remnant of past deformations in order to get corroboration for a conception of nature as a ruin of the divine body (graphically expressed in the designs of recumbent island/corpses in plate 26 [28] of *Milton*; see Fig-

---

[21] *Clio*, 108.
[22] See Tuveson, "Space, Deity, and the Natural Sublime," 28 and 38.

ure 2). When Blake tells us that Albion is "the high Cliff of the Atlantic" (*J* 30[34].16) and that "All things Begin & End in Albions Ancient Druid Rocky Shore" (*J* 27), he is doing more than setting the scene of his epic. In part, he is parodying the Alpha and Omega of Revelation, displacing it from its apocalyptic context into the body of this world—a world that stretches from cliffs to more cliffs, like the rocky ends that bracket the recumbent figures in plate 26 [28] of *Milton* from one margin of the text to the other.

Yet, for all this, it is a wiser and ultimately a more hopeful stance to regard the setting of the natural sublime as a ruin rather than as a sempiternal, boundless greatness. The latter view leads only to personal humiliation, or else (as in the example of Urizen) to amassing one's own personal grandeur and thus to setting oneself up for catastrophes and self-divisions yet to come. To see ruins, on the other hand, allows us a glimpse of a former greatness that was different from what we are left with now, perhaps a greatness closer to the form of our infinite desires. If the ruin speaks of the loss of that greatness, it at least images what must be recovered. Of all ruins, however, those of the natural sublime, as we have seen, give us the shadowiest and most dubious image of the plenitude of origins; interrogating nature's present forms to discover what went before, we tend to find more of the same. This suggests that the natural setting is, at best, the ruin of a ruin. Human ruins, however, bring us a little closer to a sublime that can satisfy (which, we must not forget, must consist in "lineaments . . . that are capable of being the receptacles of intellect"), for they preserve at least some of the outlines of art. While they keep us within a sublime of material settings, we begin to perceive culture there, not mere catastrophe, and are brought that much closer to a recollection of the greatness of origins.

ARCHITECTURAL RUINS: TRACES OF THE ANCIENT MAN

The cult of ruins figures nearly as prominently as the taste for natural grandeur in the sensibility of the eighteenth-century sublime. That Blake felt the power of the ruin to take hold of the imagination is indicated by a memorable passage near the climax of *Milton*:

> I also stood in Satans bosom & beheld its desolations!
> A ruind Man: a ruind building of God not made with hands;
> Its plains of burning sand, its mountains of marble terrible:
> Its pits & declivities flowing with molten ore & fountains
> Of pitch & nitre: its ruind palaces & cities & mighty works;
> Its furnaces of affliction in which his Angels & Emanations

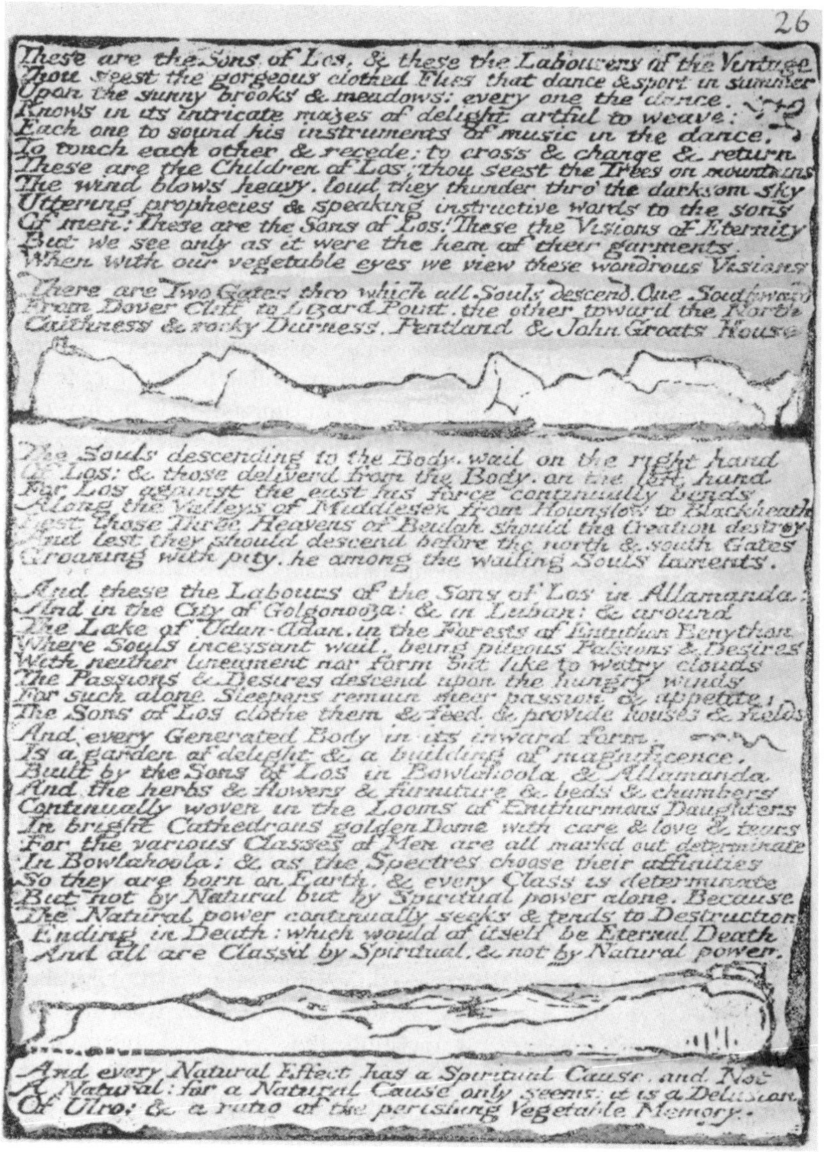

These are the Sons of Los, & these the Labourers of the Vintage
Thou seest the gorgeous clothed Flies that dance &.sport in summer
Upon the sunny brooks & meadows: every one the dance
Knows in its intricate mazes of delight: artful to weave:
Each one to sound his instruments of music in the dance.
To touch each other & recede: to cross & change & return
These are the Children of Los; thou seest the Trees on mountains
The wind blows heavy, loud they thunder thro' the darksom sky
Uttering prophecies & speaking instructive words to the sons
Of men: These are the Sons of Los! These the Visions of Eternity
But we see only as it were the hem of their garments
When with our vegetable eyes we view these wondrous Visions

There are Two Gates thro which all Souls descend. One Southward
From Dover Cliff to Lizard Point. the other toward the North
Caithness & rocky Durness, Pentland & John Groats House

The Souls descending to the Body, wail on the right hand
Of Los: & those deliverd from the Body, on the left hand
For Los against the east his force continually bends
Along the Valleys of Middlesex from Hounslow to Blackheath
Lest those Three Heavens of Beulah should the Creation destroy
And lest they should descend before the north & south Gates
Groaning with pity, he among the wailing Souls laments.

And these the Labours of the Sons of Los in Allamanda:
And in the City of Golgonooza: & in Luban: & around
The Lake of Udan-Adan. in the Forests of Entuthon Benython
Where Souls incessant wail, being piteous Passions & Desires
With neither lineament nor form but like to watry clouds
The Passions & Desires descend upon the hungry winds
For such alone. Sleepers remain meer passion & appetite ;
The Sons of Los clothe them & feed. & provide houses & fields
And. every Generated Body in its inward form.
Is a garden of delight & a building of magnificence.
Built by the Sons of Los in Bowlahoola. & Allamanda.
And. the herbs & flowers & furniture & beds & chambers
Continually woven in the Looms of Enitharmons Daughters
In bright Cathedrons golden Dome with care & love & tears
For the various Classes of Men are all markd out determinate
In Bowlahoola: & as the Spectres choose their affinities
So they are born on Earth, & every Class is determinate
But not by Natural but by Spiritual power alone. Because
The Natural power continually seeks & tends to Destruction
Ending in Death: which would at itself be Eternal Death
And all are Classd by Spiritual, & not by Natural power.

And every Natural Effect has a Spiritual Cause, and Not
A Natural: for a Natural Cause only seems: it is a Delusion
Of Ulro: & a ratio of the perishing Vegetable Memory.

Figure 2. *Milton* (Copy B), plate 26.

Labour with blackend visages among its stupendous ruins
Arches & pyramids & porches colonades & domes:

(*M* 38.15–22)

Here Blake shows, with his usual dexterity of verbal condensation, the relation of one form of ruin to another. The "ruind Man" is Albion himself, and the "ruind building of God not made with hands" is presumably the sublime world of nature, riven by catastrophe. Yet Blake is at pains to treat this world under the sign of architecture, calling it a "building," and as the passage continues, the line between nature and human construction blurs: the plains of sand evidently belong to nature, but it is less clear whether the mountains of marble are real mountains or great heaped-up architectural ruins, and the pits of ore and nitre belong ambiguously either to natural vulcanism or to human industry. At last, unmistakably human constructions emerge, "palaces & cities," and the focus ultimately narrows on a survey of their purely architectural forms, "Arches & pyramids & porches," and so forth, concentrated in a single line so as to suggest both the panoply of their grandeur and the jumbled, huddled character of their ruin. It is as if we see the monuments of human empire actually emerging before our eyes out of the substrate of a ruined nature—or conversely, and conceptually bolder, as if we gradually come to perceive the outlines of a human city anterior to and yet persisting within the eroded outlines of nature that are its material remains.

To stand "in Satans bosom" means, in one sense, to view these "mighty works" as Satan himself views them, as an opulent and "stupendous" achievement, readily capable of provoking the sublime response ("stupendous" derives from *stupeo*, the Latin verb that Burke found explicitly synonymous with the English "astonish"; see p. 18 of Chapter I). The poet's confession that he "also stood" there is a testament to his unending ambivalence about displays of the material sublime. Blake is fully aware of their delusive pretensions to infinitude and the tragic history of humiliation and destruction that they conceal, yet he is sufficiently fascinated to write about them obsessively, often in an exclamatory tone that seems as much designed to astonish the reader as to critique the premises of astonishment. Ruins are particularly a source of ambivalence; on one hand, virtually by definition, they represent loss and decay, and they call to mind the tyrannies of the past that compelled their construction and the plight of the laborers "with blackend visages" who built them.[23] On the other hand, they permit one to imagine the lineaments of a perfected, unfallen city as an inevitable rebound from the contemplation of its fallen versions—a re-

---

[23] For a study of these negative associations and related themes found in the extensive corpus of ruins literature, see Laurence Goldstein, *Ruins and Empire: The Evolution of a Theme in Augustan and Romantic Literature* (Pittsburgh: University of Pittsburgh Press, 1977).

bound that, as we have seen in other contexts, is typical of the sublime dynamic: the object of our contemplation offers a greatness that exceeds anything in our current possession, yet reminds us of our desire for an ultimate greatness that the object falls far short of supplying. Unlike the great but chaotic forms of nature, great ruins at least supply objects that resemble what we desire, for they are the products of human action. That makes them all the more tragic as testimonials to the eroding powers of time and all the more appealing to an imagination hungry for evidences of human potentiality.

The sublimity of ruins depends on their close association with two contrary forms of greatness—first, the dynamic power manifested in their construction and still locked up in some fashion in their stony remains, and second, the quantitative magnitude of time that reduces ancient structures to littleness and separates us as by a gulf from their glories. The verses on the "stupendous ruins" of Satan's bosom may echo C. F. Volney's famous treatise *The Ruins* (1791), which Blake might have read in Joel Barlow's Paris translation of 1802. Viewing a prospect of archaeological remains, Volney says, "I was struck with a scene of the most stupendous ruins: a countless multitude of superb columns, stretching in avenues beyond the reach of sight."[24] Here, the sublimity depends not on their ruinous condition but on the original glory and opulence of the structures (fine specimens of the Burkean sublime object whose bounds cannot be distinctly perceived). But Volney is soon to be impressed by opposite sensations: "The *solitude* of the place, the tranquility of the hour, the majesty of the scene *impressed on my mind* a religious pensiveness. The aspect of a *great city deserted*, the memory of *times past, compared with its present state*, all *elevated* my mind to *high* contemplations" (my emphasis).[25] As my emphasis of its key phrases shows, here it is absence and vacancy that promote a typical sublime experience of impressiveness, elevation, and inward height; silence, desertion, and a consciousness of the pastness of the past, created by the sundering gulf of time, overwhelm the observer with a new magnitude of their own. In a similar vein, Joseph Priestley remarks that "celebrated buildings and cities *in ruins* . . . present [the idea] of the length of time that hath elapsed since they flourished; and the whole sensation is greatly magnified by a comparison of their former magnificence with their present desolation."[26] Ruins, in effect, produce the sensation of great time,

---

[24] *Volney's Ruins, or Meditations on the Revolutions of Empires*, trans. Joel Barlow (New York: Dixon and Sickels, 1828), 20.

[25] Ibid., 21

[26] *Course of Lectures*, 158. Cf. Jacob Bryant (the only antiquarian to be mentioned by name in Blake's works) on the same subject: "Such were the mighty works of old, which promised to last for ever; but have been long since subverted; and their name and history oftentimes forgotten. It is a melancholy consideration, that not only in Sicily and Greece, but in all the

time as a sea or yawning space, just as the fractured cliff-faces of once-unitary continental masses demarcate oceanic expanses and airy drops. They are each site-markers of the abyss.[27]

Blake is well aware of these "dark abysses of the times remote" (*FZ* 102.33). Commentaries often suggest that the settings of his poems are "timeless," but this is a misleading formulation if it conveys the impression that Blake had no real convictions about the pastness of the past, no sense of the sublimity of receding ages, and no interest in the pursuit of cultural origins. The vertiginous effect captured, for example, in the verses "Times on times, night on night, day on day / . . . Years on years, and ages on ages" (*BL* 4.29, 31) should convince us that the poet possesses an imaginative grasp of what he is describing. Moreover, Blake is sometimes willing to confer grandeur on the modern and the momentous by garbing it in the stillness and immobility of the distant past and its remains: "Like pillars of ancient halls, and ruins of times remote they sat," he says of the National Assembly on the eve of the French Revolution (*FR* 13.258). Indeed, as his work progresses from the supposedly more "timely" early writings to the more "visionary" later ones, his interest in specifying temporal regression seems to grow. Thus, in the much–revised title to what eventually became *The Four Zoas*, Blake pointedly substituted "Ancient" for "Eternal" in the original subtitle "The Death and Judgement of the Eternal Man," and the same substitution is sporadically carried out throughout the manuscript. Likewise, in the *Descriptive Catalogue* of 1809, Blake tells us that "The British Antiquities are now in the Artist's hands; all his visionary contemplations, relating to his own country and its ancient glory, when it was as it again shall be," and he assures us that he himself has written of these antiquities: "it is voluminous, and contains the ancient history of Britain, and the world of Satan and of Adam" (E 542, 543). Again, in response to Wordsworth's attack on the Ossianic and Rowleian forgeries, Blake declares, "I Believe both Macpherson & Chatterton, that what they say is Ancient, Is so" (E 665)—a defense that would be pointless if inspiration were indeed vaguely "timeless," if it did not matter *when* a poem was written, and if the fact of genuine antiquity brought with it no luminous and distinguishing quality.

Blake's fondness for the word "ancient" and the phrase "times remote,"

---

celebrated regions of the east, the history of the pilgrim and traveller consists chiefly in his passing through a series of dilapidations; a process from ruin to ruins" (*A New System or an Analysis of Ancient Mythology*, 3d ed., 6 vols. [London: J. Walker et al., 1807], vol. 5, 213).

[27] In his essay on the sublime, Wordsworth maintains that the effect of ancient objects on the mind lies not in the objects themselves but in the notions of vast time that they provoke: "Duration is evidently an element of the sublime. . . . An object can affect us . . . when the faint sense we have of its individuality is lost in the general sense of duration belonging to the Earth itself" (*Prose Works*, 351).

his anxiety to authenticate ancient texts, and his assurances that his own works contain "ancient history" all point to his participation in a common aesthetic tendency of his time: the imagination is quickened by the glories and catastrophes of the past because they are past. Or, to describe this process more precisely, the vast quantity of time that separates us from remote events is projected onto the absent events themselves and augments their grandeur; at the same time, grandeur becomes a token of absence. Ruins serve to turn this absence into a presence, a concretized preservation of a sundering or estrangement. From another perspective, ruins are not perceived as ruins unless this feeling of estrangement takes hold.

The settings of some of Blake's designs illustrate this process succinctly. In the designs of *The Book of Job*, for example, as Job goes from prosperity to ruin, there is a strange regression in the background architecture as the series moves forward. Intact Gothic structures on the first plate give way to toppling Doric structures on the third, and then to quasi-Druidic forms that first appear on plate 4 and grow, by plate 7, to a virtual wilderness of worn and broken trilithons and megaliths that look as if they have stood ruined from "times remote" (see Figures 3–6).[28] The original Gothic building never appears ruined, but simply disappears as Job's catastrophe overtakes him; the Doric structure is never shown either intact or as an abandoned ruin, but only in the intermediate process of collapsing; the Druidic structures are shown only as ruins from their first appearance, and they seem to be the remains of buildings that never existed in the landscapes of Job's prosperity. As Blake makes no pretensions to naturalism in his background settings, we must take this curious sequence of reverse architectural history as a projection of Job's increasing estrangement from his unfallen origins—an estrangement that is registered as a sense of an ever-widening abyss of time between the present self and its originally nurturing surroundings. As his condition deteriorates, his buildings become historically more ancient until they resemble prehistoric remains. But these are the remains of buildings that never saw their prime, for they come into being in Job's world as instant ruins, like the "follies" popular on eighteenth-century country estates. And like these follies, their effect is to intensify the consciousness of time, so that Job comes to think of his catastrophe and estrangement not as recent and personal, but as ancient, immemorial, universal, and, by inference, darkly sublime.

In the *Job* designs, and in various plates of *Milton* and *Jerusalem*, megaliths, trilithons, and other remains of the ancient stone circles of Northern Europe are presented as the *ne plus ultra* of ruination. Reflecting a popular

---

[28] For a good background survey of Blake's use of architectural imagery, including the "Druidic," the classical, and the Gothic orders, see Morton D. Paley, "The Fourth Face of Man: Blake and Architecture," in *Articulate Images: The Sister Arts from Hogarth to Tennyson*, ed. Richard Wendorf (Minneapolis: University of Minnesota Press, 1983), 184–215.

Figure 3. *The Book of Job*, plate 1.

Figure 4. *The Book of Job*, plate 3.

Figure 5. *The Book of Job*, plate 4.

Figure 6. *The Book of Job*, plate 7.

theory of the day, Blake attributed a Druidic origin to these remains and believed Druidism to be the oldest of human cultures ("Adam was a Druid, and Noah" [*DC*, E 542]), but the prevalence of these ruins in his designs reflects more than anthropological interests or a desire to reinforce his own doctrinal symbolism.[29] Not only are they the oldest of all possible ruins, but they are also the earliest products of human intellect that are subject to ruin, for prior to them are the immaterial and hence undegradable pre-Adamite productions of the unfallen Man ("Albion was the Parent of the Druids" [*J* 27]). Standing as they do at the earliest threshold of time's changes, the Druidic remains serve as the quintessential embodiment of the idea that the image of the ruin creates time as a sensed experience, giving form to its abyss.

At this threshold point, as we learn from *Europe*, "was the serpent temple form'd, image of infinite / Shut up in finite revolutions" (10.21), the cycles of calendrical time. We again meet this "serpent temple" (a term borrowed from the antiquary William Stukeley, who thus designated the great stone circle at Avebury) on the full-page design that concludes *Jerusalem*—as emphatic a position as any depiction of a ruin could receive in Blake's work (see Figure 7). Here, if the consensus of commentary is correct, we see Los at a moment when "the Poets Work is Done" (*M* 29.1), turning his back on an immense Druidic remain. While based on Stukeley's fanciful reconstruction of Avebury's original form, Blake's structure exists in an indeterminate setting that is neither ancient nor contemporary; crudely shaped, apparently worn, slightly leaning, these stones seem too old to be taken for a representation of ancient Avebury in its prime, as Stukeley depicted it, with its overall intricacy of design and neat array of pillars (see Figure 8). Neither is it a representation of the Avebury of Blake's own time, where the ancient remains are fragmentary and nearly indecipherable, for the stone circle on plate 100 is complete with all its sequences of trilithons intact. Rather, the image seems to coalesce the impression of great age with that of preserved structural integrity, so that it seems to compress the whole span of ages in its stony form. As Los evidently chooses to put it behind him, one can only conclude that the serpent temple represents the entire collective mass of past time itself—the giant interval between original catastrophe and apocalypse, monumentally repetitive in the what Burke would have called the "artificial infinite" of its endless colonnades. It is a ruin, yet an intact ruin—one that persists in all its dark grandeur, which it is our fate to confront. Los may turn his back on the serpent temple, but Blake makes us gaze at it, so that even at the end of things, on the hun-

---

[29] The best account of the doctrinal significance of Druidism in Blake's thought remains Peter F. Fisher, "Blake and the Druids," *Journal of English and Germanic Philology* 58 (October 1959): 589–612.

Figure 7. *Jerusalem* (Copy D), plate 100.

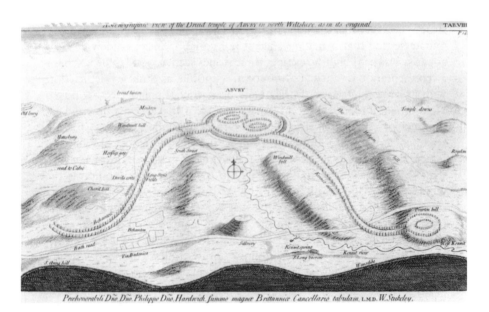

Figure 8. View of Avebury. From William Stukeley, *Abury, A Temple of the British Druids* (1743).

dredth plate of Jerusalem, we are forced to look backward into the stony abyss, the sum of all the remains of our origins. We are not allowed to forget it, for time, after all, is not yet finished for us.

But in taking us back to the idea of origins, this ruin also points us back beyond the threshold of historical time and into the lost period when all structures were new and human productive powers were in their prime. This point leads us to the other great source of the sublimity of ruins. If, on one hand, they measure the waste magnitude of time between antiquity and the present, then they testify, on the other hand, to the productive powers that men of antiquity possessed. According to Burke, "when any work seems to have required immense force and labour to effect it, the idea is grand. Stonehenge, neither for disposition nor ornament, has anything admirable; but those huge rude masses of stone, set on end, and piled each on each other, turn the mind on the immense force necessary for such a work."[30] There is a connection here to the persistent popular notion that the ancient stone circles of Britain were the work of superhuman beings—gods, giants, or demons.[31] And if the power of the giants remains memorialized in these stones, then, by an easy process of association, the ruins are in some sense what is left of the giants themselves, as if they have somehow petrified into their own products.

In his treatise on Stonehenge, Stukeley offers, in various rhetorical flourishes and scholarly asides, hints enough of this sort to activate an imagination like Blake's. Stukeley relates, for instance, the standing or "rocking" stones found at the prehistoric sites to a myth of "animated stones" devised by the god Uranus, and of Stonehenge he exclaims that "here a single stone is a ruin, and lies like the haughty carcase of *Goliath*."[32] Sometimes Stukeley provides Blake with a feast of symbolic possibilities. Thus, he says, "Stonehenge is a stone gallows, called so from the hanging parts, architraves, or rather imposts . . . So that I doubt not, *Stonehenge* in *Saxon* signifies the hanging stones. . . . The old *Britons* or *Welsh* call *Stonehenge choir gaur*, which some interpret *chorea gigantum*, the giants dance: I judge, more rightly *chorus magnus*, the great choir, round church, or temple."[33] It is not difficult to conceive the chain of dire metamorphoses that Blake could extract from these innocuous (if dubious) etymologies: giants dancing in a ring (perhaps related to the giants' dance described in *J* 63.13ff.) are trans-

[30] *Philosophical Enquiry*, 77.

[31] See Aubrey Burl, *Prehistoric Avebury* (New Haven: Yale University Press, 1979), 3.

[32] William Stukeley, *Stonehenge: A Temple Restor'd to the British Druids* (London: W. Innys and R. Manby, 1740), 52 and 12. A "rocking stone" appears next to the immense trilithon depicted on plate 6 of *Milton*, closely modeled, it seems, on Stukeley's rendering of one of the solitary Longstones at Avebury, popularly known (provocatively enough for our context) as "Adam." See Burl, *Prehistoric Avebury*, 52.

[33] *Stonehenge*, 8.

formed into a circle of stone, which in turn becomes a temple and then a system of gallows, a place for the sacrifice or dis-animation of others. Once again, *aston*ishment astonishes.

Are these Druidic remains, then, the actual bodies of the old giants? Blake hints as much on plate 70 of *Jerusalem*, where the first thing that strikes the reader's eye is the design of the immense trilithon occupying the central two-thirds of the plate (see Figure 9). The next impression is formed by the first words on the plate:

> And this the form of mighty Hand sitting on Albions cliffs
> Before the face of Albion, a mighty threatning Form.
> His bosom wide & shoulders huge overspreading wondrous
>
> (*J* 70.1–3)

Even though the verbal description goes on to give Hand other attributes that the picture cannot match, one has already sufficiently noticed a resemblance between these "mighty threatning Forms," verbal and visual, to speculate that the trilithon renders Hand's portrait (there does appear to be a clifflike drop to the left of the trilithon). And if we are skeptical about this identification, Blake encodes other hints of the interchangeability of limbs and megaliths. Given his fondness for hidden verbal-visual punning, we are not wrong to suspect deliberate planning in his layout of the plate, so that its first words are "And this the form of," and the last, "the mighty limbs of Albion." If we take these first and last words of the plate as a kind of secret caption to the towering design that occupies the center, we find ourselves gazing at the limbs themselves in petrified form.

These hinted identifications tend to blur the distinction between two kinds of man-made remains descending from the past: the ruin proper, an architectural construction, and the statue, a model of the human form, presumably imitating the race of the builders. There is a further blurring of the lines between statues in the conventional sense, imitations hewn into definite form out of an inchoate mass, and statuelike objects that, in a kind of reversal of the Galatea myth, are not imitations at all but rather transformations of the bodies of the ancient giants themselves. These latter objects are not merely the representative tokens of ancient power but the material residues of that power. Blake's work affords such examples as Lot's Wife "rendered a Permanent Statue" (*VLJ*, E 556) and the Spectre of Urthona in *Vala*, who first appears "like a statue of lead / Bent by its fall from a high tower" (*FZ* 49.13–14). These are what Keats was to call, in reference to his own fallen Titans in *Hyperion*, "natural sculpture"—beings who have, without the intervention of art, come to resemble the ruins of art.

To summarize briefly, we may say that the ruins scattered about Blake's landscapes serve to magnify the abyss of time and, simultaneously, to abolish it, by memorializing and preserving powers that otherwise would long

And this the form of mighty Hand sitting on Albions cliffs
Before the face of Albion, a mighty threatning Form.

His bo om wide & shoulders huge overspreading wondrous
Bear Three strong sinewy Necks & Three awful & terrible Heads
Three Brains in contradictory council brooding incessantly.
Neither daring to put in act its councils, fearing each other.
Therefore rejecting Ideas as nothing & holding all Wisdom
To consist in the agreements & disagreements of Ideas.
Plotting to devour Albions Body of Humanity & Love.

Such Form the aggregate of the Twelve Sons of Albion took; & such
Their appearance when combind: but often by birth pangs & loud groans
They divide to Twelve: the key-bones & the chest dividing in pain
Disclose a hideous orifice: thence issuing the Giant-brood
Arise as the smoke of the furnace, shaking the rocks from sea to sea.
And there they combine into Three Forms, named Bacon & Newton & Locke,
In the Oak Groves of Albion which overspread all the Earth.

Imputing Sin & Righteousness to Individuals; Rahab
Sat deep within him hid: his Feminine Power unreveald.
Brooding Abstract Philosophy, to destroy Imagination, the Divine-
-Humanity. A Three-fold Wonder: feminine: most beautiful: Three-fold
Each within other. On her white marble & even Neck, her Heart
Inorbd and bonified: with locks of shadowing modesty, shining
Over her beautiful Female features, soft flourishing in beauty
Beams mild, all love and all perfection, that when the lips
Recieve a kiss from Gods or Men, a threefold kiss returns
From the pressd loveliness: so her whole immortal form three-fold
Three-fold embrace returns: consuming lives of Gods & Men
In fires of beauty melting them as gold & silver in the furnace
Her Brain enlabyrinths the whole heaven of her bosom & loins
To put in act what her Heart wills; O who can withstand her power
Her name is Vala in Eternity: in Time, her name is Rahab

The Starry Heavens all were fled from the mighty limbs of Albion

Figure 9. *Jerusalem* (Copy D), plate 70.

ago have departed. They sunder us from origins and make us leap back to them. Architectural remains take on the look of eroded statues, and statues once lived as giant men. An analogy with the process of the natural sublime is apt here; looking upon the present products of time's catastrophes, we think we descry external objects wrought by ancient makers when we are actually beholding the grandeurs of our earlier selves. Yet the nature of these earlier selves remains in question. If Blake is suggesting that ruins are not what they seem, that they are not the artifacts of ancient men, but rather the fossils of ancient men, he is at the same time more profoundly suggesting the equivalence of artifacts and fossils: to show man turning into his own artifacts or into a statue of himself is a shorthand way of criticizing (under the ironic guise of sublime transformation) the notion that art is a belated, externalized derivative of an originally artless self, something to be left behind like one's bones. This may explain, to return to an earlier example, why Job starts projecting lost, ruined cities about him, looking much like a proliferation of vertebrae, as soon as he begins to suffer spiritual death. Buildings become bones—and (in the typically compensatory program of the material sublime) bones become buildings, when one has forsaken one's true intellectual grandeur, which was to have once possessed all the arts in their fullness right from the beginning.

In the face of such ironies, one must wonder in what possible way these ruined statues and statuesque ruins memorialize original powers. The answer lies perhaps in Blake's conception of ancient culture, which seems to have been as rich in sculpture and magnificent architecture as the present scene is rich in ruins. We know, for instance, of his admiration for "all the grand works of ancient art," "those wonderful originals called in the Sacred Scriptures the Cherubim, which were sculptured and painted on walls of Temples, Towers, Cities, Palaces, and erected in . . . highly cultivated states" (DC, E 531). As Morton Paley has correctly observed, "the same sculptural forms which Blake envisages as having existed historically as the cherubim exist in an eternal present in the halls of Los, the Imagination, and all true artists render their works from these archetypes."[34] Paley refers, of course, to the famous passage in Jerusalem in which the poet tells us that "All things acted on Earth are seen in the bright Sculptures of / Los's Halls & every Age renews its powers from these Works" (J 16.61–62). The "wonderful original" sculptures of Los's Halls and the ruinous sculptural forms of latter days are related to one another by an inverse reciprocity; in Los's Halls, sculptures appear as antecedent to the acts of men and as the originators of all subsequent power, whereas those sculptures that have survived into our mundane time are merely the receptacles of antecedent power and memorialize the acts of men whose living vitality has long fled.

[34] Paley, "Wonderful Originals—Blake and Ancient Sculpture," 171.

Ruins offer reminiscences of life locked in the bondage of the artifact—but in so doing, they remind us through antithesis of that ancient time when living form was sculptural in its essence.

The sublimity of the ruin, like the tropes of the bardic sublime, depends for its effect on the discontinuity of metamorphosis, the migration of power from living to inanimate objects over time. In contrast, the sublime of the "wonderful originals" of human art depends on a different sort of discontinuity, the arrest of common sense notions in the realization that these forms do their living *as* artifacts. In the ancient culture, there is a coalescence of architecture, art image, and living form, in which none is perceived as somehow the fossil or imitation of any other. The Cherubim of the ancient cities reappear in the visionary city of Golgonooza, where they offer a most striking illustration of these paradoxical coalescences:

> The Western Gate fourfold, is closd: having four Cherubim
> Its guards, living, the work of elemental hands, laborious task!
> Like Men, hermaphroditic, each winged with eight wings
> That towards Generation, iron; that toward Beulah stone;
> That toward Ulro, clay: that toward Eden, metals.

> (*J* 13.6–10)

The other three gates of Golgonooza display similar curiosities, but these may serve as representative. First, the verses leave it to us to determine whether the Cherubim are part of the architecture of the city or part of its citizenry; as living guards they suggest the latter, but Blake could not have failed to know that the carved Cherubim of actual ancient Near Eastern cities often provided not only sculptural adornment but also structural support for the gates. Second, we are deliberately forced to confront a bold paradox; the Cherubim are specifically described as "living," and yet in the very next phrase, as "the work of elemental hands" and therefore sculptural artifacts, an assumption plainly reinforced by the nature of their composition: iron, stone, clay, metals. The "elemental hands" also offer a latitude of possibilities. Since they are elemental, they seem to exclude the spiritual hands of a creator-God on high, but they may include either human hands or the shapings of nature (cf. "the work of the elements"). Moreover, since there is a crude "elemental" character to the minerals that compose the Cherubim, and yet the latter are "Like Men," there is even a suggestion present that the Cherubim create themselves, living sculptures that beget sculptures. There is no easy way, in this instance, to disentangle nature from architecture, architecture from sculpture, or sculpture from sculptors. We are close here to a fundamental unity of man, his encompassing environment, and the makings that he himself encompasses.

Golgonooza is an ideal under construction—yet in its plan, Los and his golden builders preserve the memory of the earliest and best of historical human cultures, as Blake would have understood it. It is historical in the sense that he believed that such a culture actually existed in the past, but not historical in the sense that it left any ruins behind. Although there are a number of references in the poetry to Jerusalem's fallen pillars, the only visual ruins we are actually offered are crude, simple Druidic trilithons, never anything resembling the remains of intricately carved gates and winged statuary. This suggests that our very perception of ruins as ruins also alters the perception of the culture that produced it, so that we view that ancient culture under the sign of catastrophe, a displacement from its origins. Our eyes are all too well attuned to the evidences of this displacement to perceive much else of what lies beyond its scope. But as his work progresses, Blake seems ever more concerned to investigate these more distant and dimly perceived territories. In order to follow him, we should now turn from the artifacts to the artificers, and to the important theme of the ancient unitary culture to which they belonged—a national and historical theme, for this culture left behind not only its ruins but the divided nations and regions of our present state.

Chapter VI

THE SETTING OF THE DIVIDED NATIONS

THE ANTIQUARIAN SUBLIME

BLAKE'S CATALOG description of his painting of the Ancient Britons opens up into one of the most startling outbursts of visionary enthusiasm in his prose:

> The British Antiquities are now in the Artist's hands; all his visionary contemplations, relating to his own country and its ancient glory, when it was as it again shall be, the source of learning and inspiration. Arthur was a name for the constellation of Arcturus, or Bootes, the Keeper of the North Pole. And all the fables of Arthur and his round table; of the warlike naked Britons; of Merlin; of Arthur's conquest of the whole world; of his death, or sleep, and promise to return again; of the Druid monuments, or temples; of the pavement of Watling-street; of London stone; of the caverns in Cornwall, Wales, Derbyshire, and Scotland; of the Giants of Ireland and Britain; of the elemental beings, called by us by the general name of Fairies; and of these three who escaped, namely, Beauty, Strength, and Ugliness. Mr. B. has in his hands poems of the highest antiquity. Adam was a Druid, and Noah; also Abraham was called to succeed the Druidical age, which began to turn allegoric and mental signification into corporeal command, whereby human sacrifice would have depopulated the earth. All these things are written in Eden. (*DC*, E 542–43)

Nothing better suggests Blake's association of poetic enthusiasm with antiquarian speculation than the sublime disorder of this pell-mell rush of topics, this head-spinning mix of recondite oddities that are sure to bewilder the visitors to his little exhibition at the corner of Broad Street and Golden Square. The paragraph reads like an explosion of disparate particulars that the writer is trying to contain and compress back together into singularity. One gets an impression of an open-ended series of displacements, substitutions, and restitutions, of extremities separated and rejoined. What Britain was and what "it again shall be," Arthur's first reign and his "promise to return again," are identities separated by a temporal abyss that the writer scarcely recognizes. Arthur substitutes for Arcturus, man for constellation, and the constellation figures in the stars as the residual presence of the true Keeper of the Pole, whom we learn two paragraphs later is the "giant Albion . . . Patriarch of the Atlantic. . . . The stories of Arthur are the acts of Albion" [*DC*, E 543]). Corporeal command is substituted for allegoric signification, as the Druidical age is superseded by the patriarchal; in contrast, allegorical personifications (Beauty, Strength, and Ugliness) emerge out of a battle as substitutions for apparently historical men. Substitutions and displacements create a confusion of realms normally considered discrete: the human and the natural, the terrestrial and the celestial, the factual and the figurative. As in the sublime experience, our quest for a genuine origin, for a restitution of greatness, is whetted by our glimpse of it through veils of substitution or a misty swirl of fractured particles.

This study keeps returning to the account of the Ancient Britons because it provides the nexus between a theory of the sublime per se ("The Strong man represents the human sublime") and larger concerns in Blake's work that have to do with national identity and the reconstruction of history. When Blake tells us that the sublime (along with reason and pathos) alone escaped the wreck of a historical catastrophe (Arthur's last battle), he is suggesting that the modern aesthetic life (private appropriations of greatness, after a divisive encounter with a thwarting and overpowering agency) is a residue or perhaps a displacement of transactions enacted on the global scale of the whole race at that stage in its history when the plenitude of origins still remained infused in it. Thus the modern sublime, with its transfers of power from object to subject, reenacts and privatizes such events as the transfer of greatness over geographical space, as nations divided and migrations created new bastions of glory in regions far off. Conversely, these events are sublime, even in the conventional sense, and especially so as presented by the sources that meant the most to Blake.

SYNCRETIC MYTHOGRAPHY: HISTORY AS SUBLIME TRAUMA

"All these things" are written not only in Eden but also in the works of syncretic mythographers of Blake's century, such as Jacob Bryant, William Stukeley, Edward Davies, Henry Rowlands, Rowland Jones, and others. Their imaginative impact on Blake has long been recognized. Through their mediation, according to Edward Hungerford, "Blake's visions took him to the origin of things. He saw the giants of antediluvian creation, and he moved backward in time through epochs which had preceded man."[1]

---

[1] Edward Hungerford, *Shores of Darkness* (New York: Columbia University Press, 1941), 13. For other important accounts of Blake's debt to the mythographers, see Ruthven Todd, *Tracks in the Snow: Studies in English Science and Art* (London: Grey Wall Press, 1946); A. L. Owen, *The Famous Druids: A Survey of Three Centuries of English Literature on the Druids* (Oxford: Clarendon Press, 1962); and the brief but seminally influential passage in Frye, *Fearful Symmetry*, 173–76. For a recent general overview of European tendencies to mythographic syncretism in the period, see Rossi, *The Dark Abyss of Time*, 123–270.

Yet however much criticism acknowledges the influence of the mythographers on Blake, it has had relatively little to say about the nature of their enterprise that would explain Blake's thorough and pervasive assimilation of their assumptions, especially in his later work. The tenets of cultural syncretism, particularly the curious alignments drawn between Nordic or Celtic cultures and far-flung Oriental cultures, are often regarded as mere quasi-detachable, metaphoric vehicles for Blake—but if he were only looking for vehicles, he could have found others less recondite and fantastical. It is better to begin with the clear evidence that Blake shared the general premises, values, aims, and conclusions of the syncretists, and then to inquire what this evidence has to do with the poetics of the sublime that he hoped his works would exemplify. We know that as Blake comes closer to a conscious articulation of his work as "Sublime Allegory" or "the Most Sublime Poetry," the more the settings of the works themselves rely on cultural superimpositions dear to antiquarian speculation, and this connection cannot be purely accidental. Our task, then, is to re-perceive the work of the mythographers from a perspective that is primarily literary and, in particular, germane to the discourse of the sublime.

Apart from their importance to Blake, the mythographers offer more of interest to literary history than has generally been perceived. First of all, a taste for speculative mythography often went hand in hand with a taste for the sublime mode in literature, particularly the bardic and neoprimitivist developments of the mid-century. Thus, antiquarians such as Jacob Bryant and William Stukeley involved themselves in literary controversy by championing the authenticity of Ossian and Chatterton's Rowley, while Macpherson himself dabbled in Druidic antiquities and comparative religion. Later, Richard Payne Knight shows up in literary history as both an author of an important treatise dealing with the sublime and a publicist for the theories of the French syncretist d'Hancarville.[2] Examples of such crossings might easily be multiplied, and they suggest that there is something more intrinsic in the connection of the mythographers' enterprise to the literary sublime than just the mere contemporaneity of the two vogues.

Second, the antiquarian subject matter is often tailor-made for representation as a series of sublime scenes, with a special emphasis on grand moments that have always been the staple of sublime painting and poetical description. Thus, the antiquarians dwell repeatedly on the Old Testament's two most conspicuous icons of cataclysmic sublimity—the Flood and the soaring, ever-unfinished tower of Babel—to set in motion their

[2] On Bryant and Chatterton, see Lowery, *Windows of the Morning*, 173; see also Hungerford, *Shores of Darkness*, 11 (connection of Knight and d'Hancarville); Bailey Saunders, *Life and Letters of James Macpherson* (New York: Macmillan, 1895), 199 (Stukeley's interest in Ossian).

epic machinery of human sundering, cultural dispersion, and the reestablishment of saving remnants. It is not merely the presumed "historicity" of these images that fits them to these writers' requirements; much of their attraction to the mythographers probably lies, subliminally, in the way they schematize within themselves the main coordinates of a sublime discourse: in the Deluge, they find an image of indefinite, inhuman horizontal extension; in Babel, an image of intensive, vertical human "height"; and out of both, a drama of widening spaces, high aspirations, sudden dispossessions, and longed-for recoveries unfolds.[3]

Finally, the writings of the mythographers often resonate with a sublimity of their own. The splendid opening sentence of Bryant's *New System* is a small case in point: "It is my purpose in the ensuing work to give an account of the first ages; and of the great events, which happened in the infancy of the world."[4] The simple phrasing, the vatic cadence, the sweepingly generalized terms of reference conform to canons of sublimity that Longinus had applied to the first chapter of Genesis, and they catapult the reader into a chasm of time and of mystery too vast to be measured. In the mythographers' narration of events, one often encounters the same epic sweep, as in the account of ancient migrations in Henry Rowlands's *Mona*, a work devoted to showing that Britain was the original seat of the Patriarchal religion. Rowlands shows his postdiluvian tribes journeying through a Burkean or Urizenic landscape of "huge Desarts, and over dreadful Rocks and Mountains, . . . all the Land before them being one great continued Waste or Wilderness," but these grand impediments fail to curb their migratory zeal:

> The huge stupendous Mountains, intermix'd with dreadful amazing Dens on the Western side (now *Wales*) discourag'd not these bold Adventurers from accomplishing of that Discovery; the restless unbounded Desires of those who attempted Westerly to find an End or Utmost, and to possess new Acquests . . . carried them thro' all Difficulties and dangers.[5]

It is virtually impossible to miss Rowlands's wholesale appropriation of sublime diction, as applied conventionally to both objects ("huge stupendous" heights, "dreadful amazing" depths) and subjects ("restless un-

---

[3] It is worth noting that Blake's famous letter to Butts of 6 July 1803, in which he expounds his notions of "Sublime Allegory" and "the Most Sublime Poetry," begins with a reference in the first paragraph to "Nimrods tower which I conjecture to have spread over many Countries for he ought to be reckond of the Giant brood" (E 729). Does this recollection of the most conspicuous example of sublime thwarting on record, the most thorough baffling of aspirations focused on the achievement of material grandeur, influence Blake's definition, farther into the letter, of the greatest sublimity as that which "is altogether hidden from the Corporeal Understanding"?

[4] *New System* vol. 1, v.

[5] Henry Rowlands, *Mona Antiqua Restaurata* (Dublin: Robert Owen, 1723), 19 and 23.

bounded Desires," the quest for an "End or Utmost," the transcendence of "all Difficulties"). The sublimity, however, is more than a matter of rhetoric; it is, rather, intrinsic to the events described. In a pattern now familiar to us, a catastrophe or sundering (in this case, the aftermath of the Deluge) produces both the shape of the sublime obstructive landscape and the "unbounded" desire to overcome it, a desire to restore a formerly occluded greatness within "new Acquests," a newly possessed "all."[6]

Any of these tendencies and interests, more literary or imaginative than scholarly for the most part, would have drawn Blake to the mythographers' work. But perhaps their chief value to him lies in their quest for origins and, in particular, their relentless desire to link those origins to their own native culture, to the traditions of the British homeland in which they wrote. Nearly all the mythographers relevant to Blake were preoccupied, sometimes obsessed, by the need to find parallels between the presumed patriarchal culture of the ancient Middle East and that of Britain itself, or of Northern regions in general. This idea was not particularly new to the eighteenth-century syncretists; as A. L. Owen points out, the notion that the Celtic people were descended from Gomer, the grandson of Noah, appears as early as Camden's 1586 *Britannia*, and the Gomerian connection became a commonplace thereafter.[7] What is striking about the syncretic mythography of the eighteenth and early nineteenth centuries is how the stakes are raised. The inhabitants of the British Isles need no longer trace their connection to the hallowed culture of Abraham through the belated transmission of Christianity in late antiquity; instead, the researches of the antiquaries reveal that the ancient Britons shared this hallowed culture, that it was as native to them as to Abraham himself—and in some versions of this theme, the Britons appear not merely as peers to the patriarchal culture but ultimately as its predecessors and originators.

Stukeley, for example, argued that the British Druids emigrated to their island home "during the life of the patriarch *Abraham*, or very soon afterward. Therefore they brought along with them the *patriarchal religion*, which was . . . extremely like Christianity."[8] More boldly, Rowlands declares in *Mona* that "it seems to me that GOD in those antient Times, before he determin'd his *Schekinah* and Divine Presence unto the Mosaick Taber-

---

[6] Blake may have had in mind this passage about "unbounded Desires" and "possessing new Acquests" when in *Jerusalem* he gives an ironic twist to his old dictum that "The desire of Man being Infinite the possession is Infinite" (*NNR*[b]), as Albion declares, "My mountains are my own, and I will keep them to myself!" (*J* 4.29). In *Mona*, the "huge stupendous Mountains" are those of Snowdonia in North Wales, just short of the migrating tribe's ultimate destination, the Isle of Anglesey. "Plinlimmon & Snowdon" are among the mountains that Albion designates as his possessions (*J* 4.30).

[7] See *The Famous Druids*, 67.

[8] *Stonehenge*, 2. For evidence, he offers calculations designed to show that Stonehenge answers to the dimensions and proportions of Solomon's Temple (6–7).

nacles and the *Jewish* Temple, had his sacred Places in several parts of these Countries [i.e., the British Isles], where devout Men presented themselves before him."[9] Taking an even more radical stand, Francis Wilford attempted in his "Essay on the Sacred Isles of the West" (1805) and other works to prove that Britain was the site of the antediluvian culture, perhaps of the Garden of Eden itself,[10] while Rowland Jones maintained, in an astonishing series of treatises published between 1764 and 1773, that the tribes of Gomer, having escaped the confusion of tongues at Babel, preserved the original language of the world—which, for all intents and purposes, was English: English is "a language that is thus founded on revelation," and "the pretensions of the English language to universality, may be still further urged from its being in the abstract the mother of all the western dialects and the Greek, elder sister of the orientals, and in its concrete form, the living language of the Atlantics and the aborigines of Italy, Gaul and Britain."[11] Elsewhere, Jones strongly hints that God spoke English on that creating day when he called forth light from darkness, and that pictorial representations of this event survive in the shapes of the Roman alphabet of modern everyday use.[12] The stage was well prepared for Blake's dictum that "All things Begin & End in Albions Ancient Druid Rocky Shore" (*J* 27).

The mythographers, in short, made it their project not merely to discover the unitary origins of languages and cultures but also to connect the beginnings of time with its most recent limit, *our* time, and the far away with our native home.[13] In this regard, as in others, they reveal their fascination with extremes, with the peripheries of history and geography, rather than with centers. In what seems to be yet another manifestation of the sublime sensibility, the more inaccessible the actualities of the ancient

[9] *Mona*, 228. One hardly needs to spell out the relevance of this notion to Blake's relocation of Jerusalem to England's green and pleasant land.

[10] See Todd, *Tracks in the Snow*, 34–35.

[11] Rowland Jones, "Remarks on the Circles of Gomer," *The Circles of Gomer* (London: S. Crowder, 1771), 30 and 31.

[12] Jones reminds us that "the deity appears to have made use of a form of speech, previous to the formation of Adam, in giving names to the several parts of the creation," and that he taught this language (elsewhere specified as English) to the first man; see *The Origin of Languages and Nations* (London: J. Hughes, 1764), "Preface," B2. The whole of Jones's last treatise *The IO-Triads; or The Tenth Muse* (London: privately printed, 1773) is devoted to showing how the Roman alphabet pictorially encapsulates the origins and nature of the world.

[13] Discussing Stonehenge, the chief British specimen of the epoch that attracts the antiquarians' interest, Martin Price comments on the monument's function as an icon of the sublime: "the pastness of Stonehenge is of a profound sort; it is more mysterious and suggestive than that of a classical monument, and it is also more intimately related to the English present. This peculiar mixture of remoteness and nearness, of otherness and identity, is extremely important" ("The Sublime Poem," 201).

cultures under study may be, and the more improbable the connection between their widely sundered offshoots, the grander and more momentous
these obscurities appear to the mythographers. Their haunts are the fringes
of the European world. Gathering strength throughout the eighteenth
century, there is a kind of Chaldaic craze, a preoccupation with the ancient
East, that runs in tandem with a craze for the antiquities of the near Northern strands that the mythographers call home. To speak metaphorically,
the mythographers fix their gaze on twin figures, placed high on opposite
ridges, who gaze on one another like mirror images: a Druid bard on one
side and a Chaldaic or Hebraic patriarch on the other. One figure brings
with it the charisma of revealed religion, the other, the charisma of a *genius
loci*, a ghostly ancestral presence on one's own native soil. The deep purpose of the mythographers, the hidden guidance system that moves the
vast unscientific machinery of their scholarship, is their imaginative desire
to unite these two charismas and to heal the effects of what they perceive
to be an ancient cultural trauma.

The metaphor proposed in the preceding, of bardic and patriarchal
twins situated on widely separated ridges, presupposes a yawning gap or
rift valley between them. In geographical terms, this valley represents the
European continent and the Mediterranean world, which separate the
Northern lands from the Middle East. For the mythographers, these expanses were literal evidences of rift, for they measured the vast distances of
migration and dispersal following the sundering of the unitary language at
Babel. In cultural terms, the rift is occupied by Greco-Roman civilization,
which interposes its own authority between the North and its patriarchal
origins, and indeed makes of the North no more than a peripheral and
belated satellite of a metropolitan classicism. The mythographers persistently endeavor, therefore, to depress the prestige and authority of classical
sources and even to find a kind of sublimity in this endeavor. Thus James
Parsons, in his curious but not unrepresentative *Remains of Japhet*, declares,
"the education of the youth of all *Europe* consists in the study of the *Greek*
and *Latin* classics; . . . I had recourse to *Holy Writ*, and to the *Irish* records,
and there found sufficient matter to carry me many links higher, to a summit which produced me better prospects and clearer views of what I sought
after."[14] Nothing better illustrates the mind-set of many of these syncretists
than the unconscious effrontery in which "Holy Writ and the Irish records" are placed on a par with one another, the latter successfully out-
weighing all the Greek and Roman classics. Since Parsons is offering an
account of a struggle against a blocking greatness (the classical prestige)
and a restitution of power to its true, if long obscured, originators, his

[14] James Parsons, *The Remains of Japhet: Being Historical Enquiries Into the Affinity and
Origin of the European Languages* (London, 1767), 364.

resort to sublime imagery, to summits won and expanses of vision gained, is a particularly revealing touch.

Thus when Blake speaks of the "Stolen and Perverted Writings of Homer & Ovid: of Plato & Cicero" (*M* 1), when he insists that "The Greek Muses are daughters of Mnemosyne, or Memory and not of Inspiration" (*DC*, E 531), or when he exclaims that "it is the Classics . . . that Desolate Europe with Wars" (*On Homer's Poetry*, E 270), he is, in his own colorful way, saying no more than the mythographers had implied before him. That versatile man of letters John Cleland speaks of "the falsities with which the Greeks usually adulterated all their history," and Parsons alludes to "the *Greeks*, who were ever fond of the invention or mutilation of facts, as they were ignorant of their own origin, and of great prejudices to other nations." In a similar vein, Bryant implies that the Greeks were ignorant, blundering copiers of earlier cultures' sacred lore: "I have repeatedly taken notice, that the Grecians formed a variety of personages out of titles and terms unknown: many also took their rise from hieroglyphics misinterpreted."[15] A number of the syncretists, Bryant chief among them, insisted that Greek myths are distorted memories of early Old Testament history. Thus, he finds in the figure of Noah "the original Zeus," "the original of Prometheus," and the model for Cronus, who likewise divided the world among his three sons.[16] Bryant is not confused in his attributions; rather, he is trying to reveal Greek mythology not merely as a distortion of ancient truth but as a fractured distortion. The Grecian pantheon is composed of multiple shadows cast by single archetypal figures. The inference is that the Greeks could not even invent their own manifestly fictitious mythology or get correctly what they borrowed from others.

It is, of course, understandable that these writers, most of them Christian divines, should prefer Hebraic to Grecian teachings for their key to all mythologies. More noteworthy is their willingness to accept a distinctly Northern tutelage, with an attendant effect of further humiliation to classical prestige. Some of the mythographers claimed that classical civilization, so far from bestowing a patrimony on the Gothic North (as writers of the earlier Enlightenment had maintained), was in fact itself a derivative of early Northern wisdom. Thus, Stukeley tells us that from the Druids "the *Pythagoreans*, *Platonists*, and *Greek* philosophers learn'd the best things they knew"; in *Celtic Researches*, Edward Davies makes it clear that these teachers were *Northern* Druids: "The legitimate *Apollo* of *Grecian* worship," he says, is "an accredited *Hyperborean*," and "the philosophy of *Greece*, originated in the *Celtae*"; Parsons claims that Celtic migrations from Britain

---

[15] John Cleland, *The Way to Things by Words and Words by Things* (London: L. Davis and C. Reymers, 1766), 55; Parsons, *Remains of Japhet*, 48; Bryant, *New System* vol. 3, 361.

[16] See, respectively, *New System* vol. 2, 8; vol. 3, 432; vol. 4, 19–20.

gave rise to all the Indo-European languages and cultures of the continent.[17] Plainly, then, the prestige of Greek culture (and, *a fortiori*, the manifestly derivative Roman) is unearned; it is a second-rate culture trying to pass itself off as first-rate, a supposedly rich patron who turns out in fact to be a parasitical poor relation.

All this anticlassical condescension, coming from men of formidable classical learning, requires some sort of explanation that goes beyond the mythographers' stated aims of finding common linguistic and cultural roots. If one stands back from the content of the syncretic program—Druids, Greeks, the Deluge, Babel—and concentrates instead on its tone and governing method, certain important features emerge. The tone is filled with the scorn and defiance that accompanies rebellion against received authority,[18] and the method depends on the principle of displacement as the key to understanding origins and historical outcomes. Thus, Grecian achievements are displaced patriarchal wisdom, the Eastern patriarchy is displaced Druidism, and the Indo-European tongues displaced forms of native English. The mythographers, moreover, postulate trauma (Babel or the Flood) as the root of displacement and the scattering of memory. Unlike the classical model of cultural development, in which there is a steady uniform accretion of knowledge from the primitive to the civilized states—the model expounded, to cite a familiar example, by Pope in the *Essay on Man*—in the mythographers' model, history proceeds by trauma, a dismembering of the unitary group, followed by misremembering. In this scheme, the misremembered (that is, classical learning) establishes a prestige based on false claims to primacy and creates a false consciousness about origins. The work of the mythographer, then, not unlike that of the psychoanalyst, is to recover memory repressed at the moment of trauma by removing the massive blocking agents that stand in the way.

Whatever the mythographers consciously believed they were trying to achieve, their attitudes, presuppositions, and methods all appear to be stamped with the hallmark of thinking in the sublime mode. The restless urge to push beyond the bounds of received opinion, the confrontation with a blocking greatness that must be reduced and transcended, the recovery of an anterior greatness that turns into a sort of homecoming, as whatever is most ancient is enlisted to renew the glory of the diminished here and now—all these tendencies compose a familiar pattern. As scholars, the mythographers failed because they based their "factual foundations" on what were not facts at all but rather fantasies of cultural wish-

---

[17] See Stukeley, *Stonehenge*, "Preface," n. pag.; Davies, *Celtic Researches*, 182 and 184; and Parsons, *Remains of Japhet*, 48.

[18] This antiauthoritarian stance extends as well to the mythographers' handling of scholarly sources; as Hungerford notes, in their work "recondite notions buried in the most obscure of writings became more important than the usual and the well known" (*Shores of Darkness*, 15).

fulfillment. Their real achievement, as Frye sees it, was to create "a morphology of symbolism"[19]—but perhaps the morphology they instituted may turn out to have less to do with static symbols and more with dynamic sequences, patterns of antithetical power-exchanges, that have as their model the exchanges of the sublime moment. This, at any rate, appears to be what Blake most profoundly derived from their influence.

BLAKE'S ADAPTATIONS OF THE SYNCRETIC ENTERPRISE

Blake may have believed—and indeed probably did believe—in the historical accuracy of many of the antiquarian assertions. At the same time, it would be a misconception to think of him as just another mythographer or even as a syncretist of all syncretisms. It is true that when he speaks of "Albion our Ancestor patriarch of the Atlantic Continent whose History Preceded that of the Hebrews & in whose Sleep or Chaos Creation began" (*VLJ*, E 558), the reader is tempted to believe that vast revelations are at hand and that eager efforts to piece this together with similar remarks scattered elsewhere in Blake's later writings will yield a syncretic whole. But such a reader will have no more luck in eliciting a coherent history of origins from these hints than other students of Blake have had in their attempts to reduce his work to an orderly system. What Blake offers through the influence of the antiquarians is not a composite set of historical "facts," but rather an instinctive understanding of the story of origins, trauma, and repressive displacement as an outwardly projected manifestation of sublime discourse.

Thus, when Blake borrows from the mythographers, he does so eclectically, caring little for the details of their systems and still less for a harmonization of these details. Sometimes we can catch him in the minor carelessness of endorsing conflicting mythographic sources. For example, in plate 27 of *Jerusalem*, following Stukeley, he includes Abraham in a list of Druid patriarchs and identifies Druidism with the "Patriarchal Religion." But in the *Descriptive Catalogue*, Blake tells us that "Adam was a Druid, and Noah; also Abraham was called to *succeed* the Druidical age" (E 542–43; my emphasis); here he is drawing on such sources as Jones's *Circles of Gomer* or Parsons's *Remains of Japhet*, which postulate an antediluvian date for the Celtic antiquities and a withdrawal of the Druid tribes to Britain before the catastrophe of Babel and the rise of Abraham's Chaldaic culture. This sort of inconsistency occurs within the individual works of the mythographers themselves, and, taken in isolation, is of small importance. Taken, however, in the context of Blake's disposition of settings as a whole,

---

[19] *Fearful Symmetry*, 174.

where Northern scenes are typically presented as severed from and yet inescapably connected to biblical scenes, this indeterminacy of dating points to something symptomatic. History and the geographical separations that its events impose are not, for Blake, the products of unique, fixed points in a marmoreally unalterable record of past time. Rather, the pattern of a traumatic separation from origins settles freely on any given cluster of events, so that any event seems as properly the site of the original crisis as any other, and no event may appropriate to itself the privilege of absolute priority.

Thus, the crucial event, the trauma of Britain's separation from the biblical lands, is something that is not really datable in Blake's works, because it seems to occur at different and incompatible points along the chronological line of conventional history. Blake hints at a point of separation as recent as the Babylonian captivity, for his elaborate equations of the counties of Britain with the tribes of Israel in *Jerusalem* depend on the widely prevalent theory that the Britons are descended from the Ten Lost Tribes scattered after the fall of the Temple, a position traceable in part to Blake's contemporary and fellow enthusiast Richard Brothers.[20] Alternatively, the separation may have occurred through migrations at the time of Abraham, as Stukeley maintained, if we accept one Blakean text that calls Abraham a Druid, or earlier, at the time of the scattering of the nations at Babel, if we accept a different text, one that calls Abraham a successor to the Druidical Age. Earlier still, there is the separation caused by the Flood, often conflated with the myth of the sinking of Atlantis both in the work of the mythographers and implicitly at various points in Blake's work. If Albion, who is Britain personified, is also "patriarch of the Atlantic Continent"— that is, Atlantis—then the trauma of severance consists in Britain's reduction by flood from a unitary continental status to an insular remnant.[21] If one wants to push the origins of the split farther back, one finds oneself in the midst of Albion's pre-Adamic history, that "Sleep or Chaos" in which "Creation began." But even here, one has not discovered origins except in some *pro forma* sense, for this Chaos is homologous with all its subsequent forms—the crumbling of Temples, the dispersion of nations, the confounding of languages, the drowning of continents—and differs from

---

[20] See Morton D. Paley, "William Blake, the Prince of the Hebrews, and the Woman Clothed with the Sun," in *William Blake: Essays in Honour of Sir Geoffrey Keynes*, ed. Morton D. Paley and Michael Phillips (Oxford: Clarendon Press, 1973), 260–93.

[21] Blake could have discovered in John Cleland's explanation of the Flood, based partly on natural catastrophism, partly on revisionist cultural syncretism, grounds for his own myth of geographical separation: "Thus it was, that all correspondence of the north-west part of Europe became cut off. This was historically expressed in the Egyptian annals by Atlantis, an island of immense extent, being swallowed up by an earthquake, with all its inhabitants, which probably means no more than a natural or moral separation of Britain, perhaps both, from the continent" (*The Way to Things by Words*, 11–12).

them only as a general term differs from its particular exemplifications. To use some familiar terminology of the deconstructionist era, the fissure has always already happened, and the primal event is known finally to be undetectable in history precisely because history displays so many versions of it, so many scenes of apparent origin that turn out to be no more than painted veils parting to reveal something further back. Blake's technique of eclectic, self-contradicting borrowings from mythographic sources serves not to create an all-embracing final version of truth but to reinforce a paradigm of the historical process—a process that significantly coincides with the dynamic of the sublime.

The mythographers, then, empower Blake to create settings that contribute less to a precise doctrinal content than they do to an aesthetic effect. The cultural and geographical juxtapositions of which the poet is so fond, particularly in his later work, function to expose the reader to recessive vistas of time's abyss. At the same time, these juxtapositions propagate a similar consciousness of space, although not space presented as a serene field or uniform volume, but rather as a jarring discontinuity, a widening fissure or wound. For this reason, in many of the passages in which Blake mingles English or Northern with biblical place names, there is anything but a sense of a recovery of blissful unitary origins:

> . . . Come thou to Ephraim! behold the Kings of Canaan!
> The beautiful Amalekites, behold the fires of youth
> Bound with the Chain of Jealousy by Los & Enitharmon;
> The banks of Cam: cold learnings streams: Londons dark-frowning towers;
> Lament upon the winds of Europe in Rephaims Vale.
>
> (M 19.36–40)

> Till Canaan rolld apart from Albion across the Rhine: along the Danube
> And all the Land of Canaan suspended over the Valley of Cheviot
> From Bashan to Tyre & from Troy to Gaza of the Amalekite
>
> (J 63.41–43)

> The Wound I see in South Molton S[t]reet & Stratford place
> Whence Joseph & Benjamin rolld apart away from the Nations
> In vain they rolld apart; they are fixd into the Land of Cabul
>
> (J 74.55–57)

Part of the unpleasant effect of these passages comes from their dolorous tone, their ambience of cold, darkness, frowning, lament, wounds, and futility. But, the tone aside, the interfusion of widely separated regions contributes to the effect by disorienting the reader. Paradoxically, by bringing disparate places together, Blake manages to estrange them from us all the more thoroughly, removing the very ground beneath our feet and leaving us suspended—much as Asiatic Canaan hangs ominously over Northern Cheviot.

In these passages, the relation of Albion's land to the biblical land, their original unity, is presented as a phantasmagoric dance of condensations and partings, like the fleeting fragments of memory and recognition found in nightmares and states of delirium. From one persective, space yawns like the fissures of the abyss in Burnet's accounts of the Deluge. Like Joseph and Benjamin, Canaan "roll[s] apart" from Albion, and the event is presented as if it were a natural flood coursing down the chief river valleys of Europe (also the principal routes of human migration, according to a number of the mythographers). In this perspective, the European continent, itself devoid of significant interest, becomes a kind of trough or conduit for metaphoric winds and waterways of traumatic parting and even more traumatic memory, as it forms a wide gap between two newly fixed darknesses, London's "dark-frowning towers" in the Northwest and dark Cabul to the South and East.[22] From a different perspective, there is no parting after the trauma, and the separated nations continue to inhabit the same space, but only in the way that unwelcome nightmares inhabit the space of the sleeping mind. Thus Canaan hovers over Cheviot like a bat-spectre, and Blake sees the wound made by the sundered Nations on the street where he lives. Conversely, London's towers and Cambridge's halls of scholarship cannot stay where they are; they cannot escape the ghostly memorials of Rephaim's Vale[23] but are perpetually borne back into it on the East-seeking winds of mournful recollection.

Far from liberating the settings of his later poetry from the pressures of geography, as is often assumed, Blake actually forces us, in his distinctive way, to experience these pressures more acutely. The redistribution of nations after catastrophic separation is rendered as either a grotesquely accelerated widening of space or a defamiliarizing superimposition of the scattered parts, in which each separate place, bereft of its normal contiguities and supplied with strange ones, seems all the more painfully its own isolated and fragmented self. Geography is sensed only when such separations are sensed. Once sensed, however, geographical distinctions facilitate the poet's delineations of those oppositions, confrontations, and unequal

---

[22] The "dark land of Cabul," a disagreeable region of Galilee (see 1 Kings 9.13), is Jerusalem's own place of exile when she is cast off as Albion's Emanation (see *J* 79.63 and 27.51–52: "He witherd up Jerusalems Gates, / And in a dark Land gave her birth").

[23] As S. Foster Damon informs us, "The Rephaim ('ghosts') were the original inhabitants of Canaan, Edom, Moab, and Ammon. The invading Israelites called them giants. . . . According to the Jewish mythology, [the Vale of Rephaim] was the final dwelling-place of the ghosts of the wicked giants"; see *A Blake Dictionary*, 346. It is not difficult to connect these associations of fallen giants, preserved as ghosts, to the underlying story of the divided and comatose giant Albion.

distributions of power and privileges that mark the domain of the sublime. They enable Blake to follow the course of the mythographers and set the geographical extremities against the center, one extremity against the other, and, of these extremities, one of them against itself. In this process, it is the North particularly, segregated as a separate cultural space by the parting of nations, that comes to receive a special emphasis. In the unending competition to wear the mantle of the sublime, Northern and Asiatic settings are allied against the orthodoxy of classical grandeur, but it quickly appears that these settings are themselves in opposition: the North localizes to better effect the Burkean sublime of obscurity, turbulence, and natural greatness, while the East localizes the Intellectual sublime of textual determinacy and plenitude.[24] Finally, the terms of this opposition reproduce themselves within the Northern setting itself, which presents an ambivalent face throughout the whole of Blake's career, sometimes appearing as the focal scene of whatever is barren and unregenerate, and sometimes as the preserve of original powers of culture and creativity.

THE SUBLIME OF THE NORTH: REPUDIATION AND RESTORATION

In dealing with the Northern setting, Blake's challenge is twofold. First, he must accommodate the traumatizing fact of cultural disjunction and its disorienting, nightmarish recollections with the gratifying message taught by the antiquarians that the disjunction works in favor of his own northerly neighborhood. An inspiring native pride and self-esteem grow from the knowledge that the original site of human greatness was at least *here* and not *there*, not somewhere else far off; without the disjunction, there could be no such local satisfaction. Second, Blake must confront the fact that the sublimity he would like to invest in the Northern setting must displace a sublimity that already occupies it, a sublimity of the wrong sort. Ever since the success of Thomson's "Winter," the North becomes the privileged site of the natural sublime of darkness, deprivation, and terror, as the young Blake well knows:

> O Winter! bar thine adamantine doors:
> The north is thine; there hast thou built thy dark
> Deep-founded habitation.
>
>   ("To Winter," lines 1–3)

[24] Since these regional contraries are in fact aligned on a geographically diagonal axis, the conventional terms "North" and "East" must awkwardly serve as oppositional terms here. Part of the terminological problem stems from Blake's derogation of the classical center, Greece and Italy, which is conventionally South to the North of British or Celtic lands and West to the lands of the Bible.

Blake's problem is to find a way of capitalizing on the North's reputation for sublimity, garnered through eighteenth-century nature poetry, while jettisoning the associations of desolation, material obstructiveness, and cultural barrenness that go with it.

In facing these challenges, Blake was offered a precedent in the Ossianic poems, in which Macpherson attempted a pervasive accommodation of the modern taste for sublime natural gloom with his own sense of the North's antique cultural prestige. In a series of cunning substitutions, Macpherson develops this prestige by importing biblical cadences wholesale into his Northern chants, while suppressing the Hebraic specifics they once graced. This spiritually evocative style is then subjected to all the gloom, damp, and storminess of an insistent Northern setting. Such an uneasy marriage of style and setting, drawn respectively from the antipodal peripheries of mainstream European culture, does not entirely succeed in masking the incongruities it seeks to yoke together. With a far more secure poetic instinct than Macpherson's, even in the early work of *Poetical Sketches*, Blake dramatizes his conflicting interests and allegiances by posing them as dialectical alternatives, rather than trying to blend them together. Thus, he opens his Seasons poems, in "To Spring," by saturating "our clime" (line 8) with a flood of tropes commonly acknowledged to reflect the style of the Psalms and the Song of Songs, and he closes the sequence with Northern, Thomsonian tropes in "To Winter."[25] Or, against the harsh, objectified terrors of the Burkean sublime in that poem, he poses a subjective, assertive, yet equally Northern countersublime in "To Summer":

> Our bards are fam'd who strike the silver wire:
> Our youth are bolder than the southern swains:
>
> (lines 14–15)[26]

By keeping the locus of true greatness in a kind of tense suspension (East/South or West/North? Northern terrors or Northern boldness?), Blake

---

[25] Geoffrey Hartman has suggested that "To Winter" formally represents "a genuine poetry of the North," and he sees the young Blake "at the center of intersecting visions of historical progress"—one involving the spread of creativity from the cultured East, the other involving the spread of Northern vigor outward from its own bastion; see "Blake and the Progress of Poesy," *Beyond Formalism* (New Haven: Yale University Press, 1970), 202 and 203. For a closely argued view of "To Winter," which, although differing from Hartman's, also sees it in dialectical opposition to the other "Seasons" poems, see Robert F. Gleckner, *Blake's Prelude: "Poetical Sketches"* (Baltimore: Johns Hopkins University Press, 1982), 69–75.

[26] Cf. Richard Hurd on the same subject: "We are upon enchanted ground, my friend. . . . The glympse, you have had of it [i.e., Northern European literature], will help your imagination to conceive the rest. And without more words you will readily apprehend that the fancies of our modern bards are not only more gallant, but, on a change of the scene, more sublime, more terrible, more alarming than those of the classic fablers" (*Letters on Chivalry and Romance* [London: A. Millar, 1762], 54–55).

maintains the element of conflict so necessary to the sublime dynamic, with its point of confrontation and its ever-shifting aggregations of power.

After the experimental period of *Poetical Sketches*, with its ambivalent treatment of the Northern scene, Blake's career follows a course that first relegates the North to the disparaged sphere of the Burkean sublime, then partially rehabilitates this sphere and the scene that comes with it, and finally restores the North to its place as the home of origins, detached from the conventional sublime of postcatastrophic greatness. Thus, the ambivalence remains but is displayed over the stretch of Blake's whole career. In the later Lambeth books, for instance, the North is presented as the scene of dismal catastrophe. Urizen is first relegated by the Eternals to "a place in the north" (*BU* 2.3), and then he proceeds to become a deity whose antecedents are to be found in Thomson's "Winter," with accompanying Nordic connections, as mediated by Ossian.[27] In the *Book of Ahania*, Blake goes so far as to emphasize the northerliness of his setting for the catastrophic events of the poem, by effecting a deliberate clash of opposing Northern and biblical voices. The main plot of the work, depicting the *agon* of Fuzon and Urizen, draws its imagery (some biblical allusions notwithstanding) primarily from a repertoire of motifs from Norse mythology, all of which Blake could have found in a few consecutive pages of Mallet's redactions of the Prose Edda in *Northern Antiquities*.[28] In the midst of this *Sturm und Drang*, there suddenly intrudes the elegiac voice of Ahania, whose reminiscences of unfallen days are couched in the imagery of the Song of Solomon.[29] The antithesis of fallen gloom and un-

---

[27] Cf. the description of Urizen, cited in the previous chapter, in which "his ten thousands of thunders / Rang'd in gloom'd array stretch out across / The dread world, & the rolling of wheels / As of swelling seas, sound in his clouds / In his hills of stor'd snows, in his mountains / Of hail & ice" (*BU* 3.28–33), with Thomson's description of King Winter in *The Seasons*:

> Here the grim tyrant meditates his wrath;
> Here arms his winds with all-subduing frost;
> Moulds his fierce hail, and treasures up his snows,
> With which he now oppresses half the globe.
>
> ("Winter," lines 898–901)

Cf. also, in terms of action and diction, Fuzon's confrontation with Urizen, in plate 2 of *Ahania*, with the remarkably similar confrontation of Fingal and the Spirit of Loda in the Ossianic poem "Carric-thura" (*Poems of Ossian* vol. 1, 60–62). In a note, Macpherson explicitly identifies Loda with the chief of the Norse gods Odin.

[28] In the second and third chapters of *Ahania*, the sequence of Urizen's struggle with a serpent, his piercing of the beautiful youth Fuzon with a spear tipped with the serpent's venom, and the youth's subsequent crucifixion, appears to condense and modify a similar sequence in the Prose Edda (Fables 27, 28, and 31), in which Thor the thunder-god struggles with the Midgard Serpent, Baldur the beautiful is pierced with the poisonous mistletoe, and Loki the rebel, bound on pointed rocks, continously suffers the burning venom of serpents. See Mallet, *Northern Antiquities* vol. 2, 134–58.

[29] See, e.g., the following:

fallen bliss pointedly comes across as an antithesis of poetic voices, the voice of the cloudy North and West meeting that of the sunny East and South.

The voice of the North, however, soon regains its privileges as the source of an authentic sublime. In *Vala*, Blake appears less intent on imposing an outside judgment of the North's pretensions to sublimity than on assuming its characteristic vision as his own. With *Vala* principally in mind, Harold Bloom has suggested that Blake's "own true Sublime comes in . . . a Northern [mode], in the traditions of the Icelandic Eddas."[30] Without detailing the many parallels in plot and imagery between *Vala* and the Eddas, one may focus on the title of the poem and its opening line. "The Song of the Aged Mother which shook the heavens with wrath" immediately suggests affinities with the famous *Völuspá* (literally "Song of the Prophetess") of the Elder Edda and, like it, proves to be an epic chant of the origin and fate of the gods, of shadowy beginnings and apocalyptic consummations. The "Aged Mother" herself suggests the Earth-mother or "Mother of the giant brood" who prophesies to Odin in Gray's "Descent of Odin" (line 86), a poem based on a text closely related to the *Völuspá*. It is likely that Blake originally intended Vala herself to fulfill this sibylline role, for her name is perhaps linked etymologically to the Norse word for "sibyl" (some nineteenth-century glossaries offer *vola* or *vala* as interchangeable translations),[31] and the earliest decipherable readings of the opening of his poem

---

Swell'd with ripeness & fat with fatness
Bursting on winds my odors,
My ripe figs and rich pomegranates
In infant joy at thy feet
O Urizen, sported and sang

(BA 5.24–28)

The resemblance to the Song of Solomon is noted in Bloom, *Blake's Apocalypse*, 194.

[30] This seminal insight is tucked away in the headnotes of an undergraduate text, *The Oxford Anthology of English Literature*, ed. Frank Kermode, John Hollander, et al., 2 vols. (New York: Oxford University Press, 1973), vol. 2, 12. See also Bloom's comparison, in the same text, of the opening lines of Night IX of *Vala* with Fable 32 ("The Twilight of the Gods") of the Prose Edda as rendered in Mallet's *Northern Antiquities*. Regarding these passages, Bloom says, "The unique tone of Night IX stems from its displacement of the Hebrew-Christian account of the Last Things into this world of a Northern Apocalypse, where even finality is not quite final" (vol. 2, 75).

[31] Frye, *Fearful Symmetry*, 270, derives the name Vala from Vola, mentioned by Mallet as the prophetess who chants the *Völuspá* (*Northern Antiquities* vol. 2, 202). In *William Blake's "Vala": A Numbered Text* (Oxford: Clarendon Press, 1956), H. M. Margoliouth disputes this derivation (xviii) but evidently ignores the manuscript erasures that suggest Blake's early intention to make Vala the singer of the entire mythic cycle to follow. Furthermore, in the editor's notes to "The Descent of Odin" in the 1778 edition of Gray's poetry (and in various subsequent editions), Blake could have discovered yet another name for the Earth-mother prophetess—Volva—which, given a resemblance to *vulva* that Blake is not likely to have missed, would deftly connect Gray's sibyl with the genitally sexual symbolism associated with Vala in the poem as we have it (see *The Poems of Mr. Gray*, ed. W. Mason, 4 vols. [London:

suggest that Blake twice wanted to call it the "Book of Vala" (see "Textual Notes," E 819) before he finally settled for the more vague "Aged Mother." While traces of Vala's putative role as a mother of giants survives in both *Vala* itself and *Jerusalem*, it is plausible to assume that Blake conceived of her originally as a chthonic voice rather than a dramatic character and that the whole poem is her "Song"—that is to say, her vision (an assumption that makes better sense of her title role than her sporadic appearances in the story itself can do). If that is the case, then it is significant that the vision is conceived as a Northern one in its setting, sources, and literary mediations. In *Vala*, Blake seems to regard the Northern sublime not as something to satirize, as in *Urizen*, or from which to flee in an Orientalizing nostalgia, as in *Ahania*, but to employ as the most sensitive instrument for registering the shadowiness of origins, the conflicts of strengths, and the exchanges of power and loss that, in the abstract, mark the dynamic of the sublime generally.

A more obvious indicator of Blake's northward drift in *Vala* is the gradually emergence of Urthona as the true hero of the poem. It is not uncommon to discern a "north" contained anagrammatically in Urthona's name—and in *Vala*, the connection is explicitly made between Urthona and the North, conceived as incorporating the terrific blocking agencies of the Burkean sublime: "North stood Urthonas stedfast throne a World of Solid darkness / Shut up in stifling obstruction" (FZ 74.17–18). The name itself, however, like other invented proper names in Blake, probably originated in some other proper name—either of the poet's own contrivance or discovered in a literary source—and only gradually attracted, through its phonetic or orthographic character, certain secondary associations. The likely source in this case is northerly enough; in Ossian's "Cath-loda," we encounter "U-THORNO, hill of storms" and learn that it is the mountain fastness of Loda (Odin), the baleful Northern deity of the Ossianic cycle.[32] In short, the model for Urthona came to Blake as a place, not a person, and traces of this influence appear in the earliest references, in which the status of the figure as person or place is sometimes unclear (see "Urthona's

---

J. Dodsley, T. Cadell, J. Todd, 1778], vol. 1, 153). Finally, it is greatly worth inquiring what Scandinavian lexical information was available to Blake. Just twenty years after Blake's death, in his revised edition of *Northern Antiquities*, I. A. Blackwell states in his Glossary to the Eddas that "The Old N. has two generic terms for a sybil or prophetess—Volva and Vala," and he claims elsewhere that "all Teutonic nations appear to have had their Valas or prophetesses" (P. H. Mallet, *Northern Antiquities*, new ed., ed. I. A. Blackwell [London: Bohn's Antiquarian Library, 1847], 570 and 363n). A century or so after Gray's poem, Odin's descent to the Earth-mother is replayed in another great Northern prophetic epic: In act 3 scene 1 of Wagner's *Siegfried*, Wotan's first words to Erda are "Wache, Wala!" ("Vala, awaken").

[32] *Poems of Ossian* vol. 1, 29 and 14. Kathleen Raine has noted the name resemblance and discusses aspects of the Ossianic connection in *Blake and Tradition*, 2 vols. (Princeton: Princeton University Press, 1968), vol. 1, 244–46).

dens" in "A Song of Liberty" [*MHH* 25.16], or "the pillars of Urthona" [*Am* 1.16]).

As Urthona becomes more fully personified (a process that first gets underway in earnest in *Vala*), he nonetheless retains some of the characteristics of a mountain bastion, particularly in his Spectral form, in which obstructiveness and repulsion are the chief manifestations of his strength (see his spectacular attempt to block Urizen's path in Night VI (75.5–24, where topographical qualities—"the four Cliffs of Urthona" [75.22]—still seem to cling). "Strong Urthona" is, of course, a constant epithet in Blake's work from early to late (see *Eur* 3.10; *FZ* 65.3; *J* 53.1), but in *Vala* we see that strength shifting from passive to active, from self-enclosed to outgoing, as the Spectre unites with Los in Night VII (85.26–46), then gives his battle strength to Los in Night VIII (107.31), and finally emerges, free of the Spectral encumbrance, in the triumphant conclusion as the creative giant of the poem:

> & Urthona rises from the ruinous walls
> In all his ancient strength to form the golden armour of science
> For intellectual War
>
> (*FZ* 139.7–9)

In thus redeeming Urthona, the reigning spirit of the North, Blake redeems the North itself, turning its defects into virtues. He extracts from the wintry obdurateness of its setting as an object-world the living strengths that compose the sublime of the personal self, so that obstruction becomes hardiness, resistance becomes work-energy, and darkness of surroundings (dens, storms) becomes intellectual keenness of sight.

Blake's transformation of Urthona is part of his attempt, in mid-career, to appropriate the Northern sublime (and all its affiliations with Burkean ideas) to the workings of his own poetical enterprise, so that the alternating resistances and generous disseminations of strength he finds in the World of Urthona become properties of his text. If one must settle for a belated sublime while waiting for the break of day, that is, for the recovery of origins in all their plenitude, then strength becomes a poetic necessity. It is difficult to dissociate Urthona from the "Strong man" of the "Ancient Britons" design, who explicitly "represents the human sublime" (E 543). Like Urthona of Night IX, "The strong Man acts from conscious superiority, and marches on in fearless dependance on the divine decrees, raging with the inspirations of a prophetic mind" (E 545). And like Urthona, he emerges in individuated form out of the sundering and wreckage of a former unitary greatness.

We first see the emergent Urthona in Night IV of *Vala*, gathering himself in a spectral shape, "like a statue of lead / Bent by its fall from a high tower" (*FZ* 49.13–14). Perhaps we catch here a distant reminiscence of that high tower whose proud raising led to the fall of mankind's last unitary culture and the scattering, according to some of the mythographers, of the three tribes of Noah's sons, Ham, Shem, and Japhet, to the far corners of the earth (cf. the early manuscript fragment "then She bore Pale desire": "Then Babel mighty Reard him to the Skies. Babel with thousand tongues Confusion it was calld" [E 446]). This biblical scattering of the tribes seems to underlie the story of Arthur's last battle and of "three who escaped, namely, Beauty, Strength, and Ugliness" (E 542)—a story that Blake explicitly assures us is a displacement of earlier events ("The stories of Arthur are the acts of Albion, applied to a Prince of the fifth century" [E 543]).

Indeed there is a whole series of displacements in this story, as well as linkages that take us back to the origins of human cultural differentiation. Blake himself, the Northern poet writing in London and Sussex, is only the latest representative of the Human Sublime, whose attributes include acts of "conscious superiority" and the "inspirations of a prophetic mind." Earlier, the same attributes belonged to a "Strong man," the survivor of a battle on Northern soil fought under a Northern leader. The Strong man is in turn a native, belated version of Japhet, the founder of the Northern nations, and Japhet is the historical equivalent of the mythic Urthona, who at the dawn of time separates out from his warring brothers to become the embodiment of the North itself. All that is cold, dark, obstructive, and degenerate in that setting is present in Urthona, as well as all that is invigorating, expansive, and creative. Blake's strategy is to plant his territorial flag on the most unpromising and resistant soil, presumably on the theory that the very strength of its resistance is a site marker of the richest residual energies lying beneath—energies that need only to be mined and reclaimed.

These remain, however, the strategies of belatedness, the approach of a poet whose native region seems not only climatically uncongenial but also geographically peripheral and culturally secondary. We cannot return to origins by enshrining belated, regionally segregated versions of the sublime. Such strategies, moreover, would appear to question, at least implicitly, the widespread antiquarian notion that the North was the site of the earliest, richest, and most central of human cultures. For even the Strong man, the "Human Sublime" personified, was, after all, only a retainer; he survived his king, but that king made a "promise to return again." To put this in other terms, there was a North before the North that we know now, and we shall once again have access to it. "Arthur was a name for the constellation Arcturus, or Bootes, the Keeper of the North Pole" (E 542). We have returned to the enthusiastically speculative passage with which this chapter began, a passage in which antiquarian "improbabilities and impossibilities" (E 543) pile up before the reader's eyes. But perhaps now we can see it as a less chaotic accumulation than it may have appeared at the outset. The ultimate North guarded by Arcturus[33] is a place beyond cold or barren ruggedness, beyond the strength and vigor of hardy survivors; it is simply the center that organizes all spaces in a harmonious order, the pole around which the stars trace their diurnal circles in the sky, a stellar "Eden: which / Wheel within Wheel in freedom revolve in harmony & peace" (*J* 15.19–20).[34] These cosmic wheels are commemorated in what Rowland Jones called the Circles of Gomer, "for Gomer supposed the world to be a large circle composed of many homogeneous lesser circles, systems, or combinations of elements, sides, surfaces, figures, forms and parts."[35] The Pole serves the same function for the whole cosmos of earth and sky that the central point in any field provides: it organizes space into a setting of universal convergence and omnidirectional radiating expansiveness, and hence it is emblematic of whatever can satisfy our paradoxical yearnings for coherent intellectual order and unbounded freedom.

Hence, all our compasses of desire point to this Polar North. The primordial Keeper of the Pole, then, kept watch over a setting of unfallen origins. Those bereft of their connections with origins are perpetually seeking to appropriate this setting in their pursuit of the sublime mode, even though no terrestrial region, geographical sector, or cultural community can ever claim the privilege of embodying it truly. Yet these cultures continue to recreate the circles and poles of the heavens in various earthly forms, in "the fables of Arthur and his round table," in the circular "Druid monuments, or temples," in "London stone," as "all antiquaries have proved" (E 542–43).[36] But, in so doing, these cultures cannot help turning "mental signification into corporeal command," for the celestial Pole has retreated to the sky, and the nations are left with a terrestrial North invaded by cold. We have seen that in *Jerusalem*, Blake reaches a point at which he privileges neither the geographical North over the South nor vice versa,

---

[33] Arcturus (the Bear-driver) is, in fact, the most brilliant star in the constellation of Boötes and not a constellation itself. The tail of the Great Bear (the Big Dipper) points directly to Arcturus, while the never-setting Bear revolves daily around the Pole; hence the "Keeper of the Pole" association. It is perhaps significant that Boötes occupies roughly the same latitude of distance from the celestial pole as Britain does from the terrestrial North Pole.

[34] For a photographic authentication of these concentric starry wheels, see Hilton, *Literal Imagination*, 207, fig. 65.

[35] *The Circles of Gomer*, 31.

[36] "The patriarchal or Druidical temples were laid out in such figures as were hieroglyphical and intended to describe the nature of divinity; as the circle, such as that of Stonehenge; or the circle and the seraph or the winged serpent, such as that of Abiry [*sic*]. By these were represented the divine personalities of the great objects of their worship. The circle was considered expressive of Him, who is the source of all being" (William Cooke, *An Enquiry into the Patriarchal and Druidical Religion* [1754], 28; quoted in Albert J. Kuhn, "English Deism and the Development of Romantic Mythological Syncretism," *PMLA* 71 [December 1956]: 1113).

but rather tends to treat these regions as benighted when they are regarded individually and terrifying when they are juxtaposed together. He seeks restoration of the ultimate North, the organizing center, the place where separation, differentiation, and individuation begin. Since Blake is not a mystagogue of the Absolute, we need to see what this place represents in human terms—terms compatible with a faith in the primacy of our own intellectual powers. Before there were cultures, even an original unified culture, there was language, and its capacities existed in their fullness from the beginning, before the birth of individuated meanings. Let us say that the singular polar center is to the spaces of difference what our primal powers of language and sign-making are to the world of external referentiality. With such a hypothesis, we gain entry to the last of the major settings in which Blake situates his poetry.

Chapter VII

THE SETTING OF SIGNS

LANGUAGE AND THE RECOVERY OF ORIGINS

B LAKE'S SETTINGS, as one can easily observe, often appear in configurations of numerical specificity or determinate exactitude that owe little or nothing to the material or circumstantial nature of the settings themselves. Thus, city gates, Zoas, Worlds of Existence, and Faces of Humanity come in sets of four, ages and Eyes of God in sets of seven, cathedral cities in sets of twenty-four, Heavens in sets of twenty-seven, and so forth. Pairings and oppositions, shadows, reflections, counterparts, and ratios of correspondence abound. It is as if the face of external reality is shaped—or, one might almost say, edited—according to autonomously preset intellectual directives. Highly organized codes, not obviously meaningful in themselves, endow the settings with meaningful potential, the *look* of places that signify. Geometrical and numerical patterns thus operate in Blake's work like the limited sets of visual schemata that seem to organize his ever-varied pictorial designs;[1] they are like the signifiers of an unfamiliar language, one that has somehow managed to spread itself across the surface of space and time. Space and time become a field of buried signs yielding telltale traces of an underlying setting, now obscured. This setting of signs presses upon us from behind and through the setting of nature, the setting of man's architectural remains, and the setting of geographical regions and cultural divisions, and reveals a world that once consisted solely of intellectually organized forms.

THE PRIMAL LANGUAGE AND THE CATASTROPHE OF BABEL

If the face of reality is deeply informed by signifying codes that operate in the manner of language, then the quest for origins ultimately involves a quest for that state in which reality was entirely a matter of signs in free but harmonious interplay. As a corollary, it would seem that the primal

---

[1] W.J.T. Mitchell has shown that Blake employs a small alphabet of visual forms (namely the spiral, the S-curve, the circle, and the inverted U) to compose a multitude of particular designs (*Blake's Composite Art*, 62–69), and he observes that these formative shapes "are *not* symbolic forms in the iconographical sense, but rather the schematic constituents of a pervasive symbolic style" (63).

catastrophe of separation, before the catastrophes of the division of nations or the yawning of nature's wide abyss, involved the breakup of a unitary body of signs. Out of the wreck there came into being, on one hand, a universe of objects or referents, dumb in themselves, and on the other, a fragmented, ever-shifting, inadequately expressive array of ex post facto verbal systems that pass for the natural languages of man.

Blake could have easily found contemporary sanction for these ideas in the work of the mythographers and cultural syncretists of his age. Not only was it a commonplace that, in Blake's words, "All had originally one language" (E 543), but there was also a widespread opinion that this unitary language was God's own and predated the Creation. As Henry Rowlands puts it in *Mona*,

> It will seem sufficiently plain that GOD himself was the first *Author of Language*; for we find GOD using there a *Scheme of Words* (which is Language) to express the Ideas in the *Divine Mind*, in the Works of Creation, before *Adam* had a Being. . . . Adam learned this *Language* of GOD, or what is the same thing, was inspired with it, at the Instant of his Creation. . . . We may hence conclude that *Adam*, as Prince of Mankind, had Authority enough to establish the precise Signification of Words.[2]

If the original language of mankind was the same as that used by God to present to himself the "Ideas in the Divine Mind" before all Creation, before words had external referents, then the loss of such a precious gift could only be a catastrophe of the most extraordinary magnitude. Rowlands again is a useful commentator:

> That at the Dispersion of the People at *Babel* and the Confusion of that primitive Tongue, the Minds of those dispersed People under that heavy Supernatural *Stupor*, then by Divine Vengeance inflicted on them for their impious attempt, retain'd and preserv'd nevertheless in that miserable *Oblivion*, some faint Shadows of such words, and some obscure Relicks of such Objects, as had made before, the strongest, the deepest, and most durable Impressions on their Thoughts and Imaginations.[3]

In this account, we have a nearly classic representation of the sublime moment of astonishment and deprivation: the catastrophic confrontation of unequal powers, the stony "stupor," the intimation of a residual greatness that is "obscure," yet strong and deep, are all its hallmarks. So, also, is the pattern, observed earlier, of trauma, followed by oblivion, and then by the emergence of the repressed memories of one's own former greatness. Wordsworth's phrasing in *The Prelude* comes to mind: "the soul / Remem-

---

[2] *Mona*, 292–93. See also Jones, *Origin of Languages* (note 12, Chapter VI).
[3] *Mona*, 212.

bering how she felt, but what she felt / Remembering not, retains an obscure sense / Of possible sublimity, / Whereto with growing faculties she doth aspire."[4] For the syncretic mythographer of nearly a century earlier, the same scene is enacted on the field of language itself, and the "growing faculties" of aspiration are those of a speculative scholarship intent on finding in today's words the extant traces and residues of the primal divine ideation.[5]

This aspiration accounts for the eagerness with which certain antiquarians pursued the possibility that Babel's confusion of tongues was not universal and that one or more tribes had circumvented the catastrophe, thus preserving the original divine language. Whether this language was Anglo-Celtic, as some authorities (such as Jones and Parsons) believed, or Hebrew, as others (such as Rowlands) held was less important than the faith that a repository of divinely formed signs remained accessible. Blake also looked forward to a state in which all could again converse as one. At the same time, however, he appears more doubtful than some of the antiquarians that any contemporary natural language can provide an automatic access to origins. When he speaks of "Nimrods tower which I conjecture to have spread over many Countries" (E 729), the remark is not readily intelligible (a spreading tower?) unless we assume that he reads the biblical account of Babel as a mythical condensation of an event repeated in many places at the same time. In that case, there are many towers of pride, many dispersions, and little likelihood that any group preserving the original tongue could escape the catastrophe, as they might escape a purely localized event.

This interpretation is strengthened by a well-known passage in *Jerusalem*, in which Los, on a walk through London (which is also a walk through the antiquities of the nations), seeks out the Minute Particulars,

> And saw every Minute Particular of Albion degraded & murderd
> But saw not by whom; they were hidden within the minute particulars
> Of which they had possessd themselves; and there they take up
> The articulations of a mans soul, and laughing throw it down
> Into the frame, then knock it out upon the plank, & souls are bak'd

---

[4] *Prelude* (1850), 2.315–19.

[5] Rowland Jones points to this pattern of recovery when he suggests that "there was always a pure and uncorrupted language of the world, which is to become general." Armed with various scriptural citations, he adds that "God promised to return to the people a pure language, that they might be all gathered and converse together and call upon the name of the Lord to serve him with one consent, probably . . . the Japhetan language, which having escaped the Babylonian corruption, the Jewish doctors expected should be recovered" (*The IO-Triads*, 4). Cf. Blake: "And they conversed together in Visionary forms dramatic"; "& they walked / To & fro in Eternity as One Man reflecting each in each" (*J* 98.28, 38–39).

> In bricks to build the pyramids of Heber & Terah. But Los
> Searched in vain: closd from the minutia he walkd, difficult.
>
> (*J* 45[31].7–13)

There is perhaps a buried reference here to the Tower of Babel, as described by Jacob Bryant, who considered it to have been a pyramid of brick,[6] and the likelihood of allusion is reinforced by the reference to the doubly significant "articulations." Not only are the exquisitely jointed connections of man's spiritual form reduced and crushed, but so are his powers of intelligible language—and the latter sense of "articulations" seems paramount in the passage, with its stress on self-enclosure, failed access, and dumb inertness (later in the same passage we find Los "enquiring in vain / Of stones and rocks" [lines 26–27]). If the Minute Particulars refer on one level to the particulars of language, then this is a new account of the effects of Babel, one considerably more dire than the version in Genesis. The loss is universal ("every Minute Particular") and the agency of destruction obscure and insidious: no conspicuous force of countersublimity, no "Divine Vengeance," but rather a kind of inner malfunction or the invasion of an agent that appropriates and destroys its host, like a virus inside a cell. As a final irony, the Tower of Pride is presented in this account not as the external occasion for the loss of articulateness but as its concretized fulfillment. The tower comes into being only when the loss has taken place; it is nothing more than a huge pile of dead words, dead intellectual desires and potentialities, which passes itself off as a new form of greatness. To revert to the idiom of sublime discourse, magnitude, height, and mass take the place of suppressed intellectual energy. After finding on his walk that "Every Universal Form, was become barren mountains of Moral Virtue" (lines 19–20), Los comes "To where the Tower of London frownd dreadful over Jerusalem" (line 23). This tower reinforces the suppressed presence of Babel in the passage and suggests further that for Blake the earlier tower represents language as we know it in its everday guise, a self-important vehicle for regulatory codes and authoritarian suppressions.

Blake's own language, as I shall argue presently, is an attempt to recreate a discourse that once flourished in our now dimly recollected time of ori-

---

[6] "The tower of Babel was probably a rude mound of earth, raised to a vast height, and cased with bricks, which were formed from the soil of the country and cemented with asphalt or bitumen. . . . They are very like the brick pyramids of Egypt" (*New System* vol. 3, 61). Bryant gets his bricks from Genesis 11.3, but the Egyptian pyramidical form and the erroneous notion that these pyramids were made of brick are apparently his own additions. Blake's "pyramids of Heber and Terah" extend the pyramid-building impulse beyond Nimrod, who was of the line of Ham, to the line of Shem and to the remainder of the Druidical Age, from Heber, the ancestor of the Hebrews, down to his descendant Terah, the father of Abraham, who as we know from the *Descriptive Catalogue* "was called to succeed the Druidical age" (E 542–43).

gin, when reality and sign formed a single being. But paradoxically, by transporting his discourse to these now–remote territories, Blake initially creates an estranging effect. Readers of Blake typically find themselves in an encompassing setting of semiotic resistances. These forms of resistance share some of the opacity or dumbness of material objects without participating in the latter's attachment to a continuum of familiar externality, and they share some of the arbitrary patternings found in linguistic signifiers without participating in the attachment of such signifiers to known signifieds. Hence, when we start reading Blake, we are immediately made aware of our separation from a readily accessible body of unified meaning, and this situation is a precise mirror of our actual situation in the setting of the world at large. The second effect of such a reading, however, releases us from that world, for whenever we are confronted with an array of forms that are inscrutable, detached from a familiar continuum, and yet apparently patterned with an internal consistency, we are inevitably inclined to believe that we are in the presence of code, and the temptation to decipher it becomes aroused. At this point, our sense of the Blakean world turns inside out, and it suddenly flares forth with omnipresent possibilities of accessible meaning; in the words of the Americanist critic John Irwin (regarding Poe's analogous situation), "the image of 'writing' expands until all physical shapes become obscurely meaningful forms of script, forms of hieroglyphic writing."[7]

THE HERMETIC AND KABBALISTIC BACKGROUND

The idea that the world is a kind of divine book or set of hieroglyphic symbols is hardly original to Blake. To go back no further than the seventeenth century, it flourishes in the works of such Hermetic thinkers as Robert Fludd and the German Athanasius Kircher, who, in the words of Paolo Rossi, "found in rocks geometrical figures, letters of the Greek and Roman alphabets, depictions of celestial bodies, and the outlines of trees, animals, and men; mysterious symbols springing from profound religious meanings, each one of which could offer a way to the revelation of the divine significance that permeates the world."[8] In the eighteenth century, such views become connected to the special literary milieu of the the sublime through the nexus of Druidism: this nexus provided not only an ambience of the ancient, the Northern, the mysterious, and the agreeably terrifying, but also associations with concerns that might be called, in the loose sense

---

[7] John Irwin, *American Hieroglyphics: The Symbol of the Egyptian Hieroglyphics in the American Renaissance* (New Haven: Yale University Press, 1980), 61.

[8] *The Dark Abyss of Time*, 7.

used by eighteenth-century writers, Kabbalistic.[9] The Welsh antiquary Evan Evans spoke openly of the "Druidical Cabbala," and Henry Rowlands asserts that "the deliver'd and taught Philosophy and Learning of this *Druidical* Sect, seem'd in the general Air of it, to be mostly Symbolical and Aenigmatical, . . . agreeing in that with the Traditional *Cabala* of the *Jews*."[10] For anyone who believed, as Blake did, that Albion and Adam were Druids, there were, in short, sources readily available to suggest that they possessed a code of signification "as antient as the World"[11]—a code that was, moreover, as indigenous to Northern climes as to the Hebrew.

Yet there is more than its appropriation of the garments of Druidical solemnity to make Kabbalistic modes of thinking attractive to those with a taste for the sublime. First, there is the common element of difficulty, obscurity, and an impression of receding depth. The expositor Jacques Basnage uses terms that would be at home in the eighteenth-century discourse on sublimity (blockage, human belittlement, antagonism to Reason) when he remarks of the Jewish mystics that "there is commonly such an obscure Profoundness in their Writings, as is impenetrable. Nothing that Reason dictates can be reconciled with the Terms their Books abound with: After a long and useless Search, a Man is tired."[12] But once beyond the wall of difficulty, one finds in Kabbalistic thought other characteristic

---

[9] See, e.g., Wordsworth, *The Prelude* (1850), 13.313–54, for what is probably the best-known meditation on the Druids in their dual sublime aspects of terror and transcendent wisdom. The term "Kabbalistic" is used here not in the technical sense of referring to a specific body of medieval Jewish mysticism but rather to represent a cluster of concerns that traditional Kabbalah, of all mysticisms, articulates in the most pressing way. This is also the sense of the term used by eighteenth-century English expositors, who do not often discriminate carefully between specifically Kabbalistic doctrines and those that the more general term "Rabbinic" would suit, or between doctrines of actual Jewish origin and Christian modifications or distortions. For instructive and cautionary observations on these points, see Sheila Spector, "Kabbalistic Sources—Blake's and His Critics'," *Blake/An Illustrated Quarterly* 17 (Winter 1983–1984): 84–99. Spector reports that "up to the time of Blake's death, there were over fifteen sources of Kabbalah available to the poet, though none of them accurately reflects the mysticism of the Jews" (87). An excellent and thorough critical overview of Blake's relation to Kabbalistic influences is available in Dena Bain Taylor, "Emanations of the Divine: Kabbalistic Elements in the Poetry and Designs of William Blake" (unpublished Ph.D. diss., University of Toronto, 1983). For a more recent and briefer discussion connecting Kabbalism with Blake, see Robert N. Essick, *William Blake and the Language of Adam* (Oxford: Clarendon Press, 1989), 46–48. Essick's study, which was not available to me until after the completion of my own text, in part parallels this chapter in its emphases and examples (although they are not, in his case, brought into the context of the eighteenth-century sublime).

[10] See Rowlands, *Mona*, 61, and Evan Evans, *Some Specimens of the Poetry of the Antient Welsh Bards* (London: R. J. Dodsley, 1764), 18; for the latter reference, I am indebted to my colleague Professor Dena Taylor.

[11] Jacques Basnage, *History of the Jews*, trans. Thomas Taylor (London: T. Bever, 1708), 184.

[12] Ibid., 199.

attendant lamps of the sublime: the presence of power, the supremacy of intellect, the pursuit of unity through the tracing of differentiations, and the recovery of origins. All these characteristic marks of sublimity are made possible by an extraordinary conception of universal textuality in which both the divine creative power and its artifacts, nature and history, subsist.[13] "The Rabbinic concept of language and meaning," Susan Handelman observes, "has at its center the concept of the divinity of the text. . . . The Torah is not an artifact of nature, a product of the universe; the universe, on the contrary, is the product of the Torah."[14] In a cosmic reality that is textual in character, intellect is fully present in the text's signifying potency, and power is no longer cut off from its origins, as the catastrophe-riven face of sublime nature is cut off from the original intellectual design of the creator.

In this tradition of thought, the distinction between language and setting (in the sense of a place or point situated in its surroundings), begins to blur. To quote Handelman again, "in the world of the text, rigid temporal and spatial distinctions collapse. The elements of the text are treated as much as objective reality for its students as empirical facts are by scientific observers."[15] Another, perhaps clearer, way of putting it would be to say that the text is not conceived as historically and spatially situated in an empirical world, but rather the empirical world finds itself situated in the spaces created by the differences and correspondences of the text. Such a conception tends to emphasize the formal elements of signification over the referential. It privileges the visual look of the text over aural comprehension, and hence writing over speech; signifiers over signifieds, and hence names over the objects named; and indivisible, formal base units over compound signifiers, hence letters over words and sentences. There is a historical dimension involved as well; what is thus privileged is also prior. For writers in this tradition who were interested in the questions of origins, the trail backward to the birth of writing took them from the world of created nature to the divine world of the creator, from the language of the common day to what Handelman has called the "fiery preexistent letters in which are contained the secrets of creation."[16]

---

[13] Cf. Harold Bloom, who speaks of the "sublime Kabbalistic exaltation of language, and of the arts of interpretation" and suggests that "in its glory [Kabbalah] sought and found, a power of the mind over the universe of death" (*Kabbalah and Criticism* [New York: Seabury Press, 1975], 46 and 47). Astute readers will note Bloom's self-conscious application of the language of the Wordsworthian sublime.

[14] Susan A. Handelman, *The Slayers of Moses: The Emergence of Rabbinic Interpretation in Modern Literary Theory* (Albany: State University of New York Press, 1982), 37. Handelman also quotes the Midrash (Bereishit Rabbah 1.1): "He looked into the Torah and created the world."

[15] Ibid., 47.

[16] Ibid., 38.

A writer of Blake's day who might wish to entertain such concepts did not require access to either the genuine writings of Kabbalah or the rediscoveries of modern scholars, for the general conceptual outlines were sufficiently available in English sources of the period (including translations). Blake's own assertion of the divine origin of writing at the beginning of *Jerusalem* is actually conservative: "that God . . . / Who in mysterious Sinais awful cave / To Man the wond'rous art of writing gave" (*J* 3.2–4). By accepting the traditional identification of the start of alphabetic writing with Moses' reception of the tablets of the Law on Sinai, Blake allows himself to be outstripped by more daring speculators. For example, with a multitude of ingenious arguments, Edward Davies endeavors to prove that writing is at least antediluvian, while James Parsons asserts an Adamic origin for the letters of the alphabet and the origins of culture.[17] Rowland Jones goes so far as to speculate that the primal letters were "engraved on the *bark* of the tree of knowledge of good and evil, furnishing the first pair, in their state of innocence, with two sorts of ideas or knowledge," one of them carnal knowledge.[18] Theosophical speculation could push matters farther back, as we see in Basnage's treatise on the Jews: "'Tis an Error to imagine that the Letters have no other Use than to make words by their combinations; for according to the *Cabbalists*, the World was formed by Analogy to the *Hebrew* Alphabet, and the harmony of Creatures resembles that of the Letters, which God made use of to compose the Book of Life."[19] According to this line of speculation, letters are not only coterminous with human existence but are indeed its precursors. From this position, it is a relatively easy leap to a more daring one: since God's ideas are transparent to himself, and since he scarcely needs letters to mediate communications from without, these letters can have only one source and one function—that is, they must be the precise mirror of the articulations and patternings of the Divine Mind itself.

By removing it from the realm of human artifacts, belated in derivation, and assigning it to the pre-Adamic world of divine ideas, Kabbalistically inspired thought brings writing into the orbit of the sublime. The sublime object always confronts the perceiver across a gap of discontinuity, from

[17] Davies, *Celtic Researches*, 34–35; Parsons, *Remains of Japhet*, 357–59.

[18] *Hieroglyfic; or, A Grammatical Introduction to a Universal Hieroglyphic Language* (London: John Hughes, 1763), A3. Jones proceeds quite seriously with the diverting notion that Adam and Eve received *graphic* instruction in sexual matters from the shape of the letters on the tree. For example, "the hard c also represents half the round of the posteriors, as o doth the whole of the male and female together, as the feminine or soft c doth the other half," and "the letters d and b put together, thus, db, . . . are expressive of man and woman's body part, from the thigh to the part of the body which the elbow reaches" (ibid., 17). A happy confusion of God's primordial characters with post-fifteenth-century conventions of printing minuscules underlies these conceits.

[19] Basnage, *History of the Jews*, 190.

which vantage it imparts a combination of intimidation and attraction. It intimidates because it can exercise mastery across the gap but may not itself be mastered; and it attracts because it imparts to the perceiver dim, dawning memories of another time, another place, when he and the awesome presence confronting him were masters together. Lacking external magnitude or power, writing nevertheless becomes sublime as soon as it is defamiliarized, detached from its relatively humble status as a representation of human speech, and assumes instead an autonomous a priori being. Astonishment inevitably attends this turning of the tables of priority, as one unexpectedly perceives writing not as a human instrument but as the human precursor. At the same time, there is another, more welcome shock: man recognizes his intellectual origins as most generously constituted from this script and intuits that it is his native home, to which he might return.

To cite an example, Smart's *Jubilate Agno*, that most Kabbalistically inclined of all major English poems, connects at various points the divine writing to both these kinds of astonishment—the kind that depends on defamiliarization or the raising of barriers, and the kind that comes when barriers are overthrown in a universal inclusiveness. Here, for instance, is a sample of the first kind:

For there are more letters in all languages not communicated.

. . . .

For St. Paul was caught up into the third heavens.
For there he heard certain words which it was not possible for him to understand.
For they were constructed by uncommunicated letters.
For they are signs of speech too precious to be communicated for ever.[20]

This is the divine writing at its most reclusive; not even St. Paul's rapture or his sanctity can afford him access. Letters not only are shown to have priority to speech (what Paul "heard" is preconditioned by the presence of letters that he could not see), but they operate to scramble the transparency of speech wherever they are introduced. They do not simply make referentiality hard to obtain but rather block the possibility of referentiality at the source. Their "preciousness" is a function of their privacy, like objects meant for the eyes of their owners only.

At the other extreme in the poem, one finds promiscuous identifications of humanity, divinity, and the letter such as the following:

For H is a spirit and therefore he is God.
For I is person and therefore he is God.
For K is king and therefore he is God

[20] Christopher Smart, *Jubilate Agno*, ed. W. H. Bond (Cambridge: Harvard University Press, 1954), Frag. C:40–45.

For L is love and therefore he is God.
For M is musick and therefore he is God.
For N is novelty and therefore he is God.
For O is over and therefore he is God.
For P is power and therefore he is God.

And so on through the alphabet until we read "For Christ being A and Ω is all the intermediate letters without doubt."[21] Taking the Book of Revelation literally, Smart attempts here to see all phenomena identified with an alphabetic code, indistinguishable from the Godhead itself, expressed in verse that mimics the discreteness of alphabetical symbols with its own order of identically framed but discrete syntactical units. Smart's "intricate geometry of language," as one critic has termed it,[22] mirrors the operation of the letters themselves, which act here not as a device of alienation but as one of integration; the finite plurality and abstract formality of the letters form a bridge between the human and the divine, between the indefinite plurality and play of man's attributes (his soul, his personality, affections, arts, curiosity, strengths, and so on) and an absolute and invariant unity ("therefore he is God"). Man becomes God through the mediation of the letter.[23]

Smart's genius in *Jubilate Agno* and *A Song to David* is to set up a creative tension between the unity of the letter (in which we may include such formalisms as parallelism, repetitions, alphabetical and numerical sequences, and so on) and a bewildering multiplicity of imagistic details, so that the vision is never allowed to settle in a static order. Like Blake's Golgonooza described in Chapter 1 of *Jerusalem*, which Smart's visions seem to foretell (whether or not Blake had them as models or simply repaired to a common source of influence, such as the poetics of Lowth[24]), these poems manage to assemble a vast congregation of minute particulars to be lodged within a firm architecture of recovery. At the same time, while we are riveted, even hypnotized, by the order of the overall structure, the plethora of details

[21] Ibid., Frag. C:1–8 and 18.

[22] Patricia Meyer Spacks, *The Poetry of Vision: Five Eighteenth-Century Poets* (Cambridge: Harvard University Press, 1967), 143.

[23] Moira Dearnley speaks of Smart's "philological vision of reality" and observes that "God is the Poet of the Universe, and Smart the poet of *Jubilate Agno*—and Smart adopts the divine subject matter and the divine style," the former tending toward infinite plurality, the latter dependent on a focused or "rudimentary" deployment of a limited set of signifiers; see *The Poetry of Christopher Smart* (London: Routledge and Kegan Paul, 1968), 161 and 40.

[24] For Smart's debt to Lowth's theories of parallelism and antiphonal organization in Hebraic verse, see Dearnley, *Poetry of Christopher Smart*, 138ff.; for a fruitful comparison of the ways Blake and Smart respectively adapt Lowth's prosodic ideas, see Paley, *The Continuing City*, 45–49. Paley does not rule out the possibility of Blake's direct or indirect acquaintance with *Jubilate Agno* through his friendship with Hayley, who once possessed Smart's manuscript (ibid., 47).

elude us. This tension or oscillation of perspective reflects certain conflicting emphases in the Kabbalistic exaltation of writing and the alphabet. The
image-system of the natural sublime supplies an analogy to this conflict.
We recall that greatness or magnitude resides either in forms of massy condensation or in the spaces and multiplicities born of fragmentation and
division. So, too, the divine alphabet is seen as great either because of its
unlimited distributive properties, its participation in countless differenti-
ating rearrangements; or else its greatness resides in its possession of certain limited and invariant combinations of letters that can condense within
themselves the infinite potency of the whole. These combinations are the
autonomous divine names, of which the Tetragrammaton (transliterated as
YHVH) is the preeminent. Further condensations of potency are possible,
even to the confines of a single preeminent letter within the name.[25]

Because they are determinate and invariant combinations of letters,
proper names are easily perceived as discrete objects, and because their connection to their referents is unique, admitting neither of paraphrase nor
synonym, they may be perceived as objects of a particularly aloof and private sort. When such objects are endowed with a plenary power, they raise
a troubling issue that often accompanies manifestations of the sublime:
the threat of alien control over ordinary human autonomy. A good deal of the
speculation on the power of divine names conveys an implicit or explicit
determinism. To cite examples that may have been available to Blake, we
can go from the mild "scientific" determinism of John Cleland, who attempted to derive all the radical constitutives of human language from the
names of the heathen gods, to the more splendid eccentricity of Henry
Rowlands, who held that the names of the first ten patriarchs secretly encoded "a concise and wonderful Scheme and Prophecy, in that Language
of the Restitution of deprav'd Mankind, by a Promised Messias."[26] In this

---

[25] Thus Basnage, speaking of the first letter of YHVH, *jod*, says, " 'Twas this Letter which
flowing from the primitive Light, gave being to Emanations" (*History of the Jews*, 193). In
Kabbalah, the Divine Name is an ever expanding and contracting entity, oscillating between
parameters of singularity and infinite multiplicity. Depending on one's perspective, it may
encompass four specific letters, or all the letters in the alphabet, or all the signs in a sacred
book, or all the things in the world. Speaking of the early mystical text, the *Sefer Yezirah*, the
great Judaic scholar Gershom Scholem has observed that "every existing thing somehow contains these linguistic elements and exists by their power, whose foundation is one name; i.e.,
the Tetragrammaton, or, perhaps, the alphabetical order which in its entirety is considered
one mystical name. The world-process is essentially a linguistic one, based on the unlimited
combinations of the letters"; see *Kabbalah* (New York: Times Books, 1974), 25. Elsewhere
in the same study, Scholem remarks that "from the magical belief that the Torah was composed of God's Holy Names, it was but a short step to the mystical belief that the entire Torah
was in fact nothing else than the Great Name of God Himself" (170). At the other extreme,
"the single letter is a condensed cipher of other meanings, itself a miniature inner discourse"
(Handelman, *Slayers of Moses*, 71).

[26] See Cleland, *The Way to Things by Words*, 2–10; Rowlands, *Mona*, 210. In Rowlands's

scheme, it is not the acts, but rather the names, of the patriarchs that forward the movement of history toward this restitution: if Noah ("Consolation"), for example, is offered a consoling covenant, it is because his name determined him from birth for this role. An even more overt determinism appears in the curious cosmogony of the influential commentator and sect-founder John Hutchinson:

> Moses hath shewed, and I from him, that the Eternal *Three* became Elohim, created this System, consisting of two parts, the *Names*, and the Earth and Man; and formd the *Names* into a Machine to rule Matter, constituted them Rulers, gave to each of the Three a Name, and a distinct manner of acting, so as to act jointly and separately: so that using the Name of the Substance, or the Name of each, should be in speaking, in hieroglyphical or literal Writing, to raise an Idea of the Essence of each of the Persons, the Manner of their Existence, Powers, and Actions.[27]

This is not entirely perspicuous, but the general thrust is clear enough. As if setting out to flaunt his adherence to what Swift sardonically termed in *A Tale of a Tub* "the Mechanical Operation of the Spirit," Hutchinson frankly calls the divine names "machines to rule matter," and goes further to suggest that each time these names are uttered or inscribed, their full powers are reactivated. Although Hutchinson's position is extreme, its somewhat sinister determinism may have influenced Blake when, in *Jerusalem*, he speaks of the Daughters of Albion as "Names anciently rememberd, but now contemn'd as fictions! / Although in every bosom they controll our Vegetative powers" (*J* 5.38–39). The Daughters, rightly understood, are not "goddesses" or "spirits" but deadly formal codes, designed to move our mortal parts along their destined course, and they are all the more deadly for their shadowy presence, half perceived, half disbelieved, like Ossianic ghosts moving behind a mist.

It is this alienating and oppressive side of hermetic traditions of the letter that Blake explicitly condemns when he shows the Spectre "Repeating the Smaragdine Table of Hermes to draw Los down / Into the Indefinite" (*J* 91.34–35). There is, moreover, further cause for disquiet. For Blake, sublime objects that exercise their power through mystery and aloof separation inevitably reveal themselves to be belated products of prior traumas or sunderings. In the unitary world of the text there should be no such traumas, and yet the tradition available to Blake strongly suggests that the regress

---

scheme, the names Adam, Seth, Enosh, Kainan, Mahaleel, Jared, Henoch, Methuschela, Lamech, and Noah [all Rowlands's spellings] are, by philological and other manipulations, made equivalent to the ten phrases in the sentence "Man / set or placed / in Misery / lamentable / blessed God / shall come down / teaching / that his Death will send / to humble smitten Man / Consolation" (211).

[27] John Hutchinson, *The Covenant of the Cherubim* (London: Henry Woodall, 1734), 217.

of origins operates even here. Any suggestion, for example, that a particular letter of a divine name retains a special preeminence over its fellows raises the question of relative priority and the possibility of an even more recessive *Ur*-text, of letters behind the letters. Bloom reports that "some Kabbalists spoke of a missing twenty-third letter of the Hebrew alphabet, hidden in the white spaces between the letters,"[28] a speculation that reminds us of Smart's "uncommunicated letters." As soon as the Spectre in *Jerusalem* produces the Smaragdine Table, we are told that "Los reads the Stars of Albion! the Spectre reads the Voids / Between the Stars" (*J* 91.36–37). In Basnage, we learn that "Heaven [is] considered as a *Sacred Book* . . . the characters made by the Stars are *Hebrew*," and it is inviting to speculate that Los and his Spectre are performing two kinds of Kabbalistic readings of the same heavenly text:[29] Los concentrates on the power of the fiery Minute Particulars while the Spectre, a more arcane and haunted Kabbalist, looks into "the spaces between" and sees terrifying depths within depths, and perhaps the ghosts of more ancient characters, like the receding galaxies of modern astronomy. Basnage, again, suggests that even the Beginning itself enjoys no more than a secondary status: "For Moses commencing his History with a B (Bereschit) must necessarily denote by it the Second World. The Letter B is the Number Two. Moses has put it at the beginning of Genesis; and therefore he believed that there was another World which God had created before this."[30] If the Torah cancels the certainty of the Beginning *at* the beginning, then it undermines faith in all beginnings, in both the prior world and all worlds before that, and the regress we had hoped to escape by tracing our way back to a final, divine textuality is simply reconstituted in that sphere.

If we try the opposite route, taking any given state of the text as a point of origin and then tracing its descendants, we discover that state dissolving in a flux of successively generated forms. The divine text is never a stable, marmoreal fixity; it is subject, just like the face of the sublime natural landscape, to repeated splittings and regroupings. The alleged methods of Kabbalistic analysis merely reproduce a process that theoretically occurred among the eternal letters before the beginning of time: "They separate the Letters that make up a Word, and of each Letter make another Word. They are happy when this Word happens to consist of as many Letters as the

---

[28] *Kabbalah and Criticism*, 53–54.

[29] *History of the Jews*, 244. Essick traces the stars-letters identification to Plotinus and also notes the differing modes of Los and his Spectre in *J* 91 as "two ways of interpreting a text" (*Language of Adam*, 208).

[30] Basnage, *History of the Jews*, 245. Bloom speculates that since, according to some Kabbalist texts, God contracted his being before the letters of his own name became manifest to him, and since his power is inherent in the visible letters of his name, then he himself is "belated." See *Kabbalah and Criticism*, 80.

first. . . . The Beginning which is the first Word of *Genesis* consists of six letters. Of this they make six others. . . . The Combinations and Significations infinitely multiply."[31] This process might be seen as evidence of the text's original plenitude—but if so, then this plenitude is to be revealed only in retrospect through an act of separation, through a splitting of the primordial unity and its incremental replacement by a host of belated forms.

How the external world takes shape from this wild production of letters out of letters and texts out of texts is a matter vividly expounded in the works of Rowland Jones, the most hermetic of all the syncretic antiquarians who may have influenced Blake. The absurdities of Jones's system, arising from extraordinary philological ignorance, cannot entirely mask the presence of a strong visionary imagination, one that is in good measure compatible with Blake's.[32] Jones believed that "the mundane creation seems to be the division of the elements according to the eternal patterns, ideas, or decrees, subsisting in the divine mind; with which letters seem to correspond, . . . notwithstanding Mr. Locke's assertion to the contrary, for want of a competent notion of the divine origin of human speech."[33] Jones's anti-Lockean polemic (a running theme in his works) is part of a more grandiose scheme to derive all the forms of creation from letters and all the letters from a point of singularity—or, in his words, "an emanation, separation, division, or expansion of the monad and diad into a universe and its parts." In plain terms, everything is reducible to the letters *i* and *o*, or still further, to the dot of the *i* (which encompasses the *o*) and the linear shaft below it, also derived from the dot: "a dot, point, monad, or omega, [and] a line of many smaller dots, points, diads, or omikrons."[34] From this a great deal else follows:

> For true it is, that the four lettered name Jehovah, Jove, or the five vowels, by the division of o into a e, and transposed ΕΥΟι, *the spring* of io, comprehends the symbols of I. A dark point, or intelligent omega, from whence all things flow. 2. Its fluxion, or ilation in a line or diad. 3. Its expansion, or motion, into an infinite circle or system of divine ideas, decrees or triads. 4. Its farther spring or energy, forming a tetrad, quaternion, or an io of the solar system. Its separation, or breaking off into matter, which became the fifth element . . .[35]

It is unnecessary to go into the intricacies of all this or to pursue to the end Jones's exposition, which takes us through many more letters of the alpha-

---

[31] Basnage, *History of the Jews*, 240.

[32] Jones's possible influence on Blake is noted in Owen, *The Famous Druids*, 182–86, and in Daniel Stempel, "Blake, Foucault, and the Classical Episteme," *PMLA* 96 (May 1981): 388–407.

[33] *The IO-Triads*, 10.

[34] *The Circles of Gomer*, 68 and 69.

[35] *The IO-Triads*, 8.

bet and stages of the material creation. The important points to note are that the alphabet (which is also the code of the world) is generated out of its own substance in a self-replicating and almost embryological process; that the name of God itself is constituted out of more primitive diagrammatic forms (and even that name is found in the process of temporal unfolding, the fourfold "Jove" opening into the fivefold "Je[h]ova[h]"); and finally that all is ultimately traceable to a state of forbidding and paradoxical minimalism, a point without dimension or feature that is intelligent yet "dark." The text itself is a setting constituted out of process and differentiation, and the pursuit of origins brings us ominously to the portals of nothingness where darkness reigns.[36]

BLAKE'S HUMAN TEXT

What do these arcane Hermetic speculations have to do with the sublime of William Blake? We know that he never makes alphabetic catalogs like Smart, nor does he ever derive the forms of creation from the letters of the Tetragrammaton, even though the concept itself could scarcely be unknown to him. When we consider Jones's strange self-multiplying geometry, we may recall Blake's comment in his annotations to Berkeley's *Siris*: "God is not a Mathematical Diagram" (E 664). Indeed Jones's proliferating monadic point may even remind us of these lines in *Jerusalem*:

> he is the Great Selfhood
> Satan: Worshipd as God by the Mighty Ones of the Earth
> Having a white Dot calld a Center from which branches out
> A Circle in continual gyrations.

> (*J* 29[33].17–20)

Despite these provisos, it is scarcely possible to deny Blake's attraction to schematic, largely nonreferential patternings of signs and to what Nelson Hilton has called the "sacred or numinous potency of language."[37] Thus, Blake revels in the roll-call of mysterious names—and, as has been shown

---

[36] Boehme, who appears to be Jones's master in these matters, says that "the immense Space is bottomless, . . . therefore it is like a Glass: it is all things and yet as a Nothing: it beholdeth itself, and yet findeth nothing but an A, which is its Eye." Punning on the German *Auge*, he then proceeds to fantastic diagrammatic expansions and variations of the strokes of the A until he has generated the U and a series of more complex shapes culminating in the globe of the primordial universe (see *Works* vol. 2, 11ff.). Boehme is no more embarrassed in his generation of the universe from a modern German word than Jones is in his employment of modern English nomenclature and the minuscules of modern printing fonts for a similar purpose. Once the principle is accepted that all systems of human signifiers store information encoded originally in the divine language imparted at the creation, then any set of arbitrary signifiers can be legitimately pressed to yield the same revelation.

[37] *Literal Imagination*, 13.

in more detail in Part Two of this study, the letters of his invented names tend autonomously to generate the forms of new inventions of names, much as the primordial letters in Jones's cosmos hive off from one another. If Blake does not dwell overtly on the most sublime of all names, the Tetragrammaton, it may be because fourfold schemata saturate his settings so pervasively that he has no need of overt references; the imposition of sets of four on all created things is something experienced and articulated too deeply to be relegated to mere doctrinal exposition. In any case, by the time of the Laocoön engraving, Blake is inscribing the name of God, in Hebrew, on his plate, and earlier in his career, it has been suggested, the Hebrew alphabet may have influenced the organization of one of his major works.[38] Finally, whatever aspersions Blake may cast on geometry and mathematical form, there is the omnipresent geometry of his oppositional schemata, and no shortage of numerical intricacies: "And Scofield the Ninth remain on the outside of the Eight / And Kox, Kotope, Bowen, One in him, a Fourfold Wonder / Involv'd the Eight"; "And the Seventeen conjoining with Bath, the Seventh: / In whom the other Ten shone manifest" (J 7.47–49; 40[45].37–38). We cannot fully appreciate the humane and passionate side of Blake's Intellectual Powers unless we acknowledge the presence of a strange side, unaccommodating, hard-edged, hieratic and withdrawn, that sets the warm life off and reveals it as the precious attainment that it is. Blake always seems reluctant to endorse openly the kind of schematic thinking to which he is actually so attached, but his genius is to recognize its poetic necessity and allow it full scope in his work.

But local hieratic effects are only external indicators of a more profound impulse in Blake's poetry; his major late works proceed to culminations in which the poetic setting is ever more explicitly presented as virtually indistinguishable from a universe of textuality. *Vala* concludes with the promise of a movement of history from the "ruinous walls" of nature and time to a higher state of "intellectual War," but the specifics of this intellectual setting are left to the reader's surmise (*FZ* 139.7–9). *Milton* proceeds to a much more focused climactic vision, in which the hero becomes one with Jesus in a manifestation that is simultaneously incarnational and textual:

> The Clouds of Ololon folded as a Garment dipped in blood
> Written within & without in woven letters: & the Writing
> Is the Divine Revelation in the Litteral expression:
>
> (*M* 42.12–14)

---

[38] Joseph Wittreich views *The Marriage of Heaven and Hell* as consisting of a Prologue of twenty-two lines, a body of twenty-two plates, and an epilogue of twenty-two lines, plus final flourishes, and suggests that Blake is following a model provided by Lowth, who found biblical prophecy structured on units equivalent to the number of letters in the Hebrew alphabet. See *Angel of Apocalypse*, 195.

This is less a vision of the Word made Flesh than one of the Flesh, the living continuum of history, made Word. What the divine power reveals is the idea of the world as script—or else, since the syntax permits this construction, the world affords a vision of Divinity itself as Writing: Writing *is* the Divine Revelation (what divinity is revealed to be), and its power resides not in the message but in the letters themselves ("in the Litteral expression").

This vision takes us into *Jerusalem*—which begins, in effect, where *Milton* leaves off, with an encomium to the "wond'rous art of writing" (*J* 3.4) and an apostrophe to the reader as a "[lover] of books! [lover] of heaven!" (*J* 3.1), as if the two terms were equivalent (one recalls Jacques Basnage's characterization of heaven as a "sacred book"). This initial emphasis on textuality (enforced by the stylistic discussion on the same plate, in which it is said that "every letter is studied") returns powerfully at the apocalyptic close of the poem: Albion's first act following his recovery from his death-like torpor is to speak "Words of Eternity in Human Forms, in direful / Revolutions of Action & Passion" (*J* 95.9–10). At last, in the fulfilled state of desire, the restored Intellectual Powers "conversed together in Visionary forms dramatic," and "every Word & Every Character / Was Human" (*J* 98.28, 35–36). Daniel Stempel has aptly characterized this famous conversation as "one that restores both the order and the language of eternity; the relation between words and things is immediately visible as language and representation become one."[39] One may add that the objects of representation here are not "things," in the sense of any external forms, but rather the form-making powers of language itself. Everything that follows, right up to the conclusion of the enormous vision—jewels, chariots, living creatures, flaming colors—are experiences not of things but of words: "[I] saw the Words of the Mutual Covenant Divine," the poet says of these opulent manifestations (*J* 98.41). The thrust of the whole vision is toward the apotheosis of the monadic signifier:

And I heard the Name of their Emanations they are named Jerusalem

(*J* 99.5)

The final revelation of the poem, then, is not of Jerusalem herself, but of her name—and in this one name the differentiated names of all disparates find their harbor and their self-annihilation.

Here at last, then, is the promised return to origins, the place where the Intellectual Powers know themselves fully and finally—beyond the barriers and abysses of nature, the ruins of time, the separation of North and South, and the broken towers of languages uncomprehended—a place where pattern is fused with passion, where names precede objects and signifiers pre-

---

[39] "Blake, Foucault, and the Classical Episteme," 398.

cede signifieds, and where desire is the matrix of rational thought. All Blake's sublime "spaces" are designed to project, either through antitype or analogy, the form of this purely conceptual space, where the full range of possible sublimities is generated. But what precisely is this space? It is legitimate to press the inquiry, for if the answer shows it to be none other than the dark, undifferentiated monadic signifier of occult speculations, then a final obscurantism resides at the heart of Blake's vast and vibrant system. Fortunately, the inquiry points in another direction. If the Emanations of all things harbor in the name Jerusalem, we should recall that this name itself has a name: "JERUSALEM IS NAMED LIBERTY / AMONG THE SONS OF ALBION" (*J* 26). The final harbor (and thus the point of departure) is, then, not a monadic stasis or unmoved mover, but a region of flux, unpredictability, and open possibilities—in short, "liberty" (and we may note in this word the embedded *liber*, "book"—textuality and freedom in close embrace). It is the region from which human beings feel cut off, and yet crave (as the Sons of Albion are cut off from yet crave what Jerusalem represents), and to which the potencies of language, the quintessential human gift, still give access, no matter how dull and fallen our mundane tongues may be. However much Blake may draw on mystical traditions of the letter, he remains a secularist of the sublime, if we understand "secularist" to mean one who seeks to demystify the concept of divine inscription as unapproachable ruling letters suspended in the void. The letters are divine precisely because they are expressions of human desire, taken in its most exalted sense. This is why the "Words of Eternity" have "Human Forms" and why "every Word & Every Character" is—and must be—"Human."

This vision of the humanized letters itself finds support in the speculative tradition that upholds the divinity of the text, however far Blake may take the vision beyond the positions of orthodoxy. Even the reading of a text that is sacred, yet within the world, may raise the human reader to a participation in divinity; in his *True Christian Religion*, Emanuel Swedenborg declares, for example, that the Bible is "Holy in every Verse, in every Word, and in some cases in every Letter; and hence the Word joineth Man with the Lord, and openeth Heaven."[40] In more inventive versions of this joining, the human form is made to coincide with or reside in the heavenly letters themselves, as in some Rabbinic commentary or in the work of Christian Kabbalists who may have been influenced by such commentary. Rowland Jones and his zestfully inventive attempts to equate the letters with various parts of the human anatomy also come to mind.[41] The more

---

[40] Emanuel Swedenborg, *True Christian Religion; Containing the Universal Theology of the New Church*, trans. John Clowes, 2 vols. (London, 1781), vol. 1, 267.

[41] Citing a midrash on a phrase in Genesis, Susan Handelman notes, "The letters of the alphabet here are personified—they speak and complain against God. This personification is

direct step of actually showing letters in human form (or human forms fitting themselves to the shapes of letters) is left to Blake, who enters drawings of several such "living letters" in his Notebook.[42] In *Jerusalem*, the coincidence of letters and living figures is implicit rather than overt: the poem virtually begins with a declaration that "every word and every letter is studied and put into its fit place" (*J* 3), and it virtually ends with a vision of forms that walk "To & fro in Eternity as One Man reflecting each in each & clearly seen / And seeing: according to fitness & order" (*J* 98.39– 40). It takes a reading of the whole poem, including the *seeing* of thousands of letters in terrifying ranks, to come to the recognition that the two "fitnesses" are the same and that what seems at first like an almost obsessive concern for literal exactitude has turned into a revelation of an authentically human greatness. The alphabetic letters of the text converge finally upon the hieroglyph, that ancient form of picture writing, which, according to Bishop Warburton (its first major investigator), was designed not so much to represent objects as to represent gestures or "speaking by action."[43] The entire human body and its repertoire of gestures was held to be an organ of communication in the earliest ages, a living letter in a sense scarcely metaphoric.[44] In Blake's own version of this concept, the Intellectual Powers reveal their order through the expressive freedom of human limbs—and, if that is the case, then there is no reason to limit the range of "human letters" to the repertoire of postures contained in any given formal alphabet, for the same powers of formal ordering must shine through all

---

meant to indicate that they are not arbitrary signs, but have a life-force of their own" (*The Slayers of Moses*, 72). For Jones's superimposition of letters on the various parts of the human anatomy, see, e.g., *Hieroglyfic*, 13 and 16–17; *The IO-Triads*, 11; and note 18, this chapter.

[42] Speaking of these Notebook drawings, W.J.T. Mitchell remarks, "The point is not that a human figure or other graphic form must look like a character in the English or Hebrew alphabet, but that it must be repeated often enough to be differentiated and recognized as a 'character' in an ensemble of symbolic forms"; see "Visible Language: Blake's Wond'rous Art of Writing," in *Romanticism and Contemporary Criticism*, ed. Morris Eaves and Michael Fischer (Ithaca: Cornell University Press, 1986), 85.

[43] William Warburton, *Works*, 7 vols. (London, 1788), 409; quoted in Rossi, *Dark Abyss of Time*, 242. Rossi (236–45) provides a useful overview of Warburton's theories. For a connection of these theories to Blake's work, see Tannenbaum, *Biblical Tradition in Blake's Early Prophecies*, 56–57.

[44] Speaking of writers such as Poe, Emerson, and Whitman, whose fascination with the power of the letter is analogous to Blake's, John Irwin discusses the belief that hieroglyphs originated as a duplication of the human form: "for many of these writers it was an appealing, indeed a compelling, myth to imagine that origin as a form of 'hieroglyphic' doubling in which a prelinguistic creature saw the outline of his shadow on the ground or his reflection in water and experienced both the revelation of human self-consciousness (the differentiated existence of self and world) and the revelation of language, the sudden understanding that his shadow or reflection was a double of himself and yet *not* himself, that it was somehow separate and thus could serve as a substitute that would by its shape evoke recognition of what it stood in place of" (*American Hieroglyphics*, 61–62).

Blake's gestural depictions, including the pictures in the text. In other words, the series of human forms shown in his pictures are simply an extension of the series of living letters that make up his verbal text. Text and pictures converge, then, toward a common hieroglyphic status.[45]

The assertion of an original identity of human forms and "literal" forms, later reproduced in the hieroglyphs and still later in Blake's special composite art, provides an escape from the dilemma of priority. It endorses neither the common-sense, rationalist position that human intellect historically preceded the origin of language and letters (and therefore once did without them) nor the occult tradition that letters preceded humanity, which would turn them into those dismal Hutchinsonian "Machines to rule matter." In short, there was never a time when intellect lacked embodied form, or when its embodiment lacked intrinsic "litteral expression," or when that intrinsic expression lacked determinate and ordered shape; and neither did this determinate order ever hinder the manifestation of desire in a free flow of gesture and movement. These concepts are difficult to visualize, of course—and, limited as he is to two-dimensional paper, ink, and pigments, even Blake himself can only approximate such a state for us. He perhaps comes closest to such an approximation in one of his last artistic works, the second version of the title page to his unfinished illuminated transcription of Genesis, now in the drawings collection of the Huntington Art Gallery. This title page is arguably the most striking example in all of Blake's work of a purely iconic sublime of the signifier, in which alphabetic letters, iconographical pictorial shapes, and their visual arrangements with one another combine in an interplay that is complex and multi-expressive, yet tightly concentrated in its diagrammatic coherences and balances (see Figure 10). What is chiefly important about the design for the present discussion is its celebration of origins as something located in a setting composed entirely of a field of signs, with a *literally* embodied human intellect at its center.

The title page itself is the beginning of a book, a book about the Beginning, and is thus an iconic realization of its own referential content. Moreover, it displays the word *GENESIS* in so visual a fashion (distributing its giant, strangely shaped letters to the centers of all four quarters of the page and to the horizontal and vertical median lines) that a facile reading of the word is prohibited, and it is seen more as an object, losing referentiality and gaining a self-subsistent grandeur. Most important of all, the *I* of *GENESIS* is given a human form, with a vigorous disporting of limbs, and a central position distinctly apart from the arrangement of the other letters.

---

[45] For more on this point, see Mitchell, "Visible Language," 62: "Blake treats his pictorial art as if it were a kind of writing and summarizes the entire history of writing from pictogram to hieroglyphic to alphabetic script in the pages of his illuminated books."

Figure 10. Title Page, Illustrated Genesis.

The primacy of intellect within this complex setting is stressed by the position of the human head (the dot of the *i*), augmented by a great halo, at the center of the entire design. External associations and analogues come to mind at this point: *I* for Intellect and Identity, Smart's "For I is a person and therefore he is God," Jones's comment that "the i also expresses man as an upright line placed in the centre of all worldly beings and substances, to whom they bear a relation,"[46] and even Blake's buried pun in the first line of the last textual plate of *Jerusalem*, "All Human Forms *I*-dentified."

What the Genesis title page recovers so richly for us, with its human *I* at the origin and center of a setting of proliferating intellectual forms, is the preeminence of the First Person. It involves a recognition that the exaltation of something called the "Human Form" is a meaningless abstraction, unless one can find oneself in that exalted form, unless the "human" can be brought home to what each one of us knows best and loved first, our own delight in our special inner being. This homecoming, as I have argued elsewhere in this study, is the program of the sublime. Contrary to the views of Derrida and his followers, there is for Blake no contradiction between a transcendental subjectivity and the autonomy of the signifier, and this is what makes his distinctive effort to evoke the sublime through the route of the text possible. For Blake, too, as for Derrida, there may be nothing outside of text—but for the poet, this text is not a Spectral vision out of the Burkean sublime, an abyss of receding origins, but rather the ground of our being, the place of true beginnings, where, as the Genesis design so forcefully suggests, we are most ourselves.

.   .   .   .   .

We cannot speak, however, of the "setting" of the Genesis title page as a place of recovered origins within a field of signs without giving due thought to its other setting: inside a usually closed room in a library in California, unseen by and no doubt unknown to the many hundreds who roam daily through the famous gardens outside—to say nothing of the thousands in the traffic stream of the Foothill Freeway a few miles to the north, as it crosses a region slated (according to modern-day apocalyptic speculators) for the catastrophic sunderings of earthquakes and the production of Volneian ruins. Literary criticism does not usually deal with such external settings of texts. But Blake himself is all too aware of such settings, and they compel him to explore the catastrophes of nature and the chaos of the post-Babel world in which we live. The stars, which may once have been sacred letters, have fled from the limbs of Albion, and he is mute, or else speaks words too much in servitude to a chimerical referentiality. In

---

[46] *Hieroglyfic*, 16.

such a setting, the text that actually sets out to restore our sense of our true intellectual origins, by providing us with an approximation of their very image, is often destined to be fragile, disregarded, and hidden away in the midst of Babel's din.

But if language as we know it is universally fallen—or, worse, falsely raised into a monument of dead prescriptions—it remains true that language is our only strength against the residual effects of the old catastrophe. Blake is fully aware that we remain in the midst of these residual effects, which may be why he locates one of the most famous passages about language in his work not at the beginning or end of *Jerusalem* but in its rugged middle, within a chapter devoted largely to various unsuccessful attempts by Los to rescue Albion from his plight. Referring to Bowlahoola and Allamanda, Blake says:

> (I call them by their English names: English, the rough basement.
> Los built the stubborn structure of the Language, acting against
> Albions melancholy, who must else have been a Dumb despair.)

> (*J* 36[40].58–60)

If, in his explorations of London, Los encounters towers or mountains or pyramidical heaps of dead articulation, here he asserts a countersublime, establishing the foundations of a new tower perhaps, more enduring ("stubborn") than its ill-starred predecessor at Babel because the new structure incorporates fundamental principles of human intellect. As an antidote to Albion's aphasia, Los provides not a catalog of meanings but a structure that Albion can inhabit, a place where the order of language is made perpetually visible, including its powers of generating meanings. Historically, English—like most manifestations of the sublime—is a "great object" of belated provenance, disjoined from origins. Blake refuses the temptation provided by some of the antiquarians to regard English as the original language of the world, possibly because he considers their scenario ultimately irrelevant. Babel, or aphasia, has always been, no matter how far back we track it historically—and the only antithetical term to a perpetual "then" of loss is a perpetual "now" of potential recovery, which in Blake's time and place means the resources of his language. But these resources are not an inert inheritance, a bin of goods into which the poet can dip effortlessly at any time. Hence, it is necessary for Los to "build" language, for it will not reveal its treasures unless desire and work are applied to its inchoate surfaces; it is necessary, too, for Blake the poet to build it afresh, infusing it with the new—for example, with names like "Bowlahoola" and "Allamanda," which, strange as they are, become "English" as soon as they emerge from an English poet's invention. The task of building is directed not only "against Albion's melancholy" but also for the poet's own sake, so that he may avoid the contagion of that melancholy and keep himself from becoming a "dumb despair." In the face of a world of ruins, he refuses to lapse into silence, but holds out for the chance that the stony remains can be built into a structure of words, "well contrived words, firm fixing, never forgotten, / Always comforting the remembrance" (*J* 12.35–36). These words comfort, for they alone can display intellectual acts in a lasting, determinate, and autonomous form.

EPILOGUE

BLAKE'S SUBLIME IN THE ROMANTIC CONTEXT

W E CANNOT conclude this study of Blake's sublime poetics without acknowledging that our pursuit has brought us to the verge of paradox. The human acts that, for Blake, make up the essence of the sublime experience prove to have their proper home in the still and immobile permanence of texts—which (to take a Wordsworthian phrase out of its context), if they live at all, do not live like living men. A second paradox also looms: as we explore the background imagery of Blake's poetry, the settings that in toto compose a worldview, the sublime comes to seem like a universal presence, with the face of nature, the remains of time, the patterns of history, even the structure of Eternity itself, seen as its variant manifestations—and yet this rampantly expanding circumference of the sublime's sphere of operations is discovered at last to collapse into the "I" of the poet's identity, the exuberant expression of his own individuality through the unique feats of his language. Thus there is, first, a privileging of the constructed artifact over biological vitality in what is claimed to be the genuine human center of the poet's vision, and second, more than a touch of solipsism in the claimed universality of that vision.

One can scarcely hope to resolve these paradoxes in the remaining space of this study, or in any likely larger space, since Blake never resolved them himself, and, indeed, since the their main terms—"natural" human vitality versus the reification of the poetic artifact, solipsism versus universality of vision—cast their problematic shadows on the whole of the Romantic enterprise. Issues that cannot be resolved in themselves can, however, point us in the direction of other useful kinds of understanding. In this case, they help us to deal with a large question raised at the outset of this study: once we have learned the hows and whys of Blake's sublime poetics, its premises and applications (the main tasks pursued by the preceding chapters), what can we then understand of its place in the larger framework of the eighteenth-century and Romantic sublime? And if our interest is not to remain purely historical, this question prompts another, even less likely to admit a definitive answer, yet not to be avoided: what, after all, is such a sublime poetics good for?

The briefest sketch of answers to these questions is all that is possible here. The questions themselves shade into one another (for, presumably, those elements that give Blake his distinguishing place in the sublime tradition are precisely the elements that, from his point of view, make his sublime poetics *better* than those of his contemporaries—more answerable to his own needs and those of his audience) and may appropriately be considered together. We may start with Blake's paradoxical insistence on equating the human with the textual. In asserting this equation, he shows himself to be holding a special position among theorists of the sublime. It is a position that is allied to both the idealist tradition, represented by figures such as Kant and Wordsworth, and the materially based and sensationalist conceptions of Burke—yet standing apart from either system. Blake rejects Burke's materialism but not his emphasis on sensations—which, from first to last, hold a special place of prestige in the poet's works (even in the apocalyptic discourse of the Living Creatures at the end of *Jerusalem*, the nature of the discourse is said to depend on "the Expansion or Contraction, the Translucence or / Opakeness of Nervous fibres" [*J* 98.36–37]). Blake undoubtedly realizes that no writer on the sublime provides a more exquisitely discriminated inventory of human sensations than Burke, which may be one reason why there are so many surreptitious tributes to the Burkean sublime in Blake's work. There is, after all, no more of a body-mind split in Burke's theory than there is in Blake's work. If, for Burke, all is body, then Blake seeks less to reverse this position than to infuse it with an idealist basis. He seeks an image of intellect *embodied*, and this he finds in the sensory surface offered by the text.

Like the idealists, Blake provides a scenario in which the intellect recognizes its own greatness, but in his scheme, unlike theirs, there is no diminishment of the presented sublime object and no departure of the intellect from the object into its own ineffable space. Blake's sublime of the text is incorporeal (because verbal), but not ineffable; it consists precisely of what can be *shown* in wholly definite form. No light of sense needs to go out here for the sublime to manifest itself; on the contrary, the senses are sharpened in exactitude. The sublime of the text weds the intellectual and the visible, and hence avoids what most theories of the sublime prevalent among his contemporaries seem to require—namely, a widening fissure between external forces, presented as independently powerful, and the experiencing mind seeking its own power and independence. For Blake, such a fissure is a kind of wound, and it can healed only by his asserting a common *human* denominator to both the originating sublime stimulus and the perceiver in quest of self-recognition; moreover, by insisting that this common humanity be fully embodied, he ensures that what begins as a sensory experience remains fully sensory to the last. The text is never to be abandoned, but rather to be ever better read, ever better loved, and ever more thoroughly seen. The question of whether humanity can be equated with textuality needs therefore to be considered in the light of the alternatives. If, for example, the quintessence of humanity is to be identified with something other than intellect, then no sublime is possible, and Blake is a wanderer in the materialist void along with all other idealists. But if one grants the identification, there remains the question of how best to represent it. Is that quintessence to be represented by such imagistic blanks as Pure Reason or Pure Imagination, as in those theories of the sublime that specify an ultimate departure from the sensory world, or is it to be found in a form that touches on a full range of human experience—a form that engages one's delight in sensory play, one's feeling for proportion, movement, and rhythm, and one's receptivity to moral and contemplative ideas, such as a text provides? Blake considered the alternatives and made his choice.

The second paradox involving the sublime of the text is more directly connected with its value: from one perspective, Blake's may appear to be the most egotistical of all sublimes, and from another, the most altruistic and selfless. A consideration of this point also helps to place Blake in the tradition of Romantic sublimity, for nearly all the great Romantics recognized and profoundly grappled with the twin lures of attaining an aggrandized self and of serving a common good through the articulation of a universalizing vision in which all might share. Shelley succinctly articulates the polarities and the urge to accommodate them in a single vision, when at the close of the "Hymn to Intellectual Beauty," the eponymous Spirit binds the poet "To fear [i.e., stand in awe of] himself, and love all human kind," with the clear implication that the latter feeling is dependent on the former for its accomplishment. Keats, in *The Fall of Hyperion*, in order to serve the altruistic hope that the "poet is a sage; / A humanist, physician to all men," likewise needs an aggrandizing transformation, the growth of "A power within me of enormous ken, / To see as a god sees." Perhaps the classic rationale of this Romantic focus on the aggrandized self appears at the close of *The Prelude*, as Wordsworth tries to account for his poetic preoccupation with his autobiographical transactions with a sublime Nature: "what we have loved, / Others will love, and we will teach them how."[1]

Compared to the stances of these younger contemporaries, Blake's own stance is immediately striking for its impersonality. His work deals in worldviews—domains natural and apocalyptic, near and far, past, present, and to come, that are inventoried for the knowledge they yield of our general situation and not for any overt expressionist aim. The sporadically appearing "I" of *Jerusalem* is a nominal presence only; and to state that *Milton*, with its stress on the providential moment within temporal experience,

---

[1] See "Hymn to Intellectual Beauty," line 84, in *Shelley's Poetry and Prose: Authoritative Texts and Criticism*, ed. Donald H. Reiman and Sharon B. Powers (New York: W. W. Norton, 1977); *The Fall of Hyperion*, lines 189–90 and 303–4, in John Keats, *Complete Poems and Selected Letters*, ed. Clarence DeWitt Thorpe (New York: Odyssey Press, 1935); and Wordsworth, *The Prelude* (1850) 14.446–47.

is Blake's most Wordsworthian poem serves only to reveal at once how profoundly different Blake's mode is from Wordsworth's. At the same time, most readers would agree that no impersonal poetic vision of the world is more idiosyncratic than Blake's or more stridently proclaims the unique hallmarks of its authorship. If this vision is Blake's gift to his potential readership, then it is also his challenge flung out at them, the expression of his "stubborn," authentic self, the "I" of his identity, so widely imprinted on the topics of his concern that it scarcely needs to advertise itself as "I." And beyond the desire to challenge, may we not also detect a more imperial agenda, a gesture toward the incorporation of "all" into a vast solipsistic self? If, as this study has generally shown, the structure of the world is a manifestation of the structure of the sublime, and if the sublime experience itself is structured on the experience of a text, the obvious question arises: what text? What text indeed can meet these specifications but Blake's own, with its strange machinery of discontinuous surfaces, overpowering iconic masses, its dulcet and inviting openings, and its fleeting, nearly hallucinatory glimpses of an overarching order? It is as if his vision of the world becomes one with the vision of his own text—which, in turn, is the outward manifestation of his own identity. If Blake's world seems impersonal, it may be because the First Person that is its guiding principle is so thoroughly attenuated through all its parts that it cannot be discerned in an isolatable form.

In one sense, then, Blake achieves a more "egotistical sublime" than Wordsworth himself ever manifests, despite Blake's scantier use of the first-person pronoun. The Wordsworthian "I" justifies its presence by adverting to its representative function ("what we have loved others will love"); anyone, given the right circumstances, can feel the same renovating power that the poet enjoyed through his own sublime encounters. The poet seeks to efface the gap between his own individuality and that of others; he likes to think of himself as a man speaking to men. Blake, on the other hand, presents a radical, unaccommodating face to his audience. His art makes no attempt to ingratiate itself, nor does it seek to represent the poet as an icon of typicality. Yet ironically, it is Blake's more radical and absolute "egotism" that is ultimately more altruistic, more yielding to others. The Wordsworthian "I," reaching out to other men, seeking to represent the poet's experiences as typical enough to serve as surrogates for their experiences, minimizes the risks of alienation and rejection—risks inherent in any genuine attempt to present something so fundamentally disturbing as the access of the sublime (this is one reason why Wordsworth's reputation solidified more than a hundred years before Blake's). This risk-cutting must inevitably serve that aspect of the ego that Blake calls the Selfhood. Conversely, in the aggressive and expansive self-identity that is writ large throughout Blake's works, there is no Selfhood in the baleful sense. Blake offers the whole of himself in his art and thus risks the possibility of a humiliating total rejection of his strange, uncompromising, often terrifying, and often preposterously hopeful vision; the greatest sacrifice is the one that may earn no thanks. On the other hand, there is always the chance that the offering will prove fruitful, that we his readers will find ourselves in his vision, in which case the Blakean identity attenuates itself until it becomes an identification of each of us with all, and we walk together as one.

This is not the occasion to do proper justice to the complexities and the richness of the Wordsworthian sublime, which is used here frankly as a foil to delineate what is distinctive in Blake's achievement. But if Blake could have read *The Prelude*, he probably would have seen it as an example of self-protective impulses in conflict with genuine vision. In this light, Wordsworth's rendering of his experience as common and representative seems dictated more by prudence than by altruism; by holding back a full and unsparing account of what is most unsettling and alienating in his encounters with Nature and the dark passages of his own mind, he denies his readers the full truth that they need. Encounters with such dire phenomena as a stalking mountain, a drowned man dragged up from the watery bottom, or a site where the ghosts of murder and implacable retribution haunt lead too easily and too soon to joy and feelings of elevation; such feelings seem insufficiently earned by any searching analysis of the universal substrate of catastrophe of which these phenomena are the tokens. Blake would probably consider the terror-provoking Wordsworthian spots of time less as devoid of sublimity than as premature reifications of the sublime. Their message is ostensibly to show the ultimate littleness and innocuousness of the terrific phenomena and, at the same time, the grandeur and power of the imagination—but Blake would read such scenes differently. From his assessment of existence in Nature, he would say that the mountains really *are* on the move, that murderous and retributive ghosts really do stalk us all the time, ready to descend, and that we are more vulnerable than we know. Any aesthetics that postulates a benign face to the experience of catastrophe or promises a safe elevation above it courts self-delusion and promotes the delusion of others.

The sublime of terror, identified by Burke and poeticized with such consummate power by Wordsworth, is an attempt to placate the terror by turning it into a positive value or else by hedging it about with all sorts of compensatory strategies to minimize its threats; but the underlying assumption remains that such terrors shall always be with us. It is tempting and easy for a poet to rest with such an assumption and settle for the compensatory strategies, prematurely lodging sublimity in the encounter with the terrifying object, because an exorcistic search for the buried roots of the terror and for a sublimity that can satisfy with finality seems too strenuous, too uncertain of success. It is just such a strenuous undertaking that is embodied in Blake's sublime poetics. Blake differs from his great Romantic contemporaries in degree rather than kind; like them he seeks to save himself, augmenting his strength in the face of a universe of death, and to save others as well; but he cannot remain content with premature reifications of the sublime, and the whole vast engine of his art is designed as a vehicle to push past those reifications into a difficult and dangerous unexplored territory.

This enterprise must elicit our admiration for its courage, if for nothing else. In his valuable study *Symbol and Truth in Blake's Myth* (valuable precisely because it avoids an uncritically adulatory approach to Blake), Leopold Damrosch, Jr. cautions against our "exaggerating the achieved security of [Blake's] visions of desire and minimizing the great theme of man's struggles against the internal obstacles that thwart desire," and he adds that "Blake's imaginative vision is admirable because it wrestles so honestly with the intractable facts of fallen experience."[2] These "intractable facts" are, for Blake, not so much "facts" as modes of perception, deformed versions of a deeper and more satisfying reality—but they are no less intractable for all that. It would be a mistake to believe that Blake himself was exempt from the premature reifications of the sublime mentioned above (his poetic practice would refute such a belief in any case); he, too, knows the temptation to invest with numinous power the eruptive or thwarting gestures of the fearsome Other, the oppressions of magnitude, the yawning of the abyss. Were it otherwise, he would not have been able to comprehend or enter into the fears and strategies of desperation of his fellow men, let alone with the force and brilliance that his creative work everywhere displays. And it can scarcely be otherwise; Blake's imagination is saturated in catastrophe; he sees it all about him in contemporary history, he imbibes it from a literary milieu that is half in love with terror and melancholy, and he projects it outward in his images of nature, culture, history, and cosmology. His triumph, finally, is not to submit to despair but to wrest the disruptive and discontinuous pattern of catastrophic experience out of that context and to install it in a displaced form as the driving mechanism of his own art, which works to provide a dynamic matrix that a liberated intellect can recognize as its own unrestrictive yet secure haven.

Building his great structure of words out of the ruins of a catastrophe-riven universe, Blake intends it to serve as both the expression of his unique individuality and the universal embracing and reuniting form, in which all of us can recognize ourselves and each other. Whether he realized this double dream in his art—whether, indeed, it is ever humanly realizable—is

---

[2] Leopold Damrosch, Jr., *Symbol and Truth in Blake's Myth* (Princeton: Princeton University Press, 1980), 365.

beyond the scope of this book to determine. This much, however, seems likely: at the present time, altogether as terrifying as his own, when all idealisms are suspect, when few can believe that catastrophic separations may yield sublime unifications, when even the integrity of the self is thought to be merely a construct of baleful power structures, Blake's determined insistence on hoping otherwise, and turning hope into faith, and faith into a persistent and unstinting deployment of all the resources of poetic art at his disposal, may prove that part of his legacy that serves us best. Whether the doctrinal content of his words can yield our eternal salvation remains an increasingly open question. Our earlier question—what is Blake's sublime poetics good for?—yields an answer that suffices. It is enough that the example of heroic effort incorporated and preserved in that setting of words helps us to endure.

INDEX